D0227870

THE IDEAS THAT SHAPED
POST-WAR BRITAIN

CENTRE

David Marquand is Principal of Mansfield College, Oxford.

Anthony Seldon is Founding Director of the Institute of Contemporary British History.

THE IDEAS THAT SHAPED POST-WAR BRITAIN

Edited by
DAVID MARQUAND AND
ANTHONY SELDON

FontanaPress
An Imprint of HarperCollins*Publishers*

Fontana Press
An imprint of HarperCollins*Publishers*
77–85 Fulham Palace Road
Hammersmith, London, W6 8JB

A Fontana Press Original 1996
3 5 7 9 8 6 4 2

ISBN 0 00 638449 8

Set in Linotype Sabon by
Rowland Phototypesetting Ltd,
Bury St Edmunds, Suffolk
Printed and bound in Great Britain by
Caledonian International Book
Manufacturing Ltd, Glasgow

CONTENTS

Introduction: Ideas and Policy		David Marquand and Anthony Seldon	1
1	Moralists and Hedonists	David Marquand	5
2	Politics	Albert Hirschman	29
3	The Fall of Keynesianism	Robert Skidelsky	41
4	The Keynesian Consensus	Peter Clarke	67
5	Industrial Relations	Robert Taylor	88
6	'Contract' and 'Citizenship'	Jose Harris	122
7	Social Policy	Chris Pierson	139
8	Social Democracy	Raymond Plant	165
9	Culture	Geoff Mulgan	195
10	The European Question	Jim Bulpitt	214
11	Ideas are not Enough	Anthony Seldon	257
12	The Stakeholder Society	Will Hutton	290
	Contributors		309
	Notes		311
	Index		336

Ideas and Policy

MORE YEARS have passed since 1945 than from the beginning of the century to that date. The major issues and questions in British history from 1900–45 are now fairly well established and there have been authoritative responses in many areas. In contrast, the historiography of the last fifty years is still in flux. A mass of scholarly literature has been written on particular policy areas, institutions and individuals. But the pattern and contours of post-war British history have been strangely hard to define. This is particularly true of the complex relationship between the world of ideas and the world of action. Some of the published literature refers in passing to the role of ideas, but for most authors it is very much a secondary concern.

Yet it is clear that the fifty years since the end of the Second World War have seen dramatic changes in the intellectual and cultural framework within which policy is made and implemented. The details of policy change, as well as the fluctuating fortunes of the political parties, reflect these broad changes in the subconscious of the nation and cannot be understood in isolation from them. The object of this book is to tease out the relationships between these dimensions of change. It explores the impact of transformations in the intellectual and cultural climate on the thinking and assumptions of policy makers, seeks to explain why ideas (such as privatisation or monetarism) which seemed beyond the pale in one period became the orthodoxy of another, and analyses the relationship between changing policy approaches and changes in the content of policy.

In doing so, *The Ideas that Shaped Post-War Britain* aspires to throw new light on the alleged shift from the collectivism of the post-war era to the individualism of the last decade and a half, and to place the Thatcher revolution and its aftermath, as well as the preceding thirty years, in a new and richer context.

Ideas, and the complex relationship between thought and action, provide the connecting theme of the book. However, our authors have approached the subject from very different angles. In the first chapter, David Marquand examines the rise and fall of Keynesian social democracy from the late 1940s until the mid-1970s, explores the New Right paradigm which dominated the following twenty years and speculates on the possible emergence of a third paradigm (which is itself the subject of the final chapter in the book). Marquand's distinctive approach is to provide a subtler separation than that between individualism and collectivism, and to suggest that within each dominant phase were powerful cross-cutting political languages, at one time active and moralistic, at another passive and hedonistic.

Albert Hirschman, the seminal American political economist, next measures the British post-war experience against the propositions of two of his recent books, *Shifting Involvements* (1981) and *The Rhetoric of Reaction* (1992). Hirschman's work is well known to social scientists in Britain, but historians have paid too little attention to it. His *oeuvre* provides the inspiration for several chapters that follow.

Chapters three and four provide the opportunity for two of our leading historians of economic thought to examine the impact of the ideas of Keynes, the single most powerful and influential thinker of the period, on post-war British history. Robert Skidelsky finds that Keynesian economics lost out in the 1970s to Friedmanism because the former failed to renew itself intellectually when it still held sway. A different perspective is provided by Peter Clarke in his chapter on the argument over macroeconomic policy in Britain since 1945. Robert Taylor in chapter five explores another aspect of economic policy in his story of the uneven abandonment of the voluntarist tradition in British industrial relations.

The book then moves on to consider social policy. Jose Harris, the biographer of William Beveridge, the other main influence on post-war British history, examines the theoretical underpinning of the British welfare state as it emerged in the 1940s. Chris Pierson brings the story up to the present day in his chapter on the post-war welfare state. Social policy, he finds, by the 1990s was profoundly different to how it was conceived by Beveridge fifty years before. Raymond Plant examines the social-democratic tradition in British politics, grounding his analysis in the work of C. A. R. Crosland, before moving on to consider the neo-liberal reaction to it.

The book broadens out beyond economic and social policy at this point. Geoff Mulgan considers in chapter nine British culture and its relation with society since 1945, while Jim Bulpitt explores the tortuous but central question of the motives for Britain's changing stance on Europe in chapter ten. In chapter eleven, Anthony Seldon brings together the strands of the book in his analysis of the key turning points in post-war policy across a broad area, and weighs the relative influence of ideas, individuals, interests and circumstances in bringing about change. In the final chapter, Will Hutton explores some of the ideas behind 'New Labour'. The book does not aim to be comprehensive. We are painfully aware that several key areas, such as environmentalism and feminism, have been neglected. The book is sponsored by the two organisations to which the editors belong, the Political Economy Research Centre and the Institute of Contemporary British History. The editors wish to thank colleagues at these bodies, especially Andrew Gamble and Sylvia McColm at the former, and Peter Catterall and Virginia Preston at the latter. They also wish to thank Annemarie Weitzel for her secretarial skills in bringing the book together, and Philip Gwyn Jones and Toby Mundy at HarperCollins for their enthusiasm and support.

David Marquand and Anthony Seldon, October 1996

CHAPTER 1

Moralists and Hedonists[1]

David Marquand

[T]he ideas of economists and political philosophers, both
when they are right and when they are wrong, are more
powerful than is commonly understood. Indeed, the world
is ruled by little else. Practical men, who believe
themselves to be quite exempt from any intellectual
influence, are usually the slaves of some defunct
economist. Madmen in authority, who hear voices in the
air, are distilling their frenzy from some academic scribbler
of a few years back . . . [S]oon or late, it is ideas, not vested
interests, which are dangerous for good or evil.
J. M. Keynes.[2]

[T]he supremacy of a social group manifests itself in two
ways, as 'domination' and as 'intellectual and moral
leadership' . . . A social group can, and indeed must,
already exercise 'leadership' before winning governmental
power.
Antonio Gramsci.[3]

K EYNES'S heroic intellectualism dazzles more than it per-
suades. The notion that ideas rule the world, or shape
societies, implies a platonic philosopher king, legislating for
society from the outside. No such creature appears in this
book. It is based on the assumption that, if thought influences

action, action also influences thought. Madmen in authority may distil the frenzy of academic scribblers, but academic scribblers respond to the pressures of the society around them, and their scribbles resonate only when they speak to social forces. If practical men are apt to be enslaved by defunct economists, living economists inhabit a world managed by practical men. As Gramsci knew, intellectual leadership precedes domination, but as he also knew, successful intellectual leaders tailor their appeals to inherited traditions. Belief and behaviour, ideas and policies, visions of the future and legacies of the past, form a seamless web; attempts to unpick it, to give primacy to thought over action, or to action over thought, confuse more than they illuminate.

This web provides the subject matter of the chapters that follow. In different ways, they all explore different facets of the complex and fluctuating relationship between thought and action in post-war Britain. The remaining chapters examine particular aspects of that relationship. In this chapter, I try to pull some of the threads together. I trace the rise and fall of two clusters of ideas and assumptions, through which two sets of claimants for power have sought Gramsci's 'intellectual and moral leadership', and I speculate about the possible emergence of a third cluster, as yet only half-formed. I begin by describing the varied fates of these clusters and discussing the ideas they contained. I then offer an interpretation of the courses they have followed.

It is a story that falls into three broad phases. From the late 1940s to the mid-1970s, governments of right and left alike adhered to a form of liberal collectivism, sometimes known as 'Keynesian social democracy'.[4] As that formulation implies, liberal collectivism or Keynesian social democracy was not the preserve of any single political party. Nor was it the product of any single ideological tendency. Its intellectual ancestry was too rich and diverse to fit the pigeon-holes of left and right; and it owed more to the crises, contingencies and compromises of the early post-war period than to the doctrines championed by either major party at the beginning of the period. The Attlee Government, under which its essentials were embodied in legislation and (much more importantly) in administrative practice, set out in 1945 with quite different intentions. So did the Conservative opposition under Churchill. Yet by the early 1950s at the latest, it had become the lodestar of the two front benches in the House of Commons, of the Whitehall mandarinate, of the leaders of organised capital and organised labour and of the academic and journalistic apologists and interpreters of this nexus of interests. Dissenters – Aneurin Bevan and his followers in the Labour Party; Peter Thorneycroft, Enoch Powell and Nigel Birch in the Conservative Party – were either marginalised or obliged to recant.

For Labour, the Keynesian social-democratic moment came gradually. In the two years from 1947 to 1949, ministers slowly abandoned their original vision of a socially-controlled economy – in which resources would be allocated by political decisions rather than market-place haggling – in favour of a mixed economy centred upon Keynesian demand management. The fact that the retreat from social control was headed by Sir Stafford Cripps, the arch-visionary of 1945, only made it all the more poignant. The equivalent Conservative moment was more compressed. It came in 1952, when the Cabinet rejected the Treasury's so-called 'Robot' plan for a floating pound, sterling convertibility and a return to market disciplines, on the grounds that it would lead to higher unemployment and, as Lord Cherwell argued, 'put the Conservative Party out for a generation. Even a Government with a large majority could not survive such a sudden, complete reversal of policy'.[5] Thereafter, on both sides of the party divide, the heirs of the practical men whom Keynes had teased took it for granted that they could exercise power only within Keynesian social-democratic parameters, and lead successfully only by showing that they were better Keynesian social democrats than their rivals.

The Keynesian social-democratic phase terminated amid the confusion and crises of the 1970s. In classic Gramscian fashion, it ended in the realm of ideas well before corresponding changes took place in the realm of governmental power. By the middle of the decade, at the latest, the authoritarian individualists of the New Right, with their emphasis on market freedom, social and monetary discipline and a tightly concentrated state, were making the ideological running. Keynesian social democrats still controlled the commanding heights of Whitehall, but the intellectual system on which they based their claim to power was patently crumbling. In a profound sense, they no longer knew what to do. Ministers waited in vain for coherent official advice; officials waited in vain for firm ministerial decisions.[6] It was as though a sleek ocean liner had suddenly become a rudderless raft. The New Right offered an alternative craft, and for the best part of twenty years this was the only vessel following a confident course. To be sure, New Right politicians never won a majority of the popular vote. They did not need to. With dazzling political skill, they constructed a new social coalition, distributed in such a way as to procure them decisive parliamentary majorities in spite of their comparatively low levels of popular support. More important still, the New Right paradigm shaped the political agenda and controlled the intellectual weather.

How far it still does is a moot question. Little remains of the confident and decisive Conservative regime of the 1980s. Since Britain's forced departure from the European Exchange Rate Mechanism, the Major Government has been as rudderless as were the Wilson and Callaghan Governments of the 1970s. By the early months of 1996, the Conservative Party was riven by internal disputes as savage as those which tore the Labour Party apart in the early 1980s, and most observers took it for granted that a Labour Government was only a matter of time. But this does not necessarily betoken the end of the New Right paradigm, any more than the sad *diminuendo* of the second Attlee Government between February 1950 and October 1951 betokened the end of its Keynesian social-democratic predecessor. New Right ideology and Conservative statecraft have been symbiotically connected for nearly two decades, but they are not the same thing, and the disarray of the latter proves nothing about the former. On the structure of the British state and its place in an increasingly proto-federal European Union, Tony Blair's 'New Labour' Party offers a decisive break, not just with Conservative policy, but with the governing assumptions of New Right politics. Yet on the only slightly less crucial issue of taxation and public expenditure it whistles an essentially New Right tune. It seems to be groping for a vision of the political economy as distinct from authoritarian individualism as authoritarian individualism was from Keynesian social democracy. It would be rash to assume that it will find what it is groping for.

Yet intimations of a possible new intellectual and policy paradigm are not difficult to detect – on the political right as well as on the left. The fall of communism has taken the zest out of the old battles of state against market, and socialism against capitalism. The simplistic universalities of the Cold War no longer resonate; the focus now is on complexity and difference. Persistent divergencies in the fortunes of market economies have focused attention on the varieties of capitalism, and on their moral and cultural dimensions.[7] Endemic unemployment in Europe, the rise of the working poor in the United States, the transformation of labour markets everywhere and the associated threat of fragmentation and anomie have fostered a new concern with the dangers of social exclusion and the *a priori* necessity for social cohesion.[8] Classic themes from the eighteenth and nineteenth centuries – the role of trust in a market economy; the prerequisites of civil society; the meaning of citizenship; the relationship between duties and rights; the need for and scope of a public domain; the threats to and demands of community – have been rediscovered.[9] On the right there is talk of a new 'civic conservatism'; on the left, of a 'stakeholder economy'.[10] The differences between them are real and important, but they spring from a shared experience and a common fear. As John Gray, one of the most passionate and original exponents of the new mood, puts it in an anguished pamphlet,

> Communities are scattered to the winds by the gale of creative destruction. Endless 'downsizing' and 'flattening' of enterprises fosters ubiquitous insecurity and makes loyalty to the company a cruel joke. The celebration of consumer choice, as the only undisputed value in market societies, devalues commitment and stability in personal relationships and encourages the view of marriage and the family as vehicles of self-realisation. The dynamism of market processes dissolves social hierarchies and overturns established expectations. Status is ephemeral, trust frail and contract sovereign. The dissolution of communities promoted by market-driven labour mobility weakens, where it does not entirely destroy, the informal social monitoring of behaviour which is the most effective preventive measure against crime.[11]

These intimations are still tentative and inchoate (not to say confused). Only time will tell if they can provide the basis for the kind of intellectual and moral leadership I have been discussing. Through the fog, however, it is possible to discern the outlines of a third phase and a new political divide. This new divide cuts across the divides of the last fifty or even one hundred years, and the political vocabulary of the twentieth century does not capture it. On one side are those, of left and right alike, who believe that institutions are the guarantors of freedom, and collectivities the schools of individuality. On the other are those, also of left and right, who see institutional pressures as harbingers of tyranny, and who put their faith in the spontaneous mutual adjustment of unconstrained individuals. As Robert Skidelsky has suggested, it may perhaps be a divide between political and economic liberals, or on a deeper level between pessimists and optimists.[12] Be that as it may, it is clear that, just as the final act of a play can give unforeseen meaning to the earlier acts, the tentative emergence of this new divide puts those that have preceded it in a new and unexpected light.

So far, perhaps, so obvious. The final chapter of this story may be unfamiliar, but the first two are well-known. The inner meaning, however, is not obvious at all. Three sets of arguments underpinned post-war Keynesian social democracy, each with a long pedigree. The first was economic. As Keynes put it in his famous essay, 'The End of Laissez-Faire',

> The world is *not* so governed from above that private and social interests always coincide. It is *not* so managed here below that in practice they coincide. It is *not* a correct deduction from the Principles of Economics that enlightened self-interest always operates in the public interest. Nor is it true that self-interest generally *is* enlightened; more often individuals acting separately to promote their own ends are too ignorant or too weak to attain even these. Experience does *not* show that individuals, when they make up a social unit, are always less clear-sighted than when they act separately.[13]

In short, markets fail. Their failures are systemic, not accidental. They fail because market actors cannot know enough to maximise their interests in the way that market economics postulates. They fail because they cannot, by themselves, ensure that social costs are borne by those who incur them. And, as Adam Smith knew, they fail because they cannot secure the production of public goods. Because they fail, they have to be both regulated and supplemented; and it is the state that has to regulate and supplement them. The Keynesian social-democratic paradigm left plenty of room for debate about the extent and form of state intervention, but on two points all Keynesian social democrats were agreed. They were *for* extensive state intervention *in* the market, and *against* state suppression *of* the market. In James Meade's language, they were 'Liberal Socialists';[14] in Andrew Shonfield's, they wanted a 'mixed economy', in which 'supplies of goods and services are largely determined by market processes', but in which the state and its agencies 'have a large capacity for economic intervention'.[15]

The second set of arguments was moral and political. To make a reality of civil and political rights, Keynesian social democrats insisted, social rights had to be guaranteed as well; indeed, social rights were the emblems of social progress. In his seminal 1949 essay, 'Citizenship and Social Class', T. H. Marshall offered a classic summary of the argument.[16] Citizenship, said Marshall, had three dimensions – civil, political and social. Over the preceding three centuries, the struggle for citizenship rights had shifted from the first to the second, and then from the second to the third. Civil citizenship, manifested in equal civil rights, had been established in the eighteenth century, or at any rate in the 150 years between the Glorious Revolution and the first Reform Act. Political citizenship – equality of political rights – was largely the work of the nineteenth century. In the twentieth century, the focus had shifted to social citizenship – the struggle for equal social rights. The post-war welfare state had now enshrined the principle of equal social rights in legislation.

The implications went wider than appears at first sight. The essence of citizenship lies in its autonomy: the fact that citizenship rights are held independently of market power or social status. If the domain of citizenship expands, the domain of the market-place contracts. In celebrating the extension of citizenship, Marshall was also celebrating the growth of the public domain at the expense of the market domain. In writing the history of the preceding 250 years as a history of growing citizenship, he was saying that successive aspects of social life had been ring-fenced from the operations of the market-place. In presenting that process as evidence of social progress, he was also saying that it had been right to ring-fence them: if the democratic promise of equal citizenship were to be honoured, the market domain should not be allowed to invade other domains.

Buttressing the arguments from market failure and democratic principle was an argument from historical necessity. As Albert Hirschman has suggested, one of the stock themes of 'progressive' rhetoric is an appeal to irrevocable laws of motion, carrying society, willy-nilly, in the desired direction.[17] In the eighteenth and nineteenth centuries, the founding fathers of market economics had employed that trope to devastating effect. The invisible hand of free competition, and the accompanying switch from status to contract, produced opulence; opulence produced civility; with civility came felicity; with both came progress. Not the least of the achievements of the intellectual progenitors of Keynesian social democracy – and not the least of the reasons why Keynesian social-democratic governments exercised leadership as well as power – is that they turned this historiography on its head. The irrevocable laws of motion, as depicted by them, pointed in very nearly the opposite direction – from the disorganised to the organised, from the dispersed to the concentrated, from the individual to the collective. The visible hand of oligopoly had gradually, but inexorably, replaced the invisible hand of free competition. Big firms, big unions and big government were the inescapable hallmarks of the modern age. So the maverick Conservative Harold Macmillan saw existing forms of economic organisation as 'a temporary phase in the onward march of developing social history',[18] which would, sooner or later, terminate in a planned economy. And so the Labour economist, Evan Durbin, dismissed the 'liberal' economics of Mises, Hayek and Robbins with a kind of mocking determinism. It was not, he wrote, wholly inconceivable that the politician of the future, inspired by these economists, should persuade the trade unions voluntarily to disband, and the people to accept a permanent reduction of the social services with the enthusiasm that greeted the sharp deflationary budget of 1931. It is not impossible that the British working class could be persuaded, by the compelling force of ideas, to abandon with cheerful courage the social hopes that they have entertained for generations; and thus to acquiesce in a mournful return to a world that they had left behind them for ever. It is not impossible to conceive this; but such a change is, surely, in the highest degree improbable. Social systems have rarely developed backwards.[19]

The counter-arguments which gave the New Right its victory in the struggle for intellectual and moral leadership in the late 1970s and early 1980s must be seen against this background. Their most striking feature is that they were not new at all: they consisted of more or less ingenious re-statements of very old arguments, which the rising liberal collectivists of the late nineteenth and early twentieth centuries thought they had refuted. Inequality, said the New Right, is desirable; social justice is a chimera. So are the positive freedoms embodied in social-citizenship rights and the notion of a public domain, separate from the market domain. So far from erecting boundaries between the market and other domains, market relations should be given as free a rein as possible. The invisible hand of free competition does produce opulence, state intervention in the market-place does misallocate resources and the principles that govern the finances of a private household do apply to the public finances. From this, it followed that Keynesian pump priming was inherently inflationary and state planning, even of the modest kind attempted by the governments of the 1960s and 1970s, inherently wasteful. The role of the state was to enforce contracts, to supply sound money and to ensure that market forces were not distorted. To attempt more than this was to embark on a slippery slope to inflationary crisis and collectivist oppression.

To be sure, that was only the beginning of the story. If the New Right had confined itself to a re-statement of nineteenth-century economics, no one would have listened. The originality and power of its critique of the Keynesian social-democratic system came from its politics, not from its economics. Above all, they came from its answer to the Keynesian social-democratic argument from market failure. The New Right did not, on the whole, deny that markets can fail. But it added that market failure was balanced – and more – by government failure. It followed that attempts to correct market failure through government action did more harm than good.

One reason, derived from the pessimistic Austrian anti-rationalism of Hayek, was epistemological.[20] No government or planning board, the argument ran, not even one equipped with the most sophisticated technology, can know enough to second-guess the 'spontaneous order' of the market-place. If it tries, it will fail; if it tries to compensate for its failure with further interventions (as it is inherently likely to do), it will make matters even worse. That leads on to the second reason, derived from the public-choice theorists of the so-called Virginia School. Excessive government intervention, according to this argument, is not the product of intellectual *hubris* alone. It springs from the inescapable pressures of party competition in conditions of mass democracy, and from the equally inescapable pressures of bureaucratic empire-building in the conditions created by an extended modern state. Behind all this lies the simple, not to say simplistic, premise that political processes can be reduced to economic ones: voters are like shoppers without a personal budget constraint; politicians seeking votes are like salesmen competing for custom; bureaucrats strive to maximise their bureaux as entrepreneurs strive to maximise their profits. On that key assumption rest the conclusions that politicians will always promise more than they can perform, voters will always vote for exaggerated promises, officials will ceaselessly seek to extend the scope of their activities and the extended democratic state is therefore, of necessity, a prey to self-stultifying overload.[21]

Yet even these arguments were not as new as they were sometimes thought to be. They were the latest manifestations of a long line of speculation and rhetoric, going back to the earliest apologists of the capitalist market economy and of the unconditional rights of private property.[22] The notion that markets are, in some mysterious sense, more 'spontaneous' than governments goes back to Adam Smith's famous claim that a propensity to 'truck, barter and exchange' is fundamental to human nature. The proposition that deliberate government planning cannot out-perform market spontaneity goes back to his doctrine of the invisible hand, and perhaps even to Mandeville's *Fable of the Bees*, with its sardonic claim that 'private vices' unintentionally produce 'publick benefits'. The claim that democratic party competition is bound to engender inflationary overload is a modern version of the fears that disturbed the sleep of a long line of nineteenth-century economic liberals, alarmed by the thought that a democratic suffrage would endanger the market order. On a deeper level, the assumptions behind it can be traced back to the rhetoric of the eighteenth-century Court whigs who dismissed the ideal of civic activism on the grounds that, as J. G. A. Pocock puts it, men were 'interested beings', to be policed 'by a strong central executive'.[23]

This does not prove that the arguments concerned are false, of course: old arguments may well be better than new ones. But it does raise an obvious question. Why should a set of arguments, which had seemed intellectually discredited and politically irrelevant for the first three decades after the Second World War, suddenly experience a miraculous rebirth in the fourth and fifth? Granted that the history of social thought provides plenty of examples of recycled ideas masquerading as new ones, what was it about these particular theories that made it possible to recycle them to such effect?

For many New Right sympathisers, the answer lies in a kind of inverted historicism, as deterministic as the historicism of the Keynesian social democrats and their precursors in the first part of the century. The inexorable tides of economic and social change which the Keynesian social democrats once rode, the argument runs, have changed direction. They are still there, and they are still inexorable; but they no longer run from the small to the big, from the disorganised to the organised, or from the individual to the collective. Now they run in the opposite direction. Like a de-coagulant dissolving a blood clot, the micro-electronic revolution has dissolved the great power blocks that impeded the free flow of market forces. Large organisations have broken up and social classes have merged. As a result, the state has been disempowered. For in the fluid, dynamic, rapidly-changing economy created by modern technology, the techniques of Keynesian social-democratic regulation have no purchase. Planning, corporatism, even demand management have become unnecessary, and in any case impossible. As David Howell put it during the high noon of the New Right,

> The unplanners have defeated the planners completely. There has to be less government because more government is becoming unnecessary and unworkable. The corporatists, who rested their thinking on big unionism, big government, big finance and big industry, are seeing their edifice collapse not because they have lost some temporary political power struggle (or because some other clique has won it) but because this degree of centralism has simply become outdated. The computer and micro-electronic communications disperse power and knowledge, and therefore traditional political formations, just as they disperse and alter industrial and commercial activity. So a new business landscape has emerged, and therefore a new political landscape as well.[24]

Unfortunately, there are at least two weaknesses in this answer. In the first place, its claims are too universal. The information revolution and its accompanying economic fluidity have affected the entire globe. The moral and intellectual victory of the British New Right was peculiar to Britain, or at most to the English-speaking world. If the demise of Keynesian social democracy and the rise of the New Right were the products of some inexorable technological imperative, continental Europe and Japan would have seen something similar. But although the forms of economic regulation and the rhetoric of political and intellectual leaders have changed in both, neither has experienced anything remotely comparable to the New Right ascendancy in Britain. Technological imperatives that manage to produce Margaret Thatcher in Britain, but François Mitterrand in France and Helmut Kohl in Germany, cannot be as imperious as all that.

Much the same applies to the suggestion that inexorable tides of change have disempowered the state. No one can dispute that the British state is less effective, less respected and, in important ways, less powerful today than it was in 1945. This is scarcely surprising. In 1945, it had just emerged triumphant from the most terrible test in its entire history. It had nowhere to go but down. The same is true, in varying degrees, of the other victor states of the Second World War. The Soviet Union has disappeared altogether, while the United States has suffered a decline almost as marked as that of the British state. But it is not true of the defeated states of the Second World War or, for that matter, of the other major states of western Europe. As Alan Milward has argued, the post-war history of western Europe is a history of the revival and reconstruction of the nation-state, not of its decline.[25] The German, French, Spanish and even Italian states are, by any reasonable definition, more powerful, more efficacious and more respected in the 1990s than they were in the 1940s. Indeed, most modern states have far more power over their citizens than Napoleon, Louis XIV or, for that matter,

Bismarck or Nicholas II could have dreamed of. Of course, there is much that they cannot do. In capitalist market economies, they cannot force up the long-term rate of growth by expanding demand, successfully defy the world's currency markets or make much difference to pre-tax income differentials. But they never could.

That leads on to the second weakness inherent in the New-Right world view. It purports to explain the second phase in the post-war struggle for hegemony, but it ignores the third. If it were true, there would be no cracks in the New Right's ascendancy, and no intimations of a new policy paradigm or a new ideological divide. The 1990s would be a continuation of the 1980s; the social and economic imperatives that gave the New Right hegemony in the 1970s could be relied upon to perpetuate its position into the next millennium. But, as we have seen, there are striking differences between the ideological climate of the late 1990s and that of ten years ago; that is, between Act Two of the drama and Act Three. And the transition from Act Two to Act Three is as important to the play as that from Act One to Act Two.

The key to these transitions, I shall argue, lies in a dimension which the political language of the last one hundred years does not capture. Since the late nineteenth century, it has been customary to distinguish between 'individualism' and 'collectivism' and to think in terms of transitions from one to the other. The Victorian jurist, A. V. Dicey, famously thought that the age in which he lived was dominated by a swing to collectivism, and away from the individualism of the early part of the century. More recently, W. H. Greenleaf has found the key to the British political tradition in a continuing dialectic between 'collectivism' and what he calls 'libertarianism' – essentially another word for individualism. More recently still, Robert Skidelsky has written the history of the twentieth century as a history of the rise and fall of collectivism on the one hand, and of the fall and rise of individualism on the other. Albert Hirschman's now-classic suggestion that 'involvement' swings back and forth from the public to the private sphere belongs to the same *genre*.[26]

However, despite its distinguished lineage, the distinction between individualism and collectivism is too crude to catch the full meaning of the story I have been discussing. Individualism, but for what kind of individuals? Collectivism, but for which collective goals? The abstinent, energetic, self-improving, God-fearing puritans whom Max Weber pictured as the ancestors of modern capitalism were individualists. So were (and are) the rationally-calculating utility-maximisers of Jeremy Bentham, of neo-classical economics and of the public-choice theorists of the Virginia School. But the moral and emotional meanings of these two kinds of individualism are far apart: so far, in fact, that it hinders understanding to use the same term for both. The same is true of 'collectivism'. Joseph Stalin and R. H. Tawney both held 'collectivist' values, but their conceptions of the purposes and modalities of collective action were diametrically opposed.

Plainly, no simple classification can do justice to all these nuances. Yet this does not mean that there is nothing more to be said. Cutting across the familiar distinction between collectivism and individualism is a more subtle distinction between two conceptions of the Self, of the good life and of human possibilities and purposes. On one side of the divide are those who see the Self as a static bundle of preferences, and the good life as one in which individuals pursue their own preferences without interference from others. On the other are those for whom the Self is a growing and developing moral entity, and the good life one in which individuals learn to adopt higher preferences in place of lower ones. On one side of the divide, stress is laid on satisfaction; on the other, on effort, engagement and activity. The first group is uneasy with the suggestion that some satisfactions may be morally superior to others. The second believes that it is better to be Socrates unsatisfied than a pig satisfied.

It is not easy to find labels for these two conceptions. They might be termed 'hedonist' and 'moralist', or perhaps 'passive' and 'active'. This yields a fourfold classification, in place of the simple dichotomy of individualism and collectivism. Individualism can be passive and hedonist, or active and moralist. So can collectivism. Individual liberty can be valued, in other words, because it allows individuals to satisfy freely-chosen desires, to live as they please so long as they do not prevent others from doing the same. Or it can be valued because it enables them to lead purposeful, self-reliant and strenuous lives, because it encourages them to take responsibility for their actions and, in doing so, to develop their moral potential to the full. By the same token, collective action and collective provision may be seen as instruments for maximising morally-neutral satisfaction, or as the underpinnings of personal and cultural growth, of engagement in the common life of the society and so of self-development and self-fulfilment. Anthony Crosland's collectivism was essentially passive-hedonistic. So was Nigel Lawson's individualism. Gladstone's individualism was moralist-activist, as was R. H. Tawney's collectivism.

From this perspective, the ebbs and flows in the struggle for moral and intellectual hegemony in post-war Britain acquire a much more complex significance. A stylised account of them might run like this. Instead of three Acts, the drama now contains five. In Act One, lasting from the mid-1940s to the mid-1950s, the post-war generation of Keynesian social democrats exercised moral and intellectual leadership. Their collectivism was active and moralistic. For them, rights went hand-in-hand with duties, security with activity. A just society would be a moral society – not only because its resources would be distributed fairly, but because its members would be free to lead active and fulfilling lives. Collective action and resource redistribution would rescue their beneficiaries from dependence, indignity and passivity. It would also enable them – perhaps even oblige them – to repay society for the help it had given them. An enlarged public domain held no terrors: the public domain was a place of engagement, governed by an ethic of service and commitment. Beveridge was the emblematic figure and, as Jose Harris shows in her chapter in this book, Beveridge's vision of social citizenship was quintessentially activist, drawing on a notion of civic virtue that went back to classical Greece. Social citizenship was a status, but a status that had to be earned. Its entitlements were not charitable doles granted to passive dependants, who had done nothing to help themselves. Benefits were paid out because contributions had been paid in; and Beveridge devised his system in this way because, in his own words, 'Management of one's income is an essential element of a citizen's freedom'.[27] And active citizenship was a means as well as an end. Social security had to be 'won by a democracy; it cannot be forced on a democracy or given to a democracy'.[28] The same values ran through the participatory productivism of the wartime shop stewards' movement, and inspired Stafford Cripps's conception of democratic planning as a system of moral suasion, in which 'the Government, both sides of industry and the people' worked together to achieve a common end.[29] They also underpinned Attlee's robust defence of peacetime conscription as a legitimate *quid pro quo* for the welfare state.[30]

Eventually, however, Act One gave way to Act Two. Gradually in the 1950s, and with gathering speed in the 1960s, Keynesian social democrats abandoned the austere moral activism of Attlee, Beveridge and Cripps. Keynes himself had never really shared it; though he killed himself overworking for his country, his moral vision was always suffused with the hedonistic relativism he had absorbed in the Cambridge and Bloomsbury of his youth. Later Keynesian economists saw themselves as technicians rather than moralists, or even citizens. In their eyes, their professional task was to understand the working of the economic system and to advise policy makers how to translate their preferences into action. As private individuals they might or might not make moral judgements of their own, but the realm of moral judgement and the realm of economic science were to be kept rigidly apart. What was true of post-Keynesian economic collectivism was also true, albeit for different reasons, of post-Beveridgean welfare collectivism. The notions that rights should be balanced by duties, that activity was better than dependence and the point of collective provision was to foster self-reliance and civic activism came to be seen as patronising, or elitist, or (horror of horrors) 'judgemental'. Meanwhile, the service ethic of the professional mandarinate – the twentieth-century equivalent of the 'clerisy' of the nineteenth century and, as such, the chief guardians of the moral-activist tradition – came to be seen as camouflage for illegitimate privilege.[31] On a deeper level, as Geoff Mulgan's chapter suggests, the moral and cultural presuppositions of that ethic were undermined by a loss of confidence on the part of the mandarinate itself, exacerbated by an insistent demotic relativism on the part of its critics. Among left-of-centre Keynesian social democrats, equality came to be seen as a good in itself, irrespective of the uses to which the fruits of egalitarian policies were put. Among their right-of-centre counterparts, a technocratic managerialism, in which the good life was equated with rising living standards and political leadership with the promotion of economic growth, increasingly prevailed.[32]

If the mentality of the first group was epitomised in Hugh Gaitskell's 'socialism is about equality', that of the second was summed up in Harold Macmillan's 1957 boast that the British people had 'never had it so good'. If the emblematic Keynesian social democrat of the 1940s was William Beveridge, that of the 1960s and 1970s was Anthony Crosland, with his ringing plea for an ethic of private pleasure in place of the Fabian ethic of public duty:

> We need not only higher exports and old age pensions, but more open-air cafes, brighter and gayer streets at night, later closing-hours for public houses, more local repertory

theatres, better and more hospitable hoteliers and restaurateurs, brighter and cleaner eating-houses, more riverside cafes, more pleasure gardens on the Battersea model, more murals and pictures in public places, better designs for furniture and pottery and women's clothes, statues in the centre of new housing estates, better-designed street lamps and telephone kiosks, and so on *ad infinitum* . . .

. . . To-day we are all incipient bureaucrats and practical administrators. We have all, so to speak, been trained at the L.S.E., are familiar with Blue Books and White Papers, and know our way around Whitehall . . . Now the time has come for a reaction: for a greater emphasis on private life, on freedom and dissent, on culture, beauty, leisure, and even frivolity. Total abstinence and a good filing system are not now the right sign-posts to the socialist Utopia: or, at least, if they are, some of us will fall by the wayside.[33]

Alas for riverside cafes. As Raymond Plant suggests in a later chapter, hedonistic collectivism contains a built-in flaw. By definition, the redistribution it demands makes some people better off and others worse off. Also by definition, it can offer no convincing moral argument for doing so. If rights are not balanced by duties, why should the rich make sacrifices for the poor? If collective provision is not a means to moral improvement, why should those who do not need it pay taxes to pay for it? If the public domain is not a place of engagement, governed by a service ethic, what is to prevent it from becoming a battleground for predatory vested interests? Hedonistic collectivists could not answer these questions. By the mid-1970s, Act Two was ending. It was clear that there was a moral and rhetorical vacuum at the heart of the Keynesian social-democratic system. The beginning of Act Three saw the New Right rushing in to fill it.

For the New Right attack on the Keynesian social-democratic system was moral as well as economic and political: in the last analysis, moral rather than economic or political. Market forces were better than state intervention, not just because they were more efficient, but because the market-place was quintessentially the realm of freedom, and because only free people can be moral agents. Thrift, enterprise and self-reliance were, of course, the building blocks of a prosperous economy. But that was not the chief reason for valuing them. They were also the stigmata of the 'vigorous virtues' – of virtues whose possessors were, above all, 'upright, self-sufficient, energetic, adventurous, independent-minded, loyal to friends and robust against enemies'.[34] The 'dependency culture' allegedly created by the hedonistic collectivists of the Crosland generation was condemned, not just because it ate into the public purse, but because it turned those it entrapped into 'moral cripples'.[35] 'Victorian values' were extolled, not just because they had prevailed in the days of Britain's glory, but because they were morally right. Collective action and collective provision were not only sources of inflationary overload. They were sources of moral escapism, encouraging those who took part in them to shelter from the consequences of their own actions, and so engendering a corrosive culture of guilt.[36]

But Act Three did not – could not – last. The moralistic individualism of the late 1970s and early 1980s turned out to be as fragile as the hedonistic collectivism which had preceded it. Moralistic individualists sought to resurrect the moral economy of the nineteenth century by returning to its political economy. They saw that the 'vigorous virtues' had flourished in a market economy, and they assumed that the way to reinstate them was to give freer reign to market forces. They forgot that the 'vigorous virtues' of nineteenth-century Britain had been nurtured by, and embodied in, a much older network of institutions and practices, whose origins lay far back in the pre-market past. The market economy of the nineteenth-century lived off a stock of moral capital, accumulated over long generations to which the norms of the market-place were at best alien and at worst anathema. Its apologists did not fully recognise the significance of this moral legacy. It was part of the air they breathed, and they simply took it for granted. Matters are quite different today. Today, as Mrs Thatcher and Hayek both half-recognised, a moral order capable of sustaining the vigorous virtues can no longer be taken for granted; it has to be created. But market forces cannot create it. The market is inherently amoral, antinomian, subversive of all values except the values of free exchange. In the market-place, the customer is king; and customers sooner or later get what they are prepared to pay for, irrespective of its moral quality. The New Right's moral vision was, in short, at odds with its economic vision. Act Three came to an end in the mid-1980s, with the victory of the latter over the former.

Act Four lasted from the mid-1980s until the mid-1990s. Its central theme lay in a strange mutation of policy and rhetoric, uncannily reminiscent of the mutation which had transformed the moral collectivism of the post-war period into the hedonistic collectivism of the 1960s and early 1970s. Mrs Thatcher herself continued to bang the moral-activist drum; when they remembered to, so did her ministers. But the drum-beats sounded ever-more faintly. Where early Thatcherism offered fiscal austerity, 'painful medicine' and patriotic self-sacrifice, later Thatcherism relied on easy credit, paper profits, profligate tax cuts and a consumption boom. Despite lip-service to the contrary, Alderman Roberts, with his Methodist austerities and his Grantham corner shop, ceased to be the iconic Thatcherite. He was replaced by Essex Man. Moral individualism gave way to hedonistic individualism: the vigorous virtues to the easy-going vices.

In a further twist, however, Act Four is now giving way to Act Five. Just as the hedonist-collectivist ascendancy of the 1960s and early 1970s was challenged by the moral-activist individualism of early Thatcherism, so the hedonist-individualism of late Thatcherism is now under attack from what looks suspiciously like a new kind of moral collectivism. Moral-activist drum-beats are sounding once again, but the drummers are collectivists, not individualists.

What are we to make of all this? An obvious *caveat* should be made at the outset. Ideological reductionism is as danger-ous as any other variety. My stylised account is, by definition, incomplete and over-simplified. The ideological ups and downs on which I have focused provide only part of the explanation for the political ups and downs which have accompanied them; and even the ideological ups and downs cannot be explained solely in ideological terms. Ideology is an indispensable weapon in the struggle for power, but it is not the only weapon; and even the most accomplished ideolo-gist will not get far if the structural and institutional cards are stacked against him. The arguments advanced, first by the rising liberal collectivists of the early-twentieth century, then by the rising New Right of the 1970s and now by the reborn civic activists of the 1990s have struck chords only because they have seemed to their listeners to correspond with, and to make sense of, structural changes. By the same token, the relationship between those arguments and the poli-cies followed by their proponents has been as problematic, fluctuating and confused as such relationships usually are.

That said, the arguments concerned repay study. They show, I believe, that the political culture of this country is both more complex, and less plastic, than is often imagined. The debate between what I have called 'moralists' and 'hedon-ists' – between activity and satisfaction, moral growth and utility maximisation – goes back to the dawn of the market economy, and has continued, in varying guises, ever since. To be sure, the ontological foundations of the moral-activist case have varied through time. In our day, fear of the wrath of God has been largely replaced by fear of global warming and the declining sperm count. But the continuities are as striking as the differences. Despite appearances to the con-trary – the decline of religion, the threat to the family, the spread of moral relativism, the de-legitimation of traditional elites – there is still a strong moral-activist strand in Britain's political culture. The stubborn longevity of that strand helps to explain both the triumph of Keynesian social democracy in the early post-war period, and the rise of the New Right in the late 1970s and early 1980s. It also helps to explain the disarray of the New Right today, and the tentative emergence of the new political divide I discussed earlier. For the moral activism of early Thatcherism had more in common with the moral activism of the post-war generation of Keynesian social democrats than ideologues of left or right could bring themselves to admit. In her memoirs Mrs Thatcher wrote of her upbringing: 'My "Bloomsbury" was Grantham – Methodism, the grocer's shop, Rotary and all the serious, sober virtues cultivated and esteemed in that environment'.[37] The same 'serious, sober virtues' animated the early Labour movement, haunted the pages of the Beveridge Report and shaped the culture of much of the working class. Not the least of the reasons for Mrs Thatcher's electoral success was that they gave her rhetoric a popular resonance that the hedonistic collectivists of the 1960s and 1970s could not emulate. And, to complete the story, the moral activism of the Blair generation of collectivists draws on essentially the same reservoir of virtues and traditions.

The moral activist strand in British political culture can perhaps be traced back, through the liberal collectivists of the early twentieth century, the popular radicals of the nineteenth and the Country Party of the eighteenth to the puritans of the seventeenth. But the details of its lineage need not concern us here. What matters is that the roots of the moral-activist sensibility lie deep in the history of western civilisation, in the legacy of Athens on the one hand and of Jerusalem on the other. The most striking feature of the story I have tried to tell is that in a secular, heterogeneous, supposedly multi-cultural late twentieth century society, faced with challenges almost inconceivably different from those that faced classical Greece or ancient Israel, those roots can still put forth fruit.

CHAPTER 2

Politics

Albert Hirschman

W HEN David Marquand asked me to write about the relevance to British post-war politics of two relatively recent books of mine, *Shifting Involvements* (1981) and *The Rhetoric of Reaction* (1992), I accepted rather too readily. I did have a number of points to make, or afterthoughts to formulate, about the latter book; but with respect to the former, I soon realised that some of its major propositions fitted the British case rather less well than the countries – the United States, France, and Germany – which I had primarily in mind when I wrote it. Perhaps, however, I can draw strength from this weakness: it may be of interest to present here, in a comparative vein, the quandaries and perplexities I encountered.

Let me start from the beginning. The writing of *Shifting Involvements*, so I say in my first paragraph, got underway,

    ... in June 1978 and in Paris, where a spate of articles and even books marked the tenth anniversary of the demonstrations, student uprisings, strikes and other public actions in which large masses of citizens in Western Europe, North and South America, and Japan had participated in 1968. Many commentators noted how remote this phenomenon seemed already. Indeed, the change in mood that has taken place within so short a span of time is remarkable. An important ingredient of the 'spirit of 1968' was a sudden and overwhelming concern with public issues – of war and peace, of greater equality, of participating in decision-making. This concern arose after a long period of individual economic improvement and apparent full dedication thereto on the part of large masses of people in all of the countries where these 'puzzling' outbreaks occurred. While poorly understood at the time they took place, those outbreaks are today classed as abnormal and quixotic episodes; in the course of the seventies, people returned to worry primarily about their private interests, the more so as the easy forward movement that had marked the earlier period gave place almost everywhere to uncertainty and crisis. Thus, the change from the fifties to the sixties and then to the seventies and other such alternations in earlier periods raises the question whether our societies are in some way predisposed toward oscillations between periods of intense preoccupation with public issues and almost total concentration on individual improvement and private welfare goals.

I am still rather satisfied with the way I laid out my topic in this paragraph, but upon re-reading it I immediately realised that I could never have written it in London (or Sheffield). The reason is simple: the '1968 Revolution' never took place in this country. With the exception of some minor commotions at the London School of Economics and a few anti-Vietnam War demonstrations, mostly by *American* students (such as Bill Clinton) at Oxford and Cambridge, the British student scene remained quiescent and there was no outbreak of any 'sudden and overwhelming concern with public issues'.

I am sure that this particular instance of British 'exceptionalism' has been closely studied by social scientists here. We know today that the 1968 uprisings were far less unitary than they appeared at the time and had very different specific motivations in different countries. In the United States, for example, the opposition to the Vietnam War was of course a crucial factor, whereas in Germany the students' protests were directed in part against their parents and the newly perceived responsibility of that older generation for bringing to power and supporting the Nazi regime. Nevertheless, in the background of the 1968 protests there was still a common experience: the end of the war had brought the most sustained experience on historical record of vigorous economic growth and, in particular, of the 'rise in mass consumption', so much celebrated by Walt Rostow in the fifties. This rise took place primarily in the area of durable consumer goods – automobiles, televisions, refrigerators, washing machines, and so on. In my book I argued that these famous durables have a hidden drawback: in contrast to what I called 'truly non-durables' (things such as food and fuel that actually disappear in the process of being consumed), durables are particularly good at generating waves of consumer disappointment. This view provided me with a rather novel interpretation of the events of 1968: the durables bonanza of the post-war period had exacted a delayed retribution.

Can this theory – or conjecture – be invoked to account for the 'failure' of the English students to participate in the 1968 uprisings? No doubt the growth of the English economy, while passable in the first two post-war decades, was not nearly as vigorous and sustained as in the rest of the Western world, particularly on the Continent. Could it be then that the comparatively modest expansion in the availability of durables during that period kept consumer disappointment within bounds and therefore made English society less receptive to the viruses that attacked other societies in the late sixties?

This application of my conjecture about consumer disappointment strikes me as a bit mechanical, but it does lead to a deeper question. I wonder whether British society is simply equipped with some special cultural resistance against the passion for ever more and new consumer goods that so grips other societies. Observers from the United States and the Continent have often criticised Britain or poured ridicule on it for this very reason, for its clinging, not just to traditional ways and customs, but even to traditional and 'old-fashioned' product designs, from taxis to plumbing fixtures! In *Shifting Involvements*, I pointed out at some length how Adam Smith celebrated 'opulence' and the *Wealth of Nations*, on the one hand, and denounced, on the other, in this very book and elsewhere, a whole range of consumer goods as frivolous and contemptible 'trinkets and baubles'. It looks as though this strange ambivalence is or has become a characteristic mood of the nation as a whole. In some unconscious wisdom, Britain may have acquired a resistance against the onrush of innovation, born perhaps from the hunch that various types of disappointment invariably accompany novelty.

So much for the portion of my book where I attempt to account for the movement of citizens from the pursuit of their private happiness to a sudden and intensive concern for the public interest. Let me now look at the opposite movement, the withdrawal from public affairs back to concentration on the private life and its activities. Once again, I am struck by the fact that, in this country, that movement, if it exists at all, takes a rather different shape from the one I had outlined in my book.

When I turned to the movement from the public to the private domain, one of my basic texts was Benjamin Constant's famous and luminous speech of 1820: 'De la liberté des Anciens comparée à celle des Modernes' (On the Liberty of the Ancients as Compared to that of the Moderns). Here Constant criticised Rousseau (and implicitly the French Revolution) for conceiving liberty and democracy in line with the Athenian model which was premised on the citizens' full dedication to, and participation in, public affairs. Nowadays, Constant asserted, things are very different:

> every individual is occupied by his speculations, his enterprises, and the pleasures he obtains or hopes for, so that

he wishes to be distracted from these matters only for short periods and as infrequently as possible. (Cited in *Shifting Involvements*, p. 98.)

For Constant, the basic problem of securing liberty and democracy under modern conditions lies in the tension between the desire to participate in public affairs and the pull of other affairs (or rather *affaires* – when used in French without a qualifying adjective, this term stands simply for economic interests and business operations). Constant, a perceptive observer of the contemporary French scene, saw this tension as a fact of life in post-Napoleonic France, and extrapolated this observation to 'modern society' in general. But perhaps France was actually an exception at the time: its traditional upper class, the nobility, had been decimated as a result of the Revolution, and the new ruling groups, being drawn largely from the bourgeoisie and non-aristocratic circles, may indeed have experienced the tension described by Constant. His strictures against the 'Athenian' model may apply much less to other contemporary European societies whose traditional ruling groups had not suffered any substantial depletion and displacement.

In Britain, in particular, the continuity in power of the ruling gentry was not only a fact while that country passed through *its* Revolution (I mean the Industrial one), but to assure this continuity was sensed by the gentry as both a right and even more as a *civic duty*. I am thus curious to raise the question: did any substantial voices come forward in England during the first half of the nineteenth century, to argue, like Constant did in France, that upper-class people were routinely torn between their private, commercial and money-making pursuits and their dedication to public affairs? From what little I know I doubt that this was the case. In his *English Culture and the Decline of the Industrial Spirit, 1850–1980*, the American historian Martin Wiener describes at great length the predominance of 'gentry values' throughout the

Victorian age (and beyond). The supreme value traditionally attached by the gentry to public service is impressively described by Trollope in 1864 in *Can You Forgive Her?*, the first of his Palliser novels. At the opening of a chapter he introduces Plantagenet Palliser to the reader with unusual solemnity and generality:

> Mr Palliser was one of those politicians in possessing whom England has perhaps more reason to be proud than of any other of her resources, and who, as a body, give to her that exquisite combination of conservatism and progress which is her present strength and best security for the future. He could afford to learn to be a statesman, and had the industry wanted for such training. He was born in the purple, noble himself, and heir to the highest rank as well as one of the greatest fortunes of the country, already very rich, surrounded by all the temptations of luxury and pleasure; and yet he devoted himself to work with the grinding energy of a young penniless barrister labouring for a penniless wife, and did so without any motive more selfish than that of being counted in the roll of the public servants of England. (p. 267.)

The devotion to public service is described here, with a good deal of irony, as a quirk of the upper class – but one that is presented as being quite firmly rooted just *because* it is a quirk or a 'prejudice', as Burke had put it in his *Reflections*. No trace is to be found in the novel of any concern Palliser might have over a possible neglect of business matters. Interestingly, when he is driven in the course of the plot to abandon – temporarily – his highest *public* ambition, which is to become Chancellor of the Exchequer, he does do so for a reason related to his *private* life. But this is his determination to save his marriage to Lady Glencora, rather than the pursuit of any 'base' business venture. Moreover, in the same novel, the difficult conquest of the hesitant and mercurial Alice

Vavasor by John Grey is fully accomplished only when John mentions to Alice that he too may wish to move from leading the life of a country squire to becoming a Member of Parliament (p. 795).

The counterpart to this paramount value attached by both genders of the upper strata to public service (though rendered by men only, of course) is the remarkable 'deference' to the governing class on the part of the rest of the population, as famously described around the same time by Walter Bagehot (see his Introduction to the 1872 edition of *The English Constitution*, first published in 1867).

In *Shifting Involvements* I had assembled various reasons why citizens in modern democracies often move from considerable absorption in private pursuits to throwing themselves 'body and soul' into public affairs and would then, after due disappointment with the public sphere, withdraw back to the private life. I have just shown that some major arguments for these moves – one for that from the private to the public domain and one for the opposite move – have actually not been much present in Great Britain. At the end of my book, I affirmed that the oscillations between private and public involvement have been overdone in Western societies, that these societies 'appear to to be condemned to long periods of privatisation during which they live through an impoverishing "atrophy of public meanings," followed by spasmodic outbursts of "publicness" that are hardly likely to be constructive' (p. 132). But perhaps this lament is simply not applicable to the political history of England. From the nineteenth century well into the second half of the twentieth century, this country was indeed widely considered a model of political stability, particularly in comparison to the major countries on the Continent.

The sudden outbreak of 'Thatcherism' in the not so recent past actually suggests a very different explanation: Britain may have overdone its vaunted stability. Perhaps as a result of the enormous effort furnished in the Second World War, there emerged a remarkable post-war consensus on economic and social policy based on the combined legacy and the enormous intellectual influence of Keynes and Beveridge. Eventually the consensus received a name: 'Butskellism' – a clever, slightly mocking term intimating that there was no real, deep difference any more that was separating the policy makers of the two principal parties, R. A. Butler and Hugh Gaitskell. But this convergence had a real cost which consisted in the *loss of politics as 'spectacle'* (if I may use a category whose importance has been stressed by the anthropologist Clifford Geertz). Just because of the 'deference' factor, politics had long been of considerable value in England as a spectacle. Coming on top of the loss of Empire which was another splendid spectacle – quite apart from its profitability, so long debated by economists – these losses were perhaps too much to bear: eventually they ushered into 'Thatcherism', a new spectacle of highly partisan, 'creedal' (to use Samuel Huntington's recent term), and ideology-driven politics.

Let me now briefly turn to my other, more recent book, *The Rhetoric of Reaction*. This book received its initial impetus from the appearance of a new kind of ideology-driven politics on the *American* scene in the 1980s. My reaction to the Reagan era and to its intellectual spokesmen was an attempt to present and dissect the key, invariant, and archetypal arguments used by conservatives and 'neo-conservatives' in their advocacies and polemics. The original intent of this procedure was of course to expose and mock the repetitive and simplistic nature of conservative positions. But a side-effect was to strip the basic arguments of the reactionaries – the arguments of perversity, futility, and jeopardy – down to so transparent a form that I became aware of their structural similarity to the principal arguments used, with the same monotony and exaggerations, by their traditional adversaries, the 'progressives'.

I have recently recounted how this extension of my argument to the 'progressive' side came to me as an unintended

– and originally somewhat embarrassing – afterthought. But later on I saw that afterthought as a windfall as it gave me the chance to formulate some propositions about the desirable shape of the progressive argument in the post-Reagan-Bush and post-Cold-War era. Perhaps these propositions have also some relevance for this country in its post-Thatcherite phase. (The following paragraphs are largely taken from my article 'The Rhetoric of Reaction – Two Years Later', *Government and Opposition*, 28, 3, Summer 1993, pp 310–14.)

The three archetypal reactionary positions I identify are:

- the perversity thesis, whereby any action to improve the political, social or economic order is alleged to result in the exact opposite of what is intended;
- the futility thesis, which holds that attempts at social transformation will produce no effect whatsoever and will be incapable of making a dent in the status quo; and
- the jeopardy thesis, which holds that the cost of a proposed reform is unacceptable because it will endanger previous, hard-won accomplishments.

The arguments which I then show to be progressive counterparts or equivalents of the 'reactionary' perversity, futility and jeopardy theses are essentially the following:

- We should adopt a certain reform or policy because as things are we are caught, or will shortly land in, a *desperate predicament* that makes immediate action imperative regardless of the consequences. This argument attempts to deflect the perversity thesis.
- We should adopt a certain reform or policy because such is the 'law' or 'tide' of history – this argument is the counterpart of the futility thesis, according to which attempts at change will come to naught because of various 'iron laws'.

• We should adopt a certain reform or policy because it will *solidify* earlier accomplishments – this is the progressive's retort to the jeopardy claim that the reform is bound to wreck some earlier progress.

How difficult would it be for reformers to give up this kind of rhetoric, which tends to turn the debate with their opponents into a 'dialogue of the deaf'? I believe I have just listed the arguments in decreasing order of dispensability.

The most dispensable of the three arguments is, to my mind, the alarmist claim that disaster is upon us if we fail to take this or that progressive step. This way of arguing might be called 'impending-disaster' or 'impending-revolution' blackmail. It has been a common way for various Western progressives or reformers to present their programmes, particularly since 1917, when the threat of social revolution re-appeared on the horizon of Western societies. An important variant of this way of arguing became current after the Second World War in discussions on aid for the countries of the Third World: here the disaster to be fought off – by extending generous financial aid – was revolution and the prospect of these countries being 'lost' to the Soviet zone of influence.

For some time, these ways of arguing for national or international redistribution of income have been stale from overuse. Since the events of 1989–91, they have become largely unusable as a result of the collapse of communism and the Soviet Union. As Gunnar Myrdal argued long ago, progressives can and should make a convincing case for the policies they advocate on the grounds that they are *right* and *just*, rather than by alleging that they are needed to stave off some impending imaginary disaster.

What about the argument that a certain progressive policy should be adopted because to do otherwise would be to oppose the 'tide' of history, the 'wave of the future', a futile position? This argument should also not be too difficult to discard, in part, I will admit, because, with the recent upheavals and *pace* Fukuyama, the tide of history appears to run quite strongly against the tide-of-history view of things!

Things are rather different in the case of another typical 'progressive' argument which I implicitly ask my progressive friends to use sparingly. It is the argument that a proposed reform is not only compatible with previous progressive achievements, but will actually strengthen them and will be strengthened by them. Progressives will often argue that 'all good things go together' or that there is no conceivable area of conflict between two desirable objectives (e.g. 'the choice between environmental protection and economic growth is a false one'). In itself, this is an attractive and seemingly innocuous way of arguing and my advice to reformers cannot be never to use this argument. Given their considerable interest in arguing along mutual support, rather than jeopardy lines, reformers may actually come upon, and will obviously then want to invoke, various obvious and non-obvious reasons why 'synergy' between two reforms exists or can be expected to come into being.

My point is rather that reformers should not leave it to their opponents, but should *themselves* make an effort to explore also the opposite possibility: that of some conflict or friction existing or arising between a proposed and a past reform or between two currently proposed programmes. If reformers fail to look in this direction and, in general, are not prepared to entertain the notion that any reform is likely to have some costs, then they will be ill-equipped for useful discussions with their conservative opponents.

For example, it would be disingenuous to pretend that stimulating economic growth and correcting or attenuating inequalities that arise in the course of growth require exactly the same policies. The problem rather consists in finding an optimal combination of policies that does as little damage as possible to either objective. We are more likely to find something close to this optimum if we admit from the outset that we are in the presence of two objectives between which there exists normally a good deal of tension and conflict.

CHAPTER 3

The Fall of Keynesianism

A Historian's View

Robert Skidelsky

I

The 1950s and 1960s were a capitalist golden age, even in slow-growing Britain. By historical standards, unemployment was exceptionally low, growth in real incomes exceptionally fast, economies exceptionally stable; all were achieved at a very modest cost in inflation. Although there were some sceptical voices, the consensus at the time was that this achievement was produced by something called 'Keynesianism'. In the 1970s, the golden age was replaced by a silver age of 'slumpflation', in which growth rates halved and unemployment and inflation increased simultaneously. By the end of the decade a consensus had emerged that this sorry record, too, was the result of 'Keynesianism', and the 1980s were aggressively anti-Keynesian.

Today Keynesianism is dead as policy. Most governments have inflation, not employment, targets; belief in discretionary management of the macro-economy has all but vanished. For Britain, the crucial stages in the demise of Keynesian policy can be traced in the speech of James Callaghan to the Labour Party conference in 1976, Nigel Lawson's Mais lecture of 1984, and the 1985 White Paper, *Employment: The*

Challenge to the Nation.[1] Keynesian economics, of course, continues to exist in the sense that macroeconomics is still taught to all economics students, and even monetarism can be regarded as a dissident branch of Keynesianism.[2] Moreover, the re-emergence of mass unemployment in the 1980s has stimulated a 'new Keynesian' research programme aiming to show rigorously how wage and price rigidities – central but unexplained features of the original Keynesian model – arise from the microeconomics of wage and price setting in imperfect markets.[3] However, belief in the Keynesian model of the economy, as opposed to use of Keynes's analytical framework, is confined to a minority of economists.

The problem here is to explain the 'fall of Keynesianism'. There is no doubt that Keynesianism was engulfed in what Albert Hirschman calls a 'rhetoric of reaction' and savaged in the name of futility, perversity and jeopardy.[4] The point of interest is how far this rhetoric was simply rhetorical, and how far it pointed out 'real' failures in Keynesianism. Rhetoric is the art of persuading by language rather than by argument or proofs: one can write better than one thinks. But is the central monetarist proposition that 'Changes in nominal variables have no real effects' simply a piece of rhetoric? (It is, of course, a classic example of what Hirschman calls the 'futility thesis'.) According to Donald McCloskey, economics is so impregnated with rhetoric that it makes little sense to ask which economic propositions are rhetorical and which, in some sense, are true.[5] But this begs the question of why some kinds of rhetoric flourish at some times and decay at others, or why one should prefer one kind of rhetoric to another.

I want to explore the idea that Keynesianism was undermined by real failures and not just by rhetoric. If we take Keynesianism, minimally, to be a set of ideas and policies, we have three possible sources for its failure. The first is that it misdiagnosed the causes of the social ills (such as unemployment) it set out to cure and therefore its remedies were mischievous and, in fact, created other problems (such as inflation). A sub-issue here is the extent to which Keynesian ideas, as generally accepted, were the ideas of Keynes. Secondly, one might argue that the Keynesian revolution was wrecked by policy mistakes. The ideas were right, and might have been applied with success, but in fact were not. Between the idea and the policy something intervened (such as the political process) which ensured that the idea was so badly applied that it did more harm than good. An important issue here concerns the value of ideas the fulfilment of whose promise depends on perfect application. Finally, it might be argued that the ideas and policies were right for their times, but were made obsolete by a change in the facts. In practice, these explanations are very hard to disentangle. In economic models, most of the facts a historian might wish to explain are taken as given – technically they are exogenous variables. And so it is with the typically named OPEC oil price 'shock' of 1973–4, which supposedly brought the Keynesian age to an end. But though this event, which represented a real change in the 'state of the world', was unpredicted, it was not uncaused, and part of the cause may have been the way economies were run in the 'Keynesian' age. Unexpected events are often no more than the unexpected consequences of policy decisions.

In the following section I offer some hypotheses which might explain the downfall of Keynesianism. I then test them informally by means of an opinionated history, and end with some concluding reflections.

II

Keynes himself seemed to pre-empt one answer to the question of what caused his revolution to fail when he remarked, famously, that ideas are more powerful than vested interests and strongly implied that in economics, as in all sciences, newer ideas are likely to be truer than older ones (the pro-gressive credo).[6] Both Keynesian and anti-Keynesian econom-ists have taken him at his word, the Keynesians attributing the defeat of the 'classical' system to flaws in its reasoning corrected by Keynes, and anti-Keynesians explaining the 'fall' of Keynesian ideas by flaws in Keynesian reasoning corrected by Friedman and others.

Milton Friedman says that Keynes was a great economist: he asked the right questions, but the answers he gave were wrong – they did not stand up against evidence and experi-ence.[7]Friedman's own inter-linked investigations of the con-sumption and 'demand for money' functions convinced him that economies were much more stable than Keynes believed. The severity of the Great Depression, then, was wholly the result of policy mistakes, avoidable on existing theory. There was no need for a 'Keynesian revolution'. Similarly, Harry Johnson argues that it was not wrong theory, but wrong policy, which produced Britain's mass unemployment in the 1920s.[8] More fundamentally, Hayek argues that the whole of macroeconomics was a wrong turning, made possible by Cambridge's ignorance of Austrian capital theory.[9]

The consequence of flaws in Keynes's reasoning was that the Keynesian age inevitably generated accelerating inflation, as indeed Jacob Viner predicted it would in his review of the *General Theory*.[10] The Keynesian doctors treated economies for the supposed diseases of deflation and unemployment, and this inevitably produced inflation and overfull employment. Notice that it is being assumed in all this that the *policies* pursued by governments in the Keynesian age were a more-or-less accurate application of Keynesian ideas. Ideas do not cause inflation, policies do.

The question of Keynes's relationship to the Keynesians was interestingly raised by Terence Hutchison.[11] One impor-tant contention of those who wish to defend Keynes from the Keynesians is that Keynes's *General Theory* could be made to point both ways – against inflation as well as against unemployment. John Hicks was the first to say that within the *General Theory* there were a number of possible models of the economy.[12] The implication of this line of argument is that, had he lived, Keynes would have become a 'monetarist'. That Keynes would not have been an orthodox Keynesian is as indisputable as it is banal. It is a characteristic of great thinkers – Freud and Marx are other obvious examples – that they cripple the creativity of their followers, followership being precisely the state of accepting the authority of the Master religiously, rather than rationally.

Those who argue that the Keynesian revolution was ruined by policy mistakes do not deny that ideas influence policy. But they claim that they do so mainly in their rhetorical aspect. Policy is not theory-based. Politicians use ideas as weapons – to promote their interests and legitimise their policies. This is probably the view of the role of economic ideas most widely held by political scientists and historians, reinforced by their typically poor opinion of economics as a science.

It is a short step from such arguments to the notion that ideas are simply covers for 'vested interests' – a view which Keynes explicitly rejected. Marxists have argued that Keynes's ideas were taken up because they served the interests of the bourgeoisie in the 1930s, and were dropped when they started to endanger capitalist profits in the 1970s. Friedman and Hayek, Marxists say, became popular in the 1980s because they legitimised the recreation of a 'reserve army' of the unemployed.

The main thrust of this kind of argument is to rob ideas of the sovereignty Keynes gave them. Policy will only coincidentally be appropriate to the situation – when the self-interest of politicians coincides with the 'needs' of the economy. The politically-generated business cycle is said to be a classic example of the misuse of Keynesian ideas by politicians.[13] The public-choice theorists of the Virginia School have tried to demonstrate rigorously that the incentives facing politicians and bureaucrats will cause them to run budget deficits. Once deficits have been legitimised for certain purposes they will be used for any purpose.[14]

Keynesian economists have often complained that their advice was not followed, or was followed in such a politically-distorted way as to saddle them (and more generally Keynesianism) with the odium of failure. In the 1960s it was easy for the right-wing press to caricature the Hungarian-born Nicholas Kaldor as the itinerant economist whose tax-reform proposals in developing countries brought 'revolution, inflation and toppling governments'.[15] The much more serious claim is that Keynes and the Keynesians were politically naive. Interventionist ideas were bound to be misused. Classical economics, based on the idea of a self-correcting market, discouraged political intervention in economic life. Keynes's theory, by postulating an extreme instability of unmanaged economies, removed all inhibitions to intervention. From this point of view, Keynes's cures for relatively minor diseases opened the floodgates to the politicisation of the economy. An important element in the reaction against Keynesianism was the demand for fixed rules to replace discretionary policies.

The idea that it was exogenous events which brought about the downfall of the Keynesian revolution comes in at least three versions. Keynes said that the test of a good model is that it should be 'relevant to the contemporary world'.[16] It should be able to explain the 'facts of interest' at a particular time. Because these facts change, models must change with the facts. In the 1930s the problem was unemployment; from the 1960s it was inflation. But Keynesians remained trapped in the depression economics of Keynes. The *General Theory* has a theory of prices (chapter 19). But its central reasoning was not about inflation, and it was vague about the relationship between prices and output needed for a modern theory of inflation. In this view, post-war inflation is held to have occurred independently of Keynesian ideas or policies; the

Keynesian failure was a failure to adapt the Keynesian model to the new world.

It may also be argued that the world has changed in such a way as to render Keynesian *policy* inoperative even though Keynesian *theory* retains some validity. For example, neither expectations nor institutions may now be capable of supporting a Keynesian policy; a more dispersed, de-regulated, economy may be inherently more difficult to manage. However, it may be asked whether these changes in expectations and structures were really independent of ideas and policies. Sir Alan Walters wonders 'whether the economists or the economies have become less Keynesian and more monetarist'.[17] This notion, that economies may have become more monetarist, reflects the impact of the rational-expectations revolution. Expectations about the effects of policy are formed from the experience of policy. If economies became more monetarist, in the sense that agents came to expect that injections of extra spending would raise prices rather than output *and acted accordingly*, this was because of their experience of the effects of Keynesian policies. However, there is another possibility, which is that anti-Keynesian expectations were at least partly formed by the 'rhetoric of reaction' itself.

Finally, it may be argued that the long upswing of the 1950s and 1960s and the slowdown which followed were not policy-induced at all, but were different phases of the 'Kondratieff cycle' first observed in the nineteenth century. Keynesianism was unjustly credited with the upswing and unjustly blamed for the downswing. Economists and politicians fiddled away: Rome prospered or burnt despite their best efforts.

Every historian knows that ideas, policies, and events form complex explanatory wholes. It would be naive to look for a single explanation for the demise of Keynesianism. The historical record may throw some light on the relationships between the explanatory variables and the extent to which one or other dominated at any single time.

III

The most basic, but also least tractable, question is: to what extent was the 'golden age' of the 1950s and 1960s the fruit of recognisably 'Keynesian' ideas and policies? Angus Maddison can do no better than to say that it 'was due in considerable measure to enlightened policy, but it was helped by temporarily favourable opportunities for fast growth and modest inflation'.[18] The field of enquiry can be narrowed by concentrating on the British experience, leaving aside for the moment the question of international factors.

Keynesianism was a collection of ideas, policies, and institutions designed to maintain full employment. In Britain, the Employment White Paper of 1944 committed governments to a 'high and stable level of employment'. (Similarly, the 1946 Employment Act in the USA pledged the Federal government to use all its 'plans, functions, and resources' to maintain 'maximum employment, production, and purchasing power'.) Full employment became a goal, says Herbert Stein, because it had become a fact in the war.[19] I doubt if this is true: there was full employment in the First World War too, but no full employment goal after it. The goal was not the product of full employment, or even the wishes of the electorate, but of governments' belief that they knew how to get full employment and how to maintain it. This was the result of the Keynesian revolution.

This is not to deny the importance of political factors. The Keynesian policy of full employment was adopted by the two leading capitalist victors, the United States and Britain, in order to put capitalism in a stronger position to withstand revolutionary assaults, both domestic and international. In Britain, the full employment commitment was part of an implicit social contract by which the state undertook to compensate the civilian population for its wartime sacrifices. Keynesianism was also a way of being left-wing without being socialist, and of purging Conservatism from its association with inter-war unemployment. It 'became the flag around which everyone could rally'.[20] It relegated disputes between planners and anti-planners, businessmen and socialists to the background. In liberated Europe, Keynesianism was seen as a way of re-legitimating the state.[21] Keynesianism, together with the associated commitment to welfare and a mixed economy of public and private sectors, became the basis of a new 'consensus'. So the important political function of Keynesian ideas must not be neglected. The question is whether these ideas had much effect on economic performance.

After the war, Britain's Labour government initially favoured planning sectors of supply (through a licensing or rationing system) to planning components of demand. Supply-side planning more obviously pointed to public ownership. Socialists like Dalton (Britain's first post-war Chancellor), Durbin and Gaitskell were hostile to Keynes's social values. 'Durbin recognised that Keynesian policies alone would lead to a continuation of the system of private enterprise . . .'[22] However, there was some scope for reconciliation. On the one hand, demand management could be made the instrument of redistributive goals which socialists favoured, while reducing the need for extensive nationalisation. On the other side, the socialised public utilities offered increased scope for controlling aggregate investment. On this basis, a deal could be struck. Powerful anti-planning arguments were provided by the economists Denis Robertson and, intermittently, Hubert Henderson, who both spoke for Keynes's values, if not his theory, as did Hayek in his influential book, *The Road to Serfdom*.

However, the crucial factor facilitating acceptance of Keynesianism was the need to contain inflationary pressures. Here was a paradox. The Keynesian commitment of the mid-1940s was directed to saving the world from another slump. Keynesian policy was actually adopted to control the post-war boom. The technique adopted was fiscal Keynesianism.

Not only had it proved itself in the war, but the Treasury wanted to keep interest rates low to borrow more cheaply. The situation called for budget surpluses, not deficits. Thus Keynesian calculation emerged as an instrument of financial orthodoxy.

This is the plausible story told by Jim Tomlinson. As he tells it, the budget of November 1947 marked a shift within the government from the use of controls to fiscal policy and Harold Wilson began his 'bonfire of controls' in 1948. A full employment target of 3 per cent was officially announced in 1951, mainly, it seems, to encourage the United States and other countries to follow suit so as to ensure a high demand for British exports. On the other hand, a basic problem had already emerged with using the public sector as an instrument of short-term demand management, because of its disruptive effect on public sector investment programmes. This pointed to reinserting monetary policy into the armoury of instruments available to balance the economy. 'The kind of macro-economic management that began to emerge in the late 1940s, and was to dominate the 1950s and 1960s, owed little to the devices suggested in 1944. It focused on budgetary and, to a lesser extent, monetary policy, within an overall framework of buoyant private expenditure and budget surpluses.'[23]

However, this cannot be quite right. Although British budgets were always in surplus 'above the line' from 1947 onwards, loan-financed capital spending by public authorities was much greater than it had been before the war. There was a positive borrowing requirement (budget deficit) right through the Keynesian age (except for the years 1969–70) which tended to expand with time.[24] It is at least arguable that the net impact of fiscal policy during the 'golden age' was somewhat inflationary. However, the more substantial charge is not that public spending policies produced inflationary pressures in the golden age, but that Keynesian policy-makers, over-anxious about the dangers of depression, took the build-up of these pressures too lightly.

The Conservatives, who held power from 1951 to 1964, had their own political agenda, notably cutting taxes. This meant making more use of monetary policy as an instrument of short-term demand management. More importantly, demand-management under the Conservatives was directed towards maintaining the sterling-dollar exchange rate at $2.80 at all costs, and ensuring the re-election of Conservative governments. Both aims made their policies seem perverse from a 'Keynesian' perspective, without however threatening the maintenance of full employment. From the mid-1950s onwards, maintaining the value (and it was thought the world position) of sterling in face of low productivity growth and wage inflation required subjecting the British economy to frequent 'stops' in order to protect the balance of payments from the tendency to import too much at full employment. The Conservative penchant for depressing and stimulating the economy at the 'wrong' times led to them being credited with inventing the 'political business cycle'. 'Stop-Go' or 'fine-tuning' the economy may be seen as a specific British contribution to Keynesianism arising from the economic characteristics of a declining economy, the tightness of the political battle between Conservative and Labour, and the ability of the British Prime Minister to fix, within broad limits, the date of the next general election.

Although 'stop-go' policies were attacked for destabilising the economy, they did not destabilise it by much, and unemployment never exceeded 3 per cent over the whole Conservative period. This employment record was not the result of national full employment *policy* but of a global private investment boom which swept up the 'free world' in a cumulative wave of prosperity. In other words, those historians are right who claim that the 'golden age' was the product of world conditions, from which most national economies benefited, irrespective of whether their governments were imbued with Keynesian ideas or pursued Keynesian policies. (The German, French and Japanese economies were not managed according to Keynesian principles, even rhetorically.)

To this there may seem to be one important qualification. Most governments in the post-war era spent about 10 per cent more of their national incomes than they had before the war – 35 per cent, rather than 25 per cent. This probably had an important effect in steadying economic activity over the cycle; or, to put it another way, making the cycle much shallower than it would otherwise have been. But although the higher level of government spending may have had Keynesian effects, it was not undertaken for Keynesian reasons, reflecting rather the state of international relations (arms spending) and the establishment of 'welfare states' in post-war capitalist countries.

'International conditions' is an omnibus term, made up of a 'conjuncture' of market opportunities, policies and institutions. The crucial conditions for the long private investment boom seem to have been reconstruction needs, opportunities for technological catch-up with the United States, availability of cheap labour and energy, and the policies of military spending and trade and payments liberalisation associated with the *Pax Americana*. The war had also bequeathed a set of transnational institutions (the International Monetary Fund, the World Bank and GATT) designed to reconcile the national pursuit of full employment with free trade and stable exchange rates. The central idea inspiring the Bretton Woods system, as it was known, was that full employment should be secured by national policy; its achievement would make it safe to liberalise trade and payments.

Or at least this was the British view, as argued by Keynes. It was never so clear that it was the American view. The Americans attached much more importance to trade liberalisation as the *engine*, and not just the consequence, of full employment and prosperity, and were able to impose their views on a reluctant Britain and western Europe. They looked to trade expansion rather than government spending to keep demand buoyant; this was also the economic philosophy that inspired the Common Market, which was established in 1958. Trade liberalisation was a policy decision, but it had nothing as such to do with Keynes or Keynesianism. The historical comparison is with the Cobden treaties, which helped produce a similar 'golden age' in the mid-nineteenth century.

A key question we would now want to ask about the 'golden age' is why, until about 1968, there was a lack of serious wage inflation. The answer that is most consistent with the story told above falls into three parts. First, a high rate of real economic growth allowed the demand for rising real incomes to be satisfied out of productivity gains. Secondly, the adoption of mass-production technology allowed the labour market to be balanced without upsetting the 'modest traditional pay relativities between industries, and between skilled and unskilled workers'.[25] Finally, working class incomes were still very lightly taxed, so that increases in negotiated pay were reflected in increases in take-home pay. These factors account for the moderate wage behaviour, which in turn smoothed growth. All this started to change in the 1960s.

Nevertheless, inflationary pressure was building up right through the golden age. With hindsight, it would now be widely argued that financial policy should have been used more aggressively against inflation, with labour market reforms being used to keep down the 'natural' rate of unemployment. 1957 marked one turning point in British history, when the Treasury ministers Peter Thorneycroft, Nigel Birch and Enoch Powell lost the battle to rein in public spending; 1955 had been another, when prime minister Anthony Eden fail to win Cabinet support to curb trade union power.[26] But at the time, such ideas were instincts or prejudices, which got no support from the economic theory or consensual politics of the day. As Enoch Powell said:

'we were ... monetarists ... pre-Friedman'.[27]

During the golden age, mainstream Keynesian economics became 'normal' science, with a 'research programme' based on the core Keynesian assumption that the unmanaged working of capitalist economies generated insufficient levels of demand to maintain full employment. It failed to develop the key concepts necessary to cope with, much less avert, inflation.

Keynes had seemingly left an upside-down universe – a 'general theory' of employment, without money and prices. This was not, in fact, true of the *General Theory of Employment, Interest, and Money*. But it was the emphasis Keynes gave to his theory in the circumstances of the 1930s, which was inherited, with far less justification, by his disciples in the 1950s and 1960s. To compress a complicated story: what Joan Robinson called 'bastard Keynesianism' resulted from a peace treaty between Keynesian and anti-Keynesian economists – called the neo-classical synthesis – by which the anti-Keynesians (mainly Americans) accepted the possibility of short-period 'underemployment equilibrium' in return for Keynesian acceptance that downwardly rigid money wages were the necessary and sufficient condition of it. Thus the *General Theory* turned out to be a 'special case' of the classical theory after all, but with important implications for policy. A world in which money wages are rigid and business confidence is variable is still a world which requires Keynesian therapy. However, this 'treaty', which confirmed the relevance of Keynesianism as policy while leaving it bereft of any micro-theoretical underpinnings, depended to a large extent on fears of a renewed depression.[28]

The income-expenditure model was the main Keynesian policy construction. With wages and prices fixed, together with the capital stock, wealth and the state of expectations, the model exhibited a simple dependence of output and employment on expenditure. Further, the analysis readily lent itself to quantification and thus macroeconomic modelling, so that the task of securing the desired level of output and employment was made to seem deceptively easy. 'Quantities adjust, not prices' was the flag under which the early Keynesians sailed. This left them without an economic theory of inflation or, indeed, a tenable definition of full employment. There were, in the argot, no 'supply constraints'.

In place of an inflation theory there was an empirical observation dating from 1958, the Phillips curve, which showed a stable inverse relationship between the level of unemployment and the rate of change of money wages: a lower level of unemployment brings about a higher rate of increase of money wages, and vice versa. Policy-makers thus supposedly had a 'menu of choice' between degrees of inflation and of unemployment. The message of the Phillips curve for most British Keynesians was clear. Since it was considered immoral to run the country with a 'higher margin of unused capacity', the government should maintain unemployment as close as possible to zero, and use an incomes policy to control wage costs, either in agreement with the trade unions or by legislation. Wage-push at full exployment rather than excess demand was identified as the cause of inflation. The refusal of Keynesians to take supply constraints seriously left them with cost control as their only weapon against inflation. But this begged the question of how much power a government had, or should have, in a free society.[29]

It was left to Milton Friedman of Chicago University to restate the 'classical' theory of inflation – the quantity theory of money. As we have seen, Friedman's work on the consumption function (one of Keynes's own building blocks) had led him to believe that the 'demand for money', and therefore economic activity, was much more stable than Keynes had assumed. This meant that for most circumstances the quantity theory of money was a good predictor of inflation. Friedman's policy rule was to ensure just enough money in the economy to finance what the economy was capable of producing: the unfettered forces of productivity and thrift would maintain a high level of activity. It could be argued that this was the 'right kind of theory' for the world of the 1950s and 1960s, just as Keynes's had been for the world of the 1920s and 1930s.

Friedman's decisive amendment to the dominant Keynesian orthodoxy came in 1967, with his concept of the 'natural' rate of unemployment. His central idea was that in the long-run, labour markets clear at an institutionally-determined unemployment rate, and that any attempt, by expanding money demand, to maintain the actual unemployment rate below this 'natural' rate will lead only to accelerating inflation.[30] The seeds of this are to be found in Keynes's own distinction in chapter two of the *General Theory* between 'voluntary' and 'involuntary' unemployment and his chapter nineteen on prices. Broadly speaking, Keynes defined full employment as the maximum that could be reached by expansionary measures. If one tried to lower unemployment beyond this, one would run into inflationary problems.

Friedman's much sharper concept of the 'natural' rate of unemployment provided a theoretical explanation of the tendency for inflation to increase: governments had been trying to hold actual unemployment below its 'natural' rate by expanding the money supply too much. He added one argument, known in the literature as the theory of adaptive expectations. The employment-creating effects of expansionary policy depend on 'money illusion' – on employed workers not pressing for money wage increases to compensate them for higher prices. But once inflation is expected, money illusion disappears. The employment effects of expansionary policy become increasingly temporary, the price effects increasingly permanent.

It has to be said that there was nothing in this which could not have been developed from the *General Theory*, had Keynesian economists been minded to do so. In fact, it was a fervent Keynesian, Abba Lerner, who developed a distinction between 'high' and 'low' full employment in 1951, high full employment leading to demand-pull inflation, low full employment keeping prices stable, and intermediate levels creating cost-push inflation.[31] However, even though British unemployment for most of the golden age was less than 2 per cent, mainstream Keynesians denied the existence of demand-pull inflation, rejected the distinction between 'high' and 'low' full employment, and simply said that cost-push inflation should be prevented by controlling incomes. The point is that Keynesian theory might have been refashioned and extended to suit post-war problems, but Keynesian orthodoxy stood in the way. Keynesian economists, therefore, cannot simply blame their defeats on policy mistakes or unexpected events. Politicians no doubt wished to maintain the high levels of full employment achieved in the 1950s and 1960s. There was little in the theory they were being supplied with to tell them that this might be impossible in a free society. By the 1960s, Keynesian beliefs were held religiously, and Friedman was branded as the Antichrist.

In the 1960s, British economic policy was set to target not inflation but growth, a growth target of 4 per cent a year for five years being announced in 1961. The object of policy became to make the economy grow faster than it had in the 1950s. David Marquand has called this a shift from arms' length to hands-on Keynesianism.[32] But to what extent did it reflect Keynesian analysis or prescription? The answer is far from clear. On the one hand, 'growthmanship' was a political decision reflecting the view of virtually the whole of the British ruling class that Britain was 'falling behind' the more successful capitalist economies like Germany and France. For the Labour Party, which took power in 1964, the fear was that slow growth would endanger the achievement of its welfare objectives within the framework of consensual politics; that is, one that vetoed higher taxes to finance higher welfare spending. 'Economic growth sets the pace at which Labour can build the fair and just society we want to see . . .'[33] An important background factor was the (unjustified) fear that

Western capitalism was falling behind Soviet communism. Also, there was a general fear that the spontaneous sources of post-war growth were drying up – echoing, perhaps, Keynes's forecast of 'secular stagnation'. But how far was the growth strategy the product of specific Keynesian analysis and recommendation?

Orthodox Keynesians argued that growth was demand-constrained. There were two versions of this view, one emphasising the balance of payment constraint on export demand, the other the effects of 'stop-go' policies on investment demand. The remedy for the first was devaluation; for the second the long-term 'planning' of demand, in which devaluation might also figure. Kaldor's growth model, by contrast, emphasised the supply constraints on faster growth. It was not just a matter of making demand grow faster or more smoothly, but of ensuring an appropriate supply response. Kaldor believed that the main engine of growth was growth in manufacturing output. This was because of the existence of increasing returns to scale in manufacturing industry, and because output per man was higher in manufacturing than in agriculture or services. The growth of manufacturing output in turn depended on the growth of employment in manufacturing industry. But Britain had no 'surplus' supplies of labour to transfer from agriculture to manufacturing: it was suffering from 'premature maturity'. The next best thing was to transfer labour from services to manufacturing by taxing service employment more heavily than manufacturing employment.[34] The 'Keynesian' analysis found more favour with the Conservatives, the 'structural' analysis with Labour, and particularly with Labour's Prime Minister, Harold Wilson, who was a devotee of Soviet planning. The core proposition, however, which emerged from both sets of argument, was that there were no supply constraints on the growth of the British economy that could not be overcome by policy. In particular, the idea that productivity growth was a function of output growth suggested that, despite an acute labour shortage, a planned expansion of output would carry few inflationary risks, especially if an incomes policy were used to restrain wage costs.

An 'indicative' planning system was set up by Selwyn Lloyd in 1961, strengthened by the Labour government's National Plan published in 1965. In fact, as we know, the planning period, which lasted from 1961–9, brought no increase in the national growth rate. The only things which 'grew' faster were the rate of inflation and public spending. In fact, it was in the 'planning' period that both took off, setting macroeconomic policy a much more difficult task in the 1970s. The economists, of course, claimed that their policies were misapplied: in particular, they blame Wilson's 'political' decision not to devalue the pound on winning office in 1964. This view is hard to sustain. In retrospect, Wilson's decision to stop the 'dash for growth' represents the last serious, though only partially successful, attempt for ten years to control inflation; his effort to curb trade union power in 1969 foreshadowed the eventually successful efforts of Margaret Thatcher. Wilson was not really a Keynesian. He understood that the main problems of the British economy lay on the supply-side, though his vision was clouded by his commitment to planning. By contrast, Keynesian economists of this period suffered from considerable *hubris*. They made unwarranted claims to theoretical and practical knowledge. Specifically, the claim that productivity growth depends on output growth is true only up to a certain point and in particular industries. Only in the Communist economies could such a claim be tested to destruction.

It is hard to divide responsibility for policy failures in the 1960s between the economists and the politicians. Policy was more theoretically-based in the 1960s than in the 1950s, largely because the Left was mostly in power – not just in Britain – and was less sceptical of theory than the Right. But both economists and politicians were relentlessly activist. This was an almost universal mindset. Politicians wanted to do too much; but they were encouraged to do so by the Keynesian advisers. Their policies were badly conceived; but they got bad advice.

However, although Britain may have suffered somewhat from its hyperactive policy-makers in the 1960s, the fate of the 'golden age' was being settled elsewhere. It was the inflationary financing of the Vietnam war, coming on top of the Kennedy–Johnson tax cuts and social spending programmes of 1963–5, which made inflation a serious world problem, and led to a destabilising sequence of events in which macroeconomic policy was called on to play a much more central – and exposed – role. Once inflationary expectations got established, policy-makers faced a rapidly worsening trade-off between inflation and unemployment. It was no longer a matter of keeping a light hand on the tiller. Policy-makers found they needed to swerve the tiller violently from one side to another, aiming first to halt the rise in inflation, then to halt the growth in unemployment. The increasing violence of these policy 'U-turns' contributed to the slowdown in economic growth and the tendency for structural unemployment (or the 'natural' rate) to rise from cycle to cycle, which made the old full employment commitment increasingly problematic.

The full force of these problems hit the Conservative government of Edward Heath, newly elected in 1970. Heath inherited not just the Wilson, but, more importantly, the Nixon 'Stop' of 1969–70. When British unemployment reached the 'magic' figure of one million in January 1972, he decided to reflate the economy in order to reduce it by 400,000 in twelve months. This was a political decision. The Chief Adviser to the Treasury, Sir Donald MacDougall, told him that 'the attempt to reduce unemployment so quickly would be dangerous because it would lead to inflationary shortages and bottlenecks' – a sound Keynesian warning, but by now inadequate to the total situation.[35] Nevertheless, tax cuts and spending increases went ahead in Barber's 1972 budget. At the same time, the decision was taken to withdraw the pound sterling from the European 'snake' and abolish credit controls. The Bank of England's idea was to allow interest rates rather than quantitative credit restrictions to control the volume of private borrowing. The problem was that politicians then blocked the rise in interest rates. So a private sector boom was superimposed on the public sector boom. The money supply rose by 25 per cent in 1972-3, and although unemployment came down by 400,000 (in two years) the inflation rate rose from 6 per cent a year in 1972 to 13 per cent a year later.[36] The whole episode is a good example of the interaction between technical and political mismanagement. The Keynesian economists gave politicians lame advice. The Bank of England concocted a policy which presumed that the market would be allowed to set interest rates. All this was before the OPEC oil price shock.

The analytical weakness of Keynesian economics at this point was that it could offer no theoretical explanation of the acceleration of inflation between 1968 and 1973. The worldwide explosion of the money supply was attributed to monopoly pricing by labour unions and firms rather than to the financial policy of government. It was considered sufficient refutation of Keynes's own view that, at full employment, a further increase in the quantity of money is inflationary, to point out that employment was no longer full – or at least as full as it had been in the 1950s and 1960s. This ignored Keynes's own distinction between 'voluntary' and 'involuntary' unemployment, as well as Friedman's much sharper concept of the 'natural' rate of unemployment. Ironically, the Barber boom of 1972-3 was the first and last attempt to use full-blooded Keynesian policy to maintain what was then regarded as full employment. When it failed – and when the quadrupling of oil prices gave another savage twist to the inflationary spiral – all governments, including Britain's, started to give priority to inflation reduction. Rhetorically, as well as analytically, they needed monetarism.

On 22 July 1976, the Bank of England publicly announced the adoption of money-supply targets, though it had already started using them. Fiscal policy needed to be made consistent with the goal of reducing the rate of growth in the money supply. In 1976, public expenditure started to be 'cash limited' and for the first time since the Second World War was cut during a major recession. In October 1976, James Callaghan made a speech at the Labour Party conference announcing that the government no longer believed Britain could 'spend its way' back to full employment. This is widely taken to be the year when 'monetarism' was adopted and the Keynesian full employment commitment abandoned. In fact, the situation was more complicated. The reason given for the public expenditure cuts was to 'free' resources for export and private investment as the only means of 'restoring and maintaining full employment'. This was consistent with a 'Keynesian' analysis of Britain's problem, such as had been presented by Bacon and Eltis.[37] What the Labour government retreated from was the commitment to maintain 'high' full employment, accepting that in the 1970s Britain was already in a state of 'Keynesian full employment'. Finally, an incomes policy was used until 1979 alongside monetary targeting, as part of the inflation-reduction strategy. The reluctance to put the whole burden of the fight against inflation on monetary policy reflects both a vestigial political commitment to full employment and an analytic commitment to the cost-push theory of inflation. It was the collapse of incomes policy in the 'winter of discontent' in 1978–9, leading to the election of the much more ideologically intransigent Conservative Party under Mrs Thatcher, which finally put policy Keynesianism to sleep. But not too much should be ascribed to parochial British ideology, since the demise of policy Keynesianism proved to be worldwide.

IV

A number of conclusions emerge from this, admittedly opinionated, survey. The most important is that Keynesian economics failed to renew itself intellectually during the golden age. It was therefore assaulted from outside and was severely damaged in the process. Friedman's quantity theory of money approach fitted the emerging 'stagflationary' data better than the standard Keynesian models that predicted a stable 'trade-off' between inflation and unemployment. Specifically, his theory of 'adaptive expectations' explained why successive attempts to stimulate the economy had decreasing effects on output and increasing effects on prices, even with quite high unemployment.

Friedmanism was not formally inconsistent with the *General Theory*. Keynes agreed that the quantity theory of money is valid at full employment. Friedman's 'natural rate of unemployment' was an analytically more precise analogue of Keynes's 'voluntary' unemployment. Keynes did not highlight these aspects of his 'general' theory because he did not require them to explain the depression of the 1930s. Friedman's monetarism is thus not the logical opposite of Keynes's *General Theory*, but of his 'special theory', developed to explain the Great Depression of the 1930s, in which interest rates are ruled by liquidity-preference and investment demand is interest-inelastic. Hicks's 'generalised' statement of the *General Theory* retains its value as providing a logical way of thinking about a variety of macroeconomic situations. Had it been interpreted in this way from the start, the Keynesian-Monetarist controversy might have produced less heat and more light.

Though both the Keynes and Friedman 'special cases' can be subsumed in a more 'general theory', there is a different feel to them, which reflects differing political and social values, and different assumptions about the political process.

Keynes's 'special case' implied the perversity of markets and the benevolence of governments; Friedman's, the benevolence of markets, and the perversity of governments. Keynes's quantity adjustment mechanism was designed to establish the case for discretionary government interventions to maintain full employment; Friedman's assumption of self-adjustment at full employment was designed to get the government out of economic life. Friedman attributes this difference of approach to the fact that Keynes grew up in an aristocratic society with a strong tradition of public service, whereas he grew up in America where it was assumed that the political process would be dominated by political and bureaucratic self-interest.[38] But other characteristics of the situation in which the two economists found themselves were very different. Keynes was diagnosing, and prescribing for, the ills of a *laissez-faire* economy; Friedman for the ills of a state-managed economy. The behavioural patterns – the virtues and vices – of the two kinds of system are likely to be very different; it was only natural that the two economists should over-emphasise the vices of the system they knew, and exaggerate the virtues of the system they proposed. There are evidently long swings between collectivism and individualism, into which both the Keynesian revolution and the monetarist counter-revolution can be slotted.

The second major conclusion, which follows from the above discussion, is that Keynesian economics cannot be absolved from responsibility for the failures of government policy. The crude monetarist view that Keynesianism 'caused' inflation cannot be sustained. But it failed to develop an adequate theory of inflation, which might have helped governments combat it at an earlier stage, and with far less cost. The view prevailed in the 1960s that anything could be managed or fixed with the existing tools. The *hubristic* mood of the Keynesian economics profession is captured in Paul Samuelson's testimony before a Congressional Committee in 1961: a community could have 'full employment and absence of demand inflation, at a rate of capital formation it wants ... with the degree of income distribution it desires'.[39] A starker invitation to activist politicians to mismanage the economy can scarcely be imagined. It may be said that politicians choose the advisers to give them the advice they want to hear. But choice requires competition: if all the advisers are saying the same thing, it requires extraordinarily strong political nerves to go against it. A breakdown in the conventional wisdom in economics was thus a necessary condition for a shift in economic policy.

At the same time, certain features of policy, decided on non-technical grounds, made Keynesianism more difficult to operate and undermined support for it among the business and financial community. As a social philosophy, Keynesianism represented a delicate balance between capital and labour. Maintaining demand at a high level would give businessmen the confidence to invest, and guarantee labour against the heavy unemployment of the inter-war years. Moderate collectivism was traded off against greater collectivism. (A similar implicit social contract underpinned the welfare state: the wealthier classes would pay for most of it but would be entitled to its benefits.) The shift to a more collectivist politics in the 1960s and 1970s made Keynesianism increasingly controversial. It started to be associated with a growing share of national income spent by the state, growing public sector deficits, an increasing tax burden, and attempts to control supply through planning of production and incomes. Such policies, arguably, also made the market system work less well, thus creating reasons for ever more extensive interventions. At some point Keynesianism lost its political function of preserving freedom, and came to be widely seen as an agent of creeping socialism. It stopped being able to do political work.[40]

The relationship between these political/theoretical swings and changes in the structure of economies remains obscure. To what extent were the changes in cost structures which undermined the profitability of large sections of manufacturing industry in the early 1970s caused by excess demand? It is difficult to say. What is probable is that they precipitated the microelectronic revolution which brought to an end the 'Fordist' era of mass production and undermined the autonomy of national economic policy. These developments enormously strengthened the power of international capital. In the 1980s, governments lost their ability to 'choose' their national technologies and national rates of inflation, growth, employment, taxation. In short-run perspective, the shift to monetarism is best seen as the adaptation of theory and policy to the new facts. In the long run, these facts were, at least in part, brought about by the ideas and policies which dominated the Keynesian age.

Thus it is much too simple to see the fall of Keynesianism simply as a triumph of a reactionary rhetoric. The rhetoric was the result of real failures in policy and ideas, and real changes in economic structures. If 'new Keynesian' ideas are to play a part in shaping the policies of the future they will do so in a very different world and intellectual climate from those which gave birth to the Keynesian revolution.

CHAPTER 4

The Keynesian Consensus and its Enemies

The Argument over Macroeconomic Policy in Britain since the Second World War.

Peter Clarke

UNTIL THE Second World War, no government professed to have a macroeconomic policy. The concept simply did not exist. To be sure, governments had long been held responsible, in a general way, for the health of the economy and it is obvious that 'hard times' hurt the party in power. This helped to bring the heavens down on the Conservative Government in the General Election of 1880, serving as the electoral meteorology behind the rain-dance performed with such ostentation by Gladstone in his Midlothian campaign. Conversely, an uncovenanted upturn in the export trade apparently vindicated the Free Trade case in the 1906 General Election and made Joseph Chamberlain's prescient warnings about manufacturing decline look like empty scaremongering. The arguments over the Gold Standard in the 1920s were, to our eyes, unmistakably about macroeconomic issues; in this sense, the advocates of sound money, with their theory of a self-equilibrating system that was therefore 'knave-proof', were simply blinded by their own ideology to the actual consequences of what they were doing – Keynes's point, of course, in his public criticism of the return to Gold in 1925. Indeed this controversial decision inaugurated, under the prompting of continuing unemployment, a continuing debate – concerned in many different ways with the economic role of the state – which was macroeconomic *avant la lettre*.[1]

It seems that we owe the actual term 'macroeconomic' to P. De Wolff, in an article published in 1941 in the *Economic Journal* (of which Keynes was still editor). De Wolff built upon an earlier differentiation between micro-dynamic and macro-dynamic analysis and, according to the *New Palgrave*, was 'quite clear about the distinction between micro- and macroeconomics', one being valid 'for a single person or family', the other 'for a large group of persons or families'.[2] But while this is pointing in the right direction, it fails to capture the essential definition of macroeconomics as the study of the system as a whole, not simply of one sector, however great in magnitude, nor of any sub-set of economic agents, however numerous.

This distinction is in fact made much more clearly by Keynes himself, who inescapably bulks large in any discussion of macroeconomic policy. So far as I am aware, he never used the expression macroeconomics (or microeconomics) in any of his writings, though he must surely have become aware of its growing usage in the five years before his death. Look in the index of his collected writings and there is only a hop, skip and a jump from Macmillan Committee ('*see* Finance and Industry') to Magicians ('Newton, the last of the'). Yet, like M. Jourdain, Keynes's prose was unimpaired by his lack of the right word. Book Two of the *General Theory*, concerned with 'Definitions and Ideas', leads up to a clinching assertion, in its final sentence, of 'the vital difference between the theory of the economic behaviour of the aggregate and the theory of the behaviour of the individual unit.'[3]

Indeed in the preface to the French edition, Keynes tried

to pretend that this was why he had termed it 'a *general* theory. I mean by this that I am chiefly concerned with the behaviour of the economic system as a whole – with aggregate incomes, aggregate profits, aggregate output, aggregate employment, aggregate investment, aggregate saving – rather than with the incomes, profits, output, employment, investment and saving of particular industries, firms or individuals.'[4] It was this determination to seize on the aggregate dimension – not just as an analytical issue but also as a policy tool – which makes the early history of macroeconomic policy in Britain so largely synonymous with the history of Keynesianism.

Keynesian macroeconomic theory may have been devised at the bottom of a slump, but it was symmetrical in its policy implications, as its author explicitly affirmed. 'The best we can hope to achieve is to use those kinds of investment which it is relatively easy to plan as a make-weight, bringing them in so as to preserve as much stability of aggregate investment as we can manage at the right and appropriate level,' he wrote in 1937, at the peak of British economic recovery. 'Just as it was advisable for the Government to incur debt during the slump,' he argued, 'so for the same reasons it is now advisable that they should incline to the opposite policy.'[5] The irony in the administrative reception of Keynesianism is that it was 'the opposite policy' which prevailed during the 1940s. For it is now clear that the concepts of the *General Theory* were first operationalised within the administrative community in a way which spoke to the macroeconomic issue raised by the Second World War: how to control inflation.

For present purposes, it is not the administrative but the ideological impact of Keynesianism which is the focus – by ideological, I mean the social or political purchase of Keynes's ideas, or ideas attributed to him, in a particular historical argument. Since we are concerned with 'actually existing Keynesianism', it should come as no surprise to discover that ideological distortions of Keynes's original intentions were a price that had to be paid for the influence of the doctrine.[6] What I have to say here bears less upon the policy-making process, on which there is now a fine scholarly literature, than upon the justifying rhetoric in which the central ideas were couched.

I shall take a number of representative texts in the political discussion of Keynesianism and macroeconomic policy over a period of forty years, and quote them, sometimes extensively, in order to capture and illustrate strategies of argument, rather than to assess their objective validity. It will become clear that this discourse cannot simply be characterised as a conflict between progressive and conservative positions. Indeed, if the rhetoric which helped justify the post-war consensus arguably held its own nemesis, through being pitched in an over-confident and triumphalist register, such characteristics were often echoed, or even amplified, in the anti-Keynesian rhetoric which ultimately displaced it. Progressive illusions, imputing boundless competence to projects for reform, may have a timeless element, as may a conservative wisdom, tempering enthusiasm with wholesome pragmatism. The story of the rise and fall of Keynesianism in post-war Britain however, hardly suggests that one side had a monopoly on illusions and the other on wisdom.

The ideological impact of Keynesianism makes a more straightforward, less ironical story than that of its administrative reception. The enemy here was clearly unemployment rather than inflation. It was unemployment, rhetorically termed 'Idleness', which had a star billing in the Beveridge Report as one of 'five giants on the road of reconstruction', along with 'Want, Disease, Ignorance and Squalor'.[7] Beveridge reached for no elevated soubriquet to characterise inflation, which retained its lower-case pygmy status throughout his Report. Conversely, 'Want' could not be slain without first dealing with 'Idleness'. Progressive reforms marched together in a happy example of mutual support – what Hirschman identifies as 'synergy'.[8] Beveridge needed to banish mass unemployment in order to make his grand vision of social insurance viable. Hence the third assumption of the Beveridge Plan, that full employment would be maintained. True, the actuarial premise here was for an overall level of unemployment up to 8.5 per cent, which was soon to seem an unacceptably high, rather than a desirably low figure. What was required, the Report explained, was 'not the abolition of all unemployment, but the abolition of mass unemployment and of unemployment prolonged year after year for the same individual.'[9]

Beveridge adduced five reasons for this contention. One was that cash payments, while suitable for tiding workers over, would, in the longer term, have a demoralising effect. Another was that it became impossible to test unemployment by an offer of work if there were no work to offer. The availability of work, moreover, actively drew in people who would otherwise lapse into debility. These three reasons were concerned with the working of a social insurance scheme, showing its administrative inter-dependence with a buoyant labour market. 'Fourth, and most important,' Beveridge continued, 'income security which is all that can be given by social insurance is so inadequate a provision for human happiness that to put it forward by itself as a sole or principal measure of reconstruction hardly seems worth doing.' Participation in productive employment, he suggested, was a great end in itself; the ethic of work thus provided a higher symbiosis between reforms which tackled the linked evils of unemployment and poverty. Finally, Beveridge pointed to the heavy cost of his Plan, warning that 'if to the necessary cost waste is added, it may become insupportable.' For unemployment simultaneously increased claims while depleting available resources[10]

Beveridge himself soon became converted to the practicability of reducing unemployment below 3 per cent. It was this more ambitious target which defined 'full employment' in the debates of 1944, as against 'the maintenance of a high and stable level of employment after the war' which was what the Coalition Government's White Paper more prudently promised.[11] Either way, it was unemployment which was at the centre of the arguments.

The White Paper began by clearly identifying mass unemployment as a macroeconomic problem, for which the Government now accepted responsibility. True, many caveats followed. Nigel Lawson, as Chancellor of the Exchequer more than forty years on, mischievously strung some of them together in an address to economists. Not only (so he found in paragraph 56) would it be 'a disaster if the intention of the Government to maintain total expenditure were interpreted as exonerating the citizen from the duty of fending for himself', but he was able to seize upon the remarkable comment in paragraph 74 that: 'None of the main proposals contained in this Paper involves deliberate planning for a deficit in the National Budget in years of sub-normal trade activity.'[12] The provenance of the document is thus evident, as a compromise achieved through committee work. Hence paragraph 66 upholds the 'notion of pressing forward quickly with public expenditure when incomes were falling and the outlook was dark' despite the 'strong resistance from persons who are accustomed, with good reason, to conduct their private affairs according to the very opposite principle'.[13] Yet this counter-cyclical fiscal doctrine is promptly undercut by the wholly inconsistent paragraph 74, in which Lawson took comfort.

The fact is that everything else in the White Paper is by way of qualification to its central claim. Lawson knew this perfectly well in 1987, just as Keynes did in 1944, when he wrote that it was 'the general line and purpose of policy' that mattered at this stage. 'The object of the White Paper,' he affirmed, 'is to choose the pattern of our future policy.'[14] This it did, most prominently in the foreword: 'A country will not suffer from mass unemployment so long as the total demand for its goods and services is maintained at a high level.'[15] That this claim was founded on a Keynesian multiplier analysis was later made explicit.[16]

The policy to be followed included not only strictly Keynesian measures for the counter-cyclical regulation of public investment, but also parallel measures, chiefly due to Meade, for controlling swings in consumption expenditure by varying the rates of social insurance contributions. 'The ideal to be aimed at is some corrective influence which would come into play automatically – on the analogy of a thermostatic control – in accordance with rules determined in advance and well understood by the public.'[17] The analogy chosen here may seem banal and commonplace to us but must have inspired mixed feelings in the chilly British homes of an era of open fires and fuel rationing.

The general tone of the White Paper, however, is authentically that of the 1940s and did not, despite claims by some subsequent historians, hold out easy promises of a 'New Jerusalem':

> It cannot be expected that the public, after years of wartime restrictions, will find these proposals altogether palatable; and the Government have no intention of maintaining wartime restrictions for restriction's sake. But they are resolved that, so long as supplies are abnormally short, the most urgent needs shall be met first. Without some of the existing controls this could not be achieved; prices would rise and the limited supplies would go, not to those whose need was greatest, but to those able to pay the highest price. The Government are confident that the public will continue to give, for as long as is necessary, the same wholehearted support to the policy of 'fair shares' that it has given in war-time.[18]

This kind of language made an obvious appeal to the political left. This was congruent with the way that the case for macroeconomic regulation of the economy was commonly meshed into a debate about planning, the buzz-word of the 1940s. It was under this guise that Keynesianism was assimilated to conventional arguments for socialism. When John Parker was commissioned by Penguin to put the Labour case in a book published in 1947, he struck this chord in the chapter called 'A Planned Economy':

> At the back of the minds of all those who have been through the two wars is the fear of a fresh slump and of widespread unemployment. The effect of Lord Keynes' teaching and of wartime experience has been the creation of a very widespread belief in Britain that unemployment can be practically prevented by the full development of a planned economy. Booms and slumps, it is hoped, can be ironed out if a deliberate attempt is made to do so.[19]

The fact is that planning had become an essentially contested term, a Humpty-Dumpty word which was invested with glosses appropriate to the arguments in which it was currently imbricated. 'Am I a planner?' asked James Meade in 1948:

> If a planner necessarily believes in a quantitative programme of output, employment and sales for particular industries, occupations and markets and the exercise of such direct controls by the State as are necessary to carry this out, I am certainly no planner. If an anti-planner necessarily denies that the State should so influence the workings of the price mechanism that certain major objectives of full employment, stability, equity, freedom and the like are achieved, then I am a planner.[20]

This was consistent with Meade's advocacy since 1945, as head of the economic section, of the combined use of both planning and the price mechanism: a distinction between liberal (macroeconomic) and socialist (microeconomic) planning with which Sir Alec Cairncross has made us familiar.[21]

One obvious feature of the claims for post-war macroeconomic management is the claim to novelty. This even bursts through the staid prose of the White Paper: 'The Government are prepared to accept in future the responsibility for taking action at the earliest possible stage to arrest a threatened slump. This involves a new approach and a new responsibility for the State.'[22] Here was an explicit contrast with the old belief that trade depression automatically brought its own corrective. 'In these matters,' it was proclaimed, 'we shall be pioneers.'[23]

The peroration to the White Paper sets its economic aspirations within a political framework: 'The Government believe that, once the war has been won, we can make a fresh approach, with better chances of success than ever before, to the task of maintaining a high and stable level of employment without sacrificing the essential liberties of a free society.'[24] So far, so uplifting. The implicit objection here, of course, was that mounted in its classic form by F. A. Hayek's *Road to Serfdom*. As Hirschman has shown, Hayek's critique of the welfare state can be seen as an example of the argument that such a proposal, far from achieving the best, would actually *jeopardize* the good.[25] As such it is essentially political, asserting the incompatibility of regulation with liberty. The sort of planning associated with full-employment policies was equally his target: indeed more so, since he seized on the essentially macroeconomic nature of the project to bring out its danger.

Many separate plans do not make a planned whole – in fact, as the planners ought to be the first to admit – they may be worse than no plan. But the democratic legislature will long hesitate to relinquish the decisions on really vital issues, and so long as it does so it makes it impossible for anyone else to provide the comprehensive plan. Yet agreement that planning is necessary, together with the

inability of democratic assemblies to produce a plan, will
evoke stronger and stronger demands that the government
or some single individual should be given powers to act
on their own responsibility. The belief is becoming more
and more widespread that, if things are to get done, the
responsible authorities must be freed from the fetters of
democratic procedure.[26]

This gave the special reason – though of course there were
many others – 'why "liberal socialism" as most people in
the Western world imagine it is purely theoretical, while the
practice of socialism is everywhere totalitarian'.[27] The support
of the Labour Party for planning was not wholly surprising,
but Hayek hinted at the futility as well as the jeopardy which
lay in train: 'It is one of the saddest spectacles of our time to
see a great democratic movement support a policy which must
lead to the destruction of democracy and which meanwhile
can benefit only a minority of the masses who support it.'[28]
Such arguments entered into post-war Conservative propa-
ganda, albeit often in a watered-down form.[29]

If Hayek's political argument against Keynesianism was
much the same as his argument against the welfare state,
and was unsurprisingly directed against broadly the same
opponents, it should likewise be unsurprising that this famous
economist also mounted a specifically economic argument. In
its weak form this rested on the futility of trying to buck the
market; in its strong form, which should not be overlooked, it
pointed to perverse effects. Hayek contested Keynes head-on,
asserting a dichotomous view of the available economic
strategies:

Both competition and central direction become poor and
inefficient tools if they are incomplete; they are alternative
principles used to solve the same problem, and a mixture
of the two means that neither will really work and that

the result will be worse than if either system had been consistently relied upon.[30]

Keynes took issue with this view, in the course of an otherwise highly emollient private response to Hayek: 'I should say that what we want is not no planning, or even less planning, indeed I should say that we almost certainly want more.'[31] He remained wholly unmoved by Hayek's fundamental economic contention that this sort of planning was dysfunctional, whereas for Hayek a nightmare scenario was already foretold: 'if we are determined not to allow unemployment at any price, and are not willing to use coercion, we shall be driven to all sorts of desperate expedients, none of which can bring any lasting relief and all of which will seriously interfere with the most productive use of our resources.' The prospect was of 'an inflationary expansion on such a scale that the disturbances, hardships, and injustices caused would be much greater than those to be cured'.[32]

What is plainly disclosed, of course, as these spiralling counter-effects progressively cancel the early gains, is an economic situation worse than the problems which these naive expedients were designed to remedy in the first place:

There will always be a possible maximum of employment in the short run which can be achieved by giving all people employment where they happen to be and which can be achieved by monetary expansion. But not only can this maximum be maintained solely by progressive inflationary expansion and with the effect of holding up those redistributions of labour between industries made necessary by the changed circumstances, and which so long as workmen are free to choose their jobs will always come about only with some delays and thereby cause some unemployment: to aim always at the maximum of employment achievable by monetary means is a policy which is certain in the end to defeat its own purpose. It tends to lower the productivity of labour and thereby constantly increases the proportion of the working population which can be kept employed at present wages only by artificial means.[33]

Here is a different case from the political argument with which the polemical author of *The Road to Serfdom* is generally identified: a case, however, which is easily assimilated with the rest of the *oeuvre* of the great apostle of economic liberalism. Hayek's distinctive doctrinaire approach has often been contrasted with the abhorrence of rationalism which is to be found in writers like Oakeshott. Yet there is another face to Hayek's argument which is far more conservative than liberal in its justification of 'men's submission to the impersonal forces of the market' – the more so when this was justified by an appeal to such forces as superstition. Such a commendation of conservative instincts appealed to a deeper rationale than vulgar rationalism. 'It may indeed be the case that infinitely more intelligence on the part of everybody would be needed than anybody now possesses, if we were even merely to maintain our present complex civilisation without anybody having to do things of which he does not comprehend the necessity', Hayek enjoined. 'The refusal to yield to forces which we neither understand nor can recognise as the conscious decisions of an intelligent being is the product of an incomplete and therefore erroneous rationalism.'[34]

It was Keynes, not Hayek, who captured the ear of the opinion-forming elite in post-war Britain. In particular, the canonical status of the *General Theory* was now assured, as much by vague invocation as by specific citation. The White Paper went as far as was decent in making this plain:

the Government recognise that they are entering a field where theory can be applied to practical issues with confidence and certainty only as experience accumulates and experiment extends over untried ground. Not long ago, the ideas embodied in the present proposals were unfamiliar to the general public and the subject of controversy among economists. To-day, the conception of an expansionist economy and the broad principles governing its growth are widely accepted by men of affairs as well as by technical experts in all the great industrial countries.[35]

In the two post-war books commissioned by Penguin from Labour and Conservative spokesmen, giving their cases access to a mass paperback market, there are differences of emphaisis, as one would expect. Thus Quintin Hogg's account is imbued with caution:

> Unemployment can temporarily be mitigated, and perhaps eliminated in a country, notwithstanding its international character, by government action which artificially increases demand in any way. This, however, means to some extent adopting a closed economy which, internationally speaking, is anti-social, and may involve the assumption of dictatorial powers. Moreover, unless the demand is carefully selected this palliative cannot last long. It cannot in any event last indefinitely unless ultimately world conditions improve.[36]

Conversely, in John Parker's account there was a residual flavour of socialist scepticism about relying on market mechanisms – 'since it must be remembered that in one sense labour is always being "directed" by the demands of consumers' – to achieve what Cripps was now terming 'democratic' planning, as distinct from the 'totalitarian' kind.[37]

Yet Hogg's and Parker's accounts of the 1930s are on broadly similar lines. A wrong-headed approach, it was held, had been adopted in meeting the 1931 crisis; but this could be extenuated and excused in the absence of a fully articulated Keynesian agenda. According to Quintin Hogg, it was not really a partisan matter – 'The Labour Government are not to be blamed for not following this course' – and instead he cited the Keynesian claim, 'with which I, as a Conservative, agree, that given low rates of interest, high wages, and adequate social security (for this is what redistribution means) this terrible scourge can again be relegated to the category of minor nuisances and we shall be free to face the real problem of civilisation – the lifting of humanity out of the primeval slime'.[38]

Writing in the *New Fabian Essays*, five years later, John Strachey appealed to the post-war experience of both Britain and the USA to show how a democratic government could raise the standard of life – provided it had not only the will but also the expertise. 'The government of the left when installed must know how to give effect to the push of the democratic forces,' he wrote, mindful of the historical contrast with Leon Blum in France and Ramsay MacDonald in Britain. 'The techniques for making an economic system work at full power – granted one has the will to do so – were in fact only worked out in the nineteen-thirties. The elucidations of the late Lord Keynes have in this respect played a genuine historical role.'[39]

What were these much-lauded techniques? Keynes himself had a long-standing record of wishing to regulate investment so as to make full use of resources, and in the *General Theory* he accordingly suggested 'a somewhat comprehensive socialisation of investment'. The post-war nationalisation measures in Britain, however, hardly fulfilled his criteria of controlling the overall volume of investment, whether public or private – 'it is not the ownership of the instruments of production which it is important for the State to assume'.[40] Nonetheless, Labour appealed to a synergy between its nationalisation programme and a full-employment policy, under the elastic rubric of planning. They had seen the future – and it worked. Thus, looking back on the record of the Attlee Government in 1952, Austen Albu could claim that, insofar as the rationale for the nationalisation programme had lain here, it had achieved its objective: 'The dominating motive in 1945 of planning for full employment has been satisfied with only one-fifth of industry nationalised, and there is a growing view that, in so far as internal conditions are concerned, this can be continued.'[41]

In regulating the level of effective demand Keynes's instincts were always to concentrate on investment. Practically all that the *General Theory* said about consumption was: 'The State will have to exercise a guiding influence on the propensity to consume partly through its scheme of taxation, partly by fixing the rate of interest, and partly, perhaps, in other ways.'[42] Under the Labour Government, there was a commitment to macroeconomic management of the level of demand through fiscal policy, supplemented by the use of direct controls to keep inflationary pressure in check. This is how Sir Stafford Cripps explained the matter in his Budget speech of 1950: 'Excessive demand produces inflation and inadequate demand results in deflation. The fiscal policy of the Government is the most important single instrument for maintaining that balance.'[43]

By contrast, the use of monetary policy as an economic regulator smacked of the bad old deflationary days of the Gold Standard, and was abjured by Labour. In taking this line Dalton could initially claim both theoretical and practical endorsement from Keynes. Keynes repeatedly stressed the desirability of bringing down the rate to a low *and stable* level (in this sense 'fixing' the rate). Keynes's often-quoted notion of bringing about 'the euthanasia of the rentier'[44] made a natural appeal to Labour supporters, not least Dalton himself. But although the Bank of England's discount rate remained fixed at the level of only 2 per cent until the Labour Government lost office at the end of 1951, it is now clear that Gaitskell as Chancellor was ready in principle to use monetary policy in support of budgetary policy – a case which his revisionist supporter Crosland was to elaborate in *The Future of Socialism* (1956).[45]

It was in the *New Fabian Essays* (1952) that Crosland

broached his fairly complacent assessment of the post-capitalist nature of contemporary Britain:

> The trend of employment is towards a high level, and a recurrence of chronic mass unemployment is most unlikely. The Keynesian techniques are now well understood, and there is no reason to fear a repetition of the New Deal experience of a government with the will to spend its way out of a recession, but frustrated in doing so by faulty knowledge. The political pressure for full employment is stronger than ever before; the experience of the inter-war years bit so deeply into the political psychology of the nation that full employment, if threatened, would always constitute the dominant issue at any election, and no right-wing party could now survive a year in office if it permitted the figures of unemployment which were previously quite normal.[46]

Such confidence – hubris is another word – had not grown overnight. At the end of the war there had been a general expectation that the post–1945 experience would parallel that of post–1918: a couple of years inflationary boom, with a slump around the corner. This fear was implicit in the 1944 White Paper. It was a prospect which, as John Parker reported, 'most British socialists believe to be inevitable, although they are not agreed on the date when the slump is likely to arrive, nor what course it is likely to follow.'[47] True, Dalton's Budget speech in April 1947 said that inflation rather than deflation was now the immediate danger. Yet Meade, writing in 1948, when inflation was already at the front of his own mind, prefaced his arguments with the comment: 'We are all agreed that measures must be taken to stimulate total monetary demand and to prevent it from falling below the level necessary to sustain a high output and high employment when the time next comes – as sooner or later it assuredly will come – when a deficient total demand threatens to engulf us in a major depression.'[48]

It was only from 1951 that a wholly different assumption about the nature of the economic problem supplied a new context for all these arguments. This occurred initially in the context of a rearmament programme which injected a huge boost of demand into the economy; as a proportion of GNP, defence spending rose by 3.5 per cent in three years while the budget surplus was cut by nearly 5 per cent between 1951–4.[49] Little wonder that economists – *a fortiori* the Keynesian revisionists represented in *New Fabian Essays* – stopped worrying about a slump. Even so, Strachey still qualified his judgement that, in most major respects, 'our economy is exhibiting behaviour quite different from that which it exhibited during the whole of the inter-war period' with the proviso that 'it may be argued that it is as yet too early to claim that we have succeeded in eliminating trade depressions'.[50] But although it may have been judged premature to dismiss any possibility of a slump, *fear* of a slump had nonetheless disappeared because the weapons now existed to fight it – even if there should prove to be insufficient cleverness in anticipating and obviating it. The old-fashioned capitalist misery had been abolished, perhaps capitalism too. 'It is now quite clear that capitalism has not the strength to resist the process of metamorphosis into a qualitatively different kind of society' was how Crosland put it, and a further conclusion naturally followed: 'Such an economy is far more likely to give rise to chronic inflation than chronic deflation.'[51]

Out of the frying pan into the fire? Not a bit of it! Strachey peremptorily refused to admit that 'the unmistakable fact that a full employment economy generates powerful inflationary forces is a fatal defect: it is a bias in the new system which must be identified and vigorously counteracted. But granted that it is done, there is nothing fatal about it.'[52] If the great locomotive of economic expansion had exceeded expectations about the horsepower it was capable of sustaining, this was simply a condition to which its suitably skilled driver would have to adapt: 'The habitual posture of the Chancellor of the Exchequer in a full employment economy will be that of a man pulling and hauling with might and main at the brake levers of the economy. It will not be a very popular or comfortable posture. But what of it? It is his job!'[53]

The steam-Keynesianism of the Labour revisionists was superseded by a fittingly privatised image from the impresario of Conservative Keynesianism in the 1950s, Harold Macmillan: 'The real truth is that both a brake and an accelerator are essential for a motor car; their use is a matter of judgement but their purpose must remain essentially the same – to go forward safely; or, in economic terms, expansion in a balanced economy.'[54] The main difference in demand management under the Conservatives was the reinforcement of fiscal fine tuning with a monetary policy that now used interest-rate changes to the same ends. Here was the optimistic vision of progress in controlling and regulating the macroeconomic forces which could maintain full employment while keeping inflation in check. Stop-go, of course, was one name for this kind of economic policy; and 'Butskellism' for the political consensus which underpinned it. Samuel Brittan offered this summary in 1964:

> It was an interesting mixture of planning and freedom, based on the economic teachings of Lord Keynes. Planning during this period was concerned with one global total – the amount the nation was spending on goods and services – the 'level of demand' in economists' language. If production sagged, or unemployment looked like creeping up, extra purchasing power was pumped into the system through the Budget, the banks, or the hire-purchase houses. If employment was a bit too full or the pound came under strain, demand was withdrawn through these same channels.[55]

The crucial constraint was an implicit trade-off between unemployment and inflation, which was formalised in the well-known 'Phillips curve' in 1958.[56] If there was a consensus on macroeconomic policy at this time, as I believe there was, it was about this constraint on the available political options, not about whether to opt for lower unemployment at the risk of higher inflation or vice versa – issues on which Labour and Conservatives naturally differed.

It was the very existence of this constraining framework which was to be the butt of the so-called monetarist counter-attack. According to Friedman's famous homily on monetarism in 1967, 'there is always a temporary trade-off between inflation and unemployment; there is no permanent trade-off. The temporary trade-off comes not from inflation *per se*, but from unanticipated inflation, which generally means, from a rising rate of inflation'.[57] The futility of such tinkering is the obvious message and, as Hirschman has observed, one nicely calculated to provoke maximum exasperation and asperity.[58] Yet it should not be overlooked that the charge of futility levelled against Keynesian policies has often been sup-plemented – possibly in an otiose way – by the further claim that such policies produce not merely self-cancelling, but actu-ally perverse effects. Thus Friedman accused the monetary authorities of 'a propensity to overreact' which meant that 'they feel impelled to step on the brake, or the accelerator, as the case may be, too hard'.[59] Macmillan's motor-car was thus subject to disastrously erratic regulation, as at least one of its passengers – Sir Keith Joseph – ruefully testified in retrospect:

The effect of over-reacting to temporary recession has been to push up inflation to ever higher levels, not to help the unemployed, but to increase their numbers. Thus excessive injections of money, undertaken by intelligent and enlight-ened men with good intentions, have wrought great havoc in our economy and society. The benefits have been largely temporary – and in any case cruelly reversed in the inevi-table 'stop' that follows, but the evil has lived on.[60]

It is tempting to think of the monetarist critique as a mirror-image of the post-war consensus which it subverted: a rival panacea asserted with the same cocksure triumphalism of which Keynesians had been guilty a generation previously. A glance at how monetarism was sold, and thereby subjected to its own process of ideological debasement, would hardly dispel such an impression. The keen mind of Nigel Lawson, for example, was not inhibited by undue intellectual humility. When he disclosed his thoughts about the role of micro- and macroeconomic policy in his Mais lecture in 1984, he claimed that 'the proper role of each is precisely the opposite of that assigned to it by the conventional post-war wisdom. It is the conquest of inflation, and not the pursuit of growth and employment, which is or should be the objective of macroeconomic policy. And it is the creation of conditions conducive to growth and employment, and not the suppression of price rises, which is or should be the objective of microeconomic policy.'[61] If Keynes had left macroeconomic policy standing on its head, Lawson's world-historical role was evidently to turn it the right way up again.

The radical doctrines of the left may thus be mirrored by the radical doctrines of the right; but perhaps they are more tellingly countered by a sober appeal to the intractable realities of an imperfect world. In this sense, Friedman's most effective thrust was surely the general caveat which he entered about our inherent fallibility in action, because of inherent flaws in our information:

> We simply do not know enough to be able to recognise minor disturbances when they occur or to be able to predict either what their effects will be with any precision or what monetary policy is required to offset their effects. We do not know enough to be able to achieve stated objectives by delicate, or even fairly coarse, changes in the mix of monetary and fiscal policy.[62]

The futility of pitting our puny wits against the complex battery of information marshalled by the sophisticated signals of the free market was an insight which Friedman could well have learned at Hayek's knee. It proved to be the more prescient part of an economic case against macroeconomic planning, whereas Hayek's political diatribe against the spectre of serfdom, however understandable at the time, later seemed alarmist. The rhetoric of reaction was in this sense better served by arguments which struck an affinity with an authentically conservative temperament, founded on scepticism about projects for the improvement of the human condition. The polemics of progress, conversely, ultimately rang hollow in claiming too much for the macroeconomic competence of post-war government, ignoring at their peril the salutary cautions buried in the 1944 White Paper. I have already quoted its claim that 'we shall be pioneers'. This was immediately tempered with the injunction: 'We must determine, therefore, to learn from experience; to invent and improve the instruments of our new policy as we move forward to its goal. And it would be no less foolish to ignore, than to be dismayed by, the certainty that unsuspected obstacles will emerge in practice.'[63]

CHAPTER 5

Industrial Relations

Regulation Against Voluntarism

Robert Taylor

'The first and overriding responsibility of all trade unions
is to the welfare of their own members. That is their
primary commitment, not to a firm, not to an industry,
not to the nation. A union reflects its members' contributions
and demands their loyalty specifically for the purpose of
protecting their interests as they often see them, not their
alleged "true" or "best" interests as defined by others.'
Allan Flanders[1]

NO UNDERSTANDING of the evolution of Britain's
industrial relations after 1945 is possible without a recognition of its distinctive and unique character, mainly
formed during the second half of the nineteenth century.
Unlike in the countries of continental Europe, the relationship
between employers and employees has always lacked substan-
tive legal regulation. The country never had positive legal
rights provided by Parliament to underpin freedom of association in the workplace or to legitimise collective bargaining.
Agreements have not been legally binding contracts enforceable by either party through the courts. 'British industrial

relations have, in the main, developed by way of industrial autonomy', the labour-law academic Professor Otto Kahn-Freund explained in 1955. 'It means that employers and employees have formulated their own codes of conduct and devised their own machinery for enforcing them.'[2] As a result, the state appeared to take an impartial, reluctant and essentially limited attitude to the way industrial relations were conducted in the workplace. Even as late as 1966, the Trades Union Congress expressed the view that the state's role was to improve the interests of workers only as 'the second best alternative to the development of employed people themselves of the organisation, the competence, the representative capacity to bargain and to achieve for themselves satisfactory terms and conditions of employment'.[3] Where trade unions displayed a proven competence to act as bargainers, then government should stand aside. 'Its attitude is one of abstention, of formal indifference', explained the TUC.

From their beginning, Britain's trade unions did not seek positive legal rights as a means of protecting themselves from the actions of hostile employers, class-biased courts or an intrusive state. Instead, they lobbied Parliament to provide them with legal immunities as a defence against the dangers of the use of the common law, which regarded them essentially as bodies 'in restraint of trade' and a threat to the maintenance of absolute property rights. It was Parliament that ensured through legislation that trade unions enjoyed at least a negative freedom to organise workers and bargain on their behalf with employers. The defence of 'free' collective bargaining demanded that trade unions should be allowed to insist on the maintenance of those legal immunities to ensure their survival as voluntary and autonomous associations practising collective self-regulation. However, the so-called voluntarist tradition that emerged as a result was by no means as secure or unquestioned as its enthusiasts were often to claim. The 'collective *laissez-faire*' approach to industrial relations was, after all, dominant in a society which remained deeply divided by class. But while there was a strong sense of class consciousness in Britain, conflicting interests in the workplace were normally reconciled through compromise and accommodation, though not by notions of partnership or consensus.

Moreover, the state was not entirely absent from the free operations of either the labour market or the workplace, despite voluntarism's undoubted tenacity. In the nineteenth century, laws were passed by Parliament to prevent women and children from being exploited by employers, particularly in the number of hours they could work and what kind of jobs they were allowed to do. Health and safety at work questions in general also commanded Parliament's sporadic attention. During the 1890s, governments created public institutions which were designed to encourage voluntary conciliation and arbitration as a way of settling industrial disputes. It was a Conservative Government, under Lord Salisbury, that passed the Fair Wages resolution in 1891 requiring model labour standards to be upheld in publicly tendered contracts in the public services. The 1906 Liberal Government introduced statutory minimum pay rates into the so-called sweated trades, through the creation of wages councils, and also established labour exchanges to assist people in search of work. The First World War brought a stronger and more direct intervention by the state into industrial relations. In the public services, trade unionism was then actively encouraged, with official approval. The outbreak of widespread labour militancy in 1918–20 led to the passage of the Emergency Powers Act (1920), although this turned out not to be as draconian a piece of legislation in practice as it first appeared. 'Even in the case of national emergencies, a government could not impose a cooling-off period, order strikers back to work or impose a settlement.'[4] 'There has never been any reason of principle why those protections could not be pursued by collective bargaining', argued the industrial sociologist Alan Fox. 'It was expediency and historical accident rather than theory which drew these boundaries.' As he pointed out: 'The British are always prepared to accept state support or intervention when it suits their sectional purposes, yet only in dire national emergency do they invest it with "national" meaning and give it the willing submission which such an interest implies.'[5]

However, for the most part, before 1945 Britain's trade unions continued to insist the operations of both the law and the state should be kept as far away as possible from workplace activities. Such instinctive reluctance to encourage the legal regulation of the employment relationship did not mean trade union officials practised a benevolent co-operation with employers under the voluntarist tradition. They were never under any doubts that they had to work under what was always an unequal balance of power between the forces of capital and labour. The voluntarist industrial relations system may have been based on underlying assumptions of co-operation and conciliation, but there was always a widespread fear and, on occasions, hostility towards organised labour among employers, politicians and lawyers. It is true companies rarely resorted to legal coercion or even the use of the lock-out to keep labour in its place. But the lack of martyrs did not mean Britain's trade unions were secure as respectable pillars of the community, even though most of the time trade union leaders practised sober self-reliance and preached moderation as they sought to achieve influence in furthering the working class interest.

In fact, the trade unions saw no real contradiction in their position as they defended their own autonomy while, at the same time, advocated the need for a positive extension of state power in the labour cause outside the employment relationship. By the end of the nineteenth century, a growing number of trade unions favoured collectivist forms of socialism while they continued to support free trade, political pluralism and the civil rights of free born Englishmen (if not women). Trade unions began to support openly the ideological objective of the common ownership of the means of production, distribution and exchange and some even wrote that commitment into their constitutions. Such radical ideas, however, usually presupposed the creation of a powerful centralised and activist state, except among the Guild Socialists. By the 1930s, such views had hardened into orthodoxy across all sections of the labour movement. The TUC called for the 'commanding heights' of industry to be nationalised and a public welfare system established that was based on universalist principles of provision for all citizens, irrespective of their income and funded out of redistributive taxation. State controls were to be imposed on capital flows, dividends, profits, investment, rents and prices. Britain was to be turned into a state-planned autarchy. However, one crucial area was to remain untouched by the onward march of public regulation. This was the country's industrial relations system of free collective bargaining, autonomous trade unions and legal immunities.

Faith in the virtues of the voluntarist tradition continued to be admired immediately after 1945 and for understandable reasons. Despite its undoubted imperfections, it had not only survived the test of total war but many believed it was crucial in the achievement of victory over Nazism. The state did not need to resort to coercive methods to stimulate production for Britain's war effort on the home front. It thrived – for much of the time – through co-operation and consent. 'As far as possible the principle of voluntaryism was to be preserved within a framework in which the value of compulsory powers lay primarily in the indirect pressure they could be called upon to exercise', wrote H. M. D. Parker in his official history of war production. 'Workers were to be encouraged and persuaded to do what was required of them because much better results would be achieved if they could feel that, although they might have been compelled, they had of their own free will agreed to accept the employment offered to them.'[6] If the exigencies of war failed to undermine the fundamentals of voluntarism, why should anybody believe in the need for its destruction under peacetime conditions?

As a result, workplace voluntarism emerged in 1945 relatively unscathed. It is true that significant breaches in the system had taken place under the draconian powers made available to Ernest Bevin (as Minister of Labour and National Service) in Churchill's wartime coalition government for the mobilisation and direction of workers. Strikes were banned (though this was not so apparent by 1944, especially on some of the country's coal fields) and demarcation lines were suspended with an impressive mobilisation of female labour to maximise war production. But trade unions insisted on the need for them to regulate their own affairs without outside state interference in sensitive areas such as wage bargaining.

In their robust defence of their own autonomy as negotiators, the trade unions said they reflected the views as well as the interests of their members. As voluntary associations, their ultimate responsibility lay not to a wider public interest, however that was defined, but to the demands and aspirations of the rank and file they claimed to represent. However, by mid-century, the inherent tensions between voluntarism and the need for regulation in the labour market were growing more difficult to contain. Trade unions after 1945 were to find themselves divided increasingly from within over what to do about the public demands being imposed upon them by governments wrestling with the problems of a vulnerable and relatively declining economy, and the calls from their own members to press for improvements in their living standards through collective bargaining at a time of national austerity but 'full' employment.

Labour's general election victory in 1945 aroused genuine enthusiasm among the trade unions. In part, it reflected a strong sense of solidarity and social patriotism, as well as the intoxicating vision of building a 'New Jerusalem'. It also appeared to presage a dynamic extension in the use of state power in the furtherance of working class interests. 'Advances in housing, education, social security, national insurance and medical provision were a consequence of bargains developed between labour and capital under the auspices of extended state intervention in wartime conditions.'[7] The TUC had played an influential role in the development of public policy through its commitment to the concept of 'full' employment and Beveridge's social insurance scheme. Its calls for the nationalisation of public utilities were welcomed by ministers. The 'implied social contract' signed between the trade unions and Churchill's coalition government during the crisis days of mid-1940 was now to bring about a fundamental reconstruction of the country in the interests of working people and their families. An enhanced sense of what the sociologist T. H. Marshall at that time called 'social citizenship' was to be a living reality for millions, not just a theoretical abstraction.

But the trade union commitment to the extension of the public interest through legislative measures emanating from an enlightened and centralised state was never to be complete. In the proposed state-dominated economy there was to be no planning of wages. The defence of free collective bargaining after 1945 reflected the private concerns of the trade unions and above all that of their members. Workers might be regarded by academics as social citizens in the formulation of welfare policy, but in a tight labour market with low unemployment they sought understandably to maximise their strength at the bargaining table with employers. At no stage did union leaders wish to establish a full-blown corporatist system in a strategic alliance with a Labour government. Appeals to solidarity, patriotism and fairness may have made some emotional impact immediately after 1945 in temporarily restraining worker expectations, but no serious attempt was made to construct national institutions in post-war Britain that would reflect the existence of a supposedly permanent social consensus between the forces of capital and labour. The severe limitations imposed by the trade unions as well as the Labour Government on the development of corporatism were also reflected in attitudes to other labour market questions. Only limited interest was displayed in both the boardroom and the shop floor on the establishment of a comprehensive industrial training system that would replace the inadequate provision of skills with a high quality workforce. Training was to remain – as it had always been – a hallowed part of the voluntarist tradition where employers negotiated with the craft unions in meeting their specific skill needs, with little concern for the wider public interest. Moreover, the strong commitment to the creation and maintenance of 'full' employment was to be achieved by government not through its introduction of supply-side measures to improve skills and job opportunities in the labour market, but by the 'application of monetary and fiscal instruments in demand management'.[8] The Ministry of Labour and National Service under George Isaacs, the former print union leader, might have taken 'central responsibility for the whole direction of the labour economy and by extension the national economy' but instead, to the obvious satisfaction of the trade unions, it was 'accorded a much more limited role as, in effect, the ministry servicing the voluntary processes of collective bargaining and industrial relations. Within this sphere of operation, it was natural that its institutional ethos should be that of collective *laissez-faire*'.[9]

Trade union leaders in the 1940s were even ambivalent about the efficacy of workplace mobilisation through the factory-based joint production committees that proved such important instruments for worker solidarity during the war years, epecially after Hitler's attack on the Soviet Union on 22 June 1941, when the Communist Party threw its activist shop steward movement behind maximising war production. But as James Hinton pointed out, employers were able to re-establish their autocratic powers in peacetime 'against notions of shop floor citizenship', partly because of 'the appeal of voluntaristic codes of behaviour both to trade unions and the state itself'. 'The primacy given to the defence of free collective bargaining by British trade unions tended to inhibit support for that purposive partnership between workers and the state which would be the indispensable condition for any system of participatory planning', he argued. 'For many trade unionists, Bevin's championship of a limited measure of freedom from the state seemed more realistic than radical demands for power in partnership with the state.'[10]

At a time when the ideology of state collectivism went virtually unchallenged across the political spectrum, such attitudes might have seemed surprisingly complacent. But they reflected deep convictions based on traditional practice. Behind the stirring appeals to social patriotism and an avowed belief in equality of opportunity, instincts on both sides of industry remained hostile to the public regulation of the labour market and the workplace. At the same time, politicians of all parties professed an admiration for what they believed were the admirable virtues of self-restraint and responsibility trade unions had exercised during wartime in their conduct of collective bargaining. As a result, immediately after 1945 no public mood existed to pursue a *dirigiste* economic policy that threatened trade union autonomy by regulating the labour market and the workplace in what it was believed were going to be the easier years of peace.

But the increasingly severe economic troubles facing the post-war Labour Government soon began to erode the state's faith in the virtues of workplace voluntarism. It was becoming abundantly clear that governments needed to play a more active and strategic role in the management of the post-war economy than they had done before 1939. The operation of the labour market could no longer simply be left to employers and trade unions with minimalist government interference. Indeed, from its first months in office, powerful ministerial voices were being raised in Attlee's cabinet calling for the establishment of a national wages policy that would limit the level of pay settlements by exhortation (or, if necessary, through state control), encourage higher productivity and prevent soaring inflation in the national interest. In March 1948 the TUC agreed – under enormous government pressure – to devise a policy of voluntary wage restraint to be pursued by self-discipline and rhetorical appeals to collective responsibility. Remarkably it was to last, with considerable success, for just over two years, despite labour market pressures that reflected the greater bargaining power many workers had begun to experience as a result of the post-war conditions of 'full' employment. Trade union leaders may not have been keen to act as corporatists, but most were willing – often against their better instincts – to curb or dampen down the wage demands of their members in order to help a Labour government in economic trouble. However, they were unprepared to abandon voluntarism in collective bargaining as an act of loyalty for more than a very limited period of time.

The predominance of the public interest in the conduct of industrial relations conflicted with the fundamental concern among the trade unions to defend their own freedom as collective bargainers. A trade union official admitted to Ferdynand Zweig, in his classic study of British workers published in 1950, that while he welcomed the new role for the trade unions, with their enhanced status in making public policy, he warned that it would deprive them of their independence. 'We were not meant to be public servants to guard the interests of the nation', he explained. 'We were appointed to protect our members and to further their interests within the framework of the law. Does anyone ask the employer to have the national interest in mind instead of the interest of his firm? It is all right having the national interest in mind but we are not the right people to have it.'[11]

This was a genuine dilemma for the trade unions and no satisfactory answer could be found on what to do about it. The very success of Labour's economic policy after 1945 in creating conditions of 'full' employment, partly through macro-demand management, left the *laissez-faire* labour market virtually intact and made it more difficult for trade unions at national level to retain any semblance of effective authority over the behaviour of their members; industry-wide collective agreements clearly came under mounting strain in the face of an emerging articulate and self-assertive shop steward movement, especially in the private manufacturing sector.

During the early 1950s under the Conservatives, voluntarism enjoyed something of an Indian summer as state planning went out of fashion. Winston Churchill, anxious to live down his reputation as a class warrior in the 1926 General Strike, was even prepared to shelve the more paternalistic but regulatory approach of his party's 1947 Industrial Charter and allow employers, trade unions and workers to continue administering the self-regulating industrial relations system. His hands-off strategy towards the trade unions was later criticised by some historians like Andrew Roberts and Robert Rhodes-James blessed with hindsight, as misguided appeasement of organised labour. But at the time it aroused little hostility and ushered in a period of gradual improvement in the living standards of most workers. While economists worried about wage-push inflation, sluggish productivity and rising unit labour costs, One-Nation Tories like Harold Macmillan proclaimed triumphantly that people had 'never had it so good'. Working-class affluence, with its emphasis on acquisitive individualism, began to erode more high-minded assumptions that lay behind the concept of social citizenship. But the spread of prosperity among workers through the aggressive affirmation of private affluence worried many public policy-makers. The upsurge of sectionalist, unofficial strikes in the automobile industry and the outbreak of industrial unrest in engineering, ship-building and on the railways in the mid-1950s brought an end to the relative industrial peace that had lasted since the mid-1920s and led to doubts in government circles about the wisdom of the voluntarist approach. An anguished and inconclusive debate took place in Eden's cabinet during the summer of 1955 about the possibility of stimulating legislation that would require mandatory secret ballots before trade unions called strikes and to use penal sanctions against workers who took part in unofficial industrial action. Increasingly, ministers began to discuss whether they should try to achieve a measure of workplace pay restraint in the national interest by applying downward pressure on higher money wages. But faith in the system of free voluntary negotiation was not to be so easily destroyed. A firm believer in the 'middle way', Macmillan himself agonised over what he saw increasingly as the trade union 'problem'. He did so in part because of an increasing conviction in government circles that Britain's *laissez-faire* labour market was one of the reasons for the country's relative economic stagnation. Some radical Conservatives – most notably the authors of the 1958 Bow Group pamphlet, *A Giant's Strength* – called for state regulation of trade unions to make them more disciplined and responsible institutions, capable of disciplining their errant members. But such demands for greater *dirigisme* as a way of reforming industrial relations clashed with the belief of those Conservatives, who argued trade unions had grown much too strong and hostile to the freedom of individual workers and therefore needed weakening through a limitation on the breadth of their legal immunities in industrial disputes.

In the political climate of the late 1950s, such thoughts failed to convince the Government that there was an urgent need to act directly to end, through the legal regulation of organised labour, what they saw as trade union excesses. But in 1956 came the first signs of a growing impatience with the consequences of wage-push inflation in a tight, decentralised labour market. A White Paper called for the creation of 'an efficient and enlightened system of industrial relations' with a 'full and frank exchange of opinion and information' between management and employees.[12] Apparently sectionalist interests in society had to be subordinated to the economic needs of the nation. But appeals to workers and trade unions for voluntary self-restraint fell predictably on deaf ears. No government was ready at that time to abandon 'full' employment in order to introduce greater self-discipline in the labour market by discouraging wage demands that, it was alleged, priced workers out of their jobs. However, growing public concern over the country's relative economic decline encouraged ministers to adopt a more interventionist strategy towards the wider labour market. A plethora of legislative measures were passed between 1962 and 1965 which helped to bring a greater sense of security and equity to workers facing redundancy. The Contract of Employment Act (1962) laid down minimum periods of notice for workers and required employers to provide them with written statements covering the main terms of their employment contracts. The Industrial Training Act (1964) established tripartite industrial training boards funded by a compulsory levy on employers, in an attempt to make them improve the skills of their own workers. In 1965, the Labour Government introduced statutory redundancy payments to encourage labour mobility. The introduction of wage-related unemployment benefit in 1965 also represented a move by the state to stimulate a shake-out in inefficient sectors of industry by cushioning the social consequences of corporate change.

Macmillan's decision to form the National Economic Development Council in 1962 was an attempt to encourage the active involvement of the trade unions as well as employers in the making of public policy by working with government in the achievement of planned economic growth. Although the TUC agreed to join the NEDC, it refused to participate in the government-created National Incomes Commission formed later that year, which sought, in a tentative way, to deal with wage inflation through the exhortation of workers to display self-restraint in the public interest. Some union leaders began to accept that voluntarism in its purist form was no longer credible if the economy was to enjoy sustained expansion without overheating or avoiding a return to mass unemployment. But such piecemeal erosion of the voluntarist system by the state did not represent a full-scale assault on *laissez-faire* assumptions. Governments were turning to public policy remedies to try and prop up, not undermine, the traditional industrial relations system and their approach was at best half-hearted. There was still no desire to abandon voluntarism and adopt the corporatist approach admired at the time in Gaullist France and Adenauer's West Germany, where the growth of social markets in the early 1960s was proving to be highly successful.

Nonetheless, the acquisitive and individualistic pressures coming from British workers could not so easily be placated by paternalistic forms of state intervention. Self-regarding shop floor sectionalism brought a confused and grudging response from trade union leaders to the development of public regulation in the labour market. In the early 1960s, planning had once again became a fashionable concept as policy-makers worried about the country's relative economic decline and saw the need for more vigorous state action to improve its business performance. Britain was described in an influential book written by Michael Shanks, the *Financial Times*'s industrial editor, as the 'stagnant society' which was even falling behind the Communist world, wrongly regarded by many as a success because of the supposed dynamism of its statist approach to economic management and the cult of centralised planning.

Both the industrial and political wings of the Labour movement began to discuss the possibility of creating a national incomes policy under a future Labour government or what Frank Cousins, left-wing general secretary of the Transport and General Workers union liked to call euphemistically 'the planned growth of wages'.[13] But such a view still fell far short of full-blown corporatism. As in the years immediately after the war, trade unions were constrained in what they could do by the economistic demands of their rank-and-file members and the sectionalist traditions of their own organisations. 'If we do not fulfil the purposes for which members join unions, to protect and raise their real standard of living, then the unions will wither and finally die', warned Cousins.[14] On another occasion, he emphasised it was the purpose of trade unions to 'sell our labour and our skill in the open market to the best of our ability while we live under the present system'.[15] In northern European democracies during the 1960s, 'worker solidarity' was more than just a slogan, as social-market economies developed with substantial state involvement through a variety of institutional arrangements designed to harmonise the relations between capital and labour in the form of social partnership. Among British policy-makers, a similar desire to develop an activist public policy was apparent, but it failed to overcome traditional individualistic assumptions in what continued to be a predominantly diverse, fragmented and unregulated labour market.

Indeed, during the late 1960s, the upsurge of so-called 'new unionism' – symbolised by the election of left-wing leaders like Jack Jones as general secretary of the Transport and General Workers Union and Hugh Scanlon as president of the Engineering Workers – was less evidence of any socialist shop-floor offensive and more the reflection of growing worker discontent at the intrusive use of state power to control incomes and the increasing tax burden being imposed by governments to provide the finance for burgeoning public expenditure programmes. Behind the fashionable talk about 'workers control' and 'industrial democracy' lay a strong and familiar defence of traditional voluntarism. Not for the first time, trade union sectionalist policies that reflected the demands of individual workers proved far more tenacious than well-intentioned appeals by governments calling on workers to act with self-restraint in the public interest.

In fact, during the 1960s workplace voluntarism faced

threats that eroded its credibility. The demands of the economy required order and discipline in wage expectations as well as an awareness by trade unions and employers alike about the genuine dangers of wage-push inflation. Sterling was vulnerable to international speculation while anxieties over both the balance of payments and visible trade deficits compelled governments to hanker after forms of national-incomes restraint to impress overseas' financial opinion, particularly in the United States. But the lurch – in crisis conditions – into the imposition of a statutory incomes policy was carried out in an *ad hoc* fashion.

No serious attempt was made until 1969 to try and reform the industrial relations system itself through direct state intervention. But the decentralisation of power in growing parts of private manufacturing – coupled with the devolution of authority in many trade union structures to the part-time shop steward and away from the full-time union bureaucracy – focused attention on the parochial demands of specific plants. Such trends failed to generate any sense of worker solidarity, let alone increase socialist consciousness on the shop floor, but they helped to intensify tendencies to fragmentation between competing and diverse work groups. As Dr John Goldthorpe argued in his seminal study of affluent manual workers in Luton during the 1960s: 'Neither as a way to greater worker participation in the affairs of the enterprise, nor as a political force, is unionism greatly valued. Rather, one would say, the significance that unionism has for workers is very largely confined to issues arising from their employment which are economic in nature and which are local in their origins and scope.'[16] The Donovan Royal Commission report in 1968 reflected what was happening to workplace voluntarism. In its famous analysis, it argued that Britain had 'two systems of industrial relations' defined as 'formal' and 'informal'. On one side were the official public institutions – trade unions and employer bodies – bound together by industry-wide collective agreements, but on the other was the reality of shop stewards and managers in individual companies bound together by custom and practice with decentralised autonomy.[17] However, the report said little about what the relationship ought to be between the public interest as interpreted by the state and the sectionalist concerns of trade unions and their members, partly because it failed both to examine either the effects of organised labour on the economy or the dramatic growth of public-sector trade unionism that was taking place during the 1960s. But it was no longer regarded as acceptable by the end of the decade that trade unions should be left alone to practise voluntarism with employers with the state playing only a limited role on the sidelines. Their activities in the economy had become of such essential public concern that no government could afford to ignore them. As the Ministry of Labour argued in its own evidence to the Donovan Commission: 'The furtherance of the interests of union members has become dependent upon the social and economic advance of the nation. It is clearly in the interests of trade union members that trade union policies and actions should as far as possible assist the government in achieving economic conditions favourable for increased industrial output and the maintenance of full employment.'[18] Private and public interests could no longer be accommodated by a voluntarist system that had outlasted its industrial and political usefulness.

In fact, the Labour Government of 1968–70 did not believe that the enhancement of the public interest in industrial relations would necessarily weaken trade unions. On the contrary, in their differing ways, both Barbara Castle, as Employment Secretary in the Labour Government, and later Conservative Prime Minister, Edward Heath, argued that direct positive government intervention was required to reform the way in which trade unions behaved in the workplace through the stimulus of the law in order to strengthen them as responsible industrial institutions. Moreover, they argued that a *dirigiste* approach would help to introduce more social justice onto the shop floor through moves to achieve greater worker equality, rectify the inefficient use of labour and help precipitate productivity improvements. In 1969, Labour's *In Place of Strife* White Paper promised to 'encourage a more equitable, ordered and efficient system', beneficial to trade union members as well as the wider community. It went so far as to suggest: 'The need for state intervention and involvement in association with both sides of industry is now admitted by almost everybody. The question that remains, is what form should it take at the present time?'[19] The trade unions took a wholly negative view of what was being proposed. Mrs Castle's efforts to reform industrial relations through the positive use of the law collapsed in the face of determined union resistance and the Labour Government was compelled to stage an undignified retreat. Edward Heath's more comprehensive and ambitious attempt in the Industrial Relations Act (1971) to modernise voluntarism also failed to win trade union approval. Its avowed intention of turning trade unions into orderly and responsible bodies organised in a clear command structure conflicted with its libertarian desire to extend worker individualism by abolishing the closed shop and emphasising a worker's right not to join a trade union.

Those dramatic and well-publicised setbacks at the hands of trade union power for government attempts to regulate industrial relations were not, however, the whole of the story. On the contrary, on all sides there was a growing recognition that voluntarism was no longer enough and that some form of legal regulation was needed to encourage reform in both the public interest and that of workers themselves. The Equal Pay Act (1970) accepted that earnings inequalities between men and women could not be erased by collective bargaining alone but needed an external stimulus from legislation, and this was welcomed by the trade unions. Despite industrial strife over public-sector pay and the Industrial Relations Act,

Heath's government took a benevolent view of trade unions and it created new public institutions with their active support, designed to regulate important parts of the labour market in a voluntary manner. In 1973, the Manpower Services Commission was formed as a public agency designed to take over the administration of employment and training services from the Department of Employment. Here trade union and employer representatives sat together in partnership with independent nominees. In the following year the tripartite Health and Safety at Work Commission was established, along with the Advisory, Conciliation and Arbitration Service. The Equal Opportunities Commission and the Commission for Racial Equality were also to follow in the mid-1970s. All those public bodies were established to introduce an enlightened coherence to public policy by involving trade unions and employers in joint decision-making. The delegation of government responsibilities to public agencies was supported by the TUC which assisted directly in the appointment of representatives to serve on them.

Moreover, the emergence of the social contract between Labour and the TUC during the period revealed an implied acceptance by the trade unions that some degree of legal regulation was of crucial importance to them. The repeal of the Industrial Relations Act in 1974 did not mean a return to pure voluntarism. The law was to be used both to encourage good labour practice but also to uphold individual worker rights. A panoply of new public bodies was established by the Labour Government – the Central Arbitration Committee, the Employment Appeals Tribunal and the Certification Office – to develop a new public interest approach to industrial relations that was not seen by trade unions as a threat to their existing autonomy. The Employment Protection Act (1975) sought to extend in a modest way both trade union and individual worker freedoms through the creation of new legal rights. Regulations were introduced to provide minimum levels of maternity leave, to ensure paid time-off for carrying out trade union and public-service work, and to offer compensation for workers found to have suffered from unfair dismissal. That particular measure also laid down provisions for trade union recognition from employers and imposed a statutory obligation on them to observe collectively agreed terms and conditions of employment. In addition, it provided a legal right for unions to enjoy access to company information in redundancy situations and for collective bargaining purposes. 'It was modest legislation based on the practices of many good employers. Only in two areas – unfair dismissal and maternity leave – was really new ground broken', suggested John Monks, now the TUC's general secretary.[20] But critics of the trade unions saw such legislation as an unacceptable advance in the power of organised labour and against the public interest. Others asserted the modest changes fell far short of the range of regulation enjoyed by workers in northern democratic Europe. The social-contract legislation – however limited – was certainly a clear breach with the voluntarist tradition, even if union leaders continued to insist that the reforms were designed to reinforce and not provide a substitute for voluntarism. While the new laws suffered from 'problems of weak enforcement, drafting defects and narrow judicial interpretation', they revealed a more trusting attitude by trade unions towards the use of positive law to achieve their objectives.[21]

But the pressures against the use of regulation to modify voluntarism did not disappear in the era of the social contract. On the contrary, the imposition of a voluntary incomes policy after July 1975, replete with flat-rate wage awards, aroused widespread discontent especially among skilled workers in private manufacturing industry who saw their pay differentials and relativities eroded and living standards squeezed. No amount of public interest legislation was going to calm shop-floor unrest. Indeed, the greater formality in workplace unionism with the spread of the closed shop, the creation of joint multi-union combine committees, and increasing emergence of full-time shop stewards all helped to enhance the autonomy and independence of workers and weakened what remained of the social solidarity of the war years. The gap inside the unions between the leaders and the rank and file grew wider as the state tried to impose ever greater burdens on the shop floor to secure wage restraint in the public interest. What emerged at the end of the social contract period was not a trade union movement transformed into a willing corporatist partner in the management of the economy, but a highly fragmented and disintegrating structure that could not withstand the powerful upsurge for higher pay packets, driven from below by workplace activists. This did not reflect the emergence of a proletarian class consciousness but a revived self-destructive sectionalism. 'We now see a growing division of workers into sections and groups, each pursuing its own economic interest irrespective of the rest', observed Professor Eric Hobsbawm. The 'economistic militancy' of the time paralleled a sharp decline in workplace solidarity.[22]

To an alarming extent, strikes appeared to have turned into wars of all against all, where producer interests eclipsed the needs of the consumer or the community in the wider society. The ferocity of the industrial conflict culminating in the 1978–9 'winter of discontent' revealed the severe limitations that existed on the use of public regulation in the labour market. It also suggested Britain's trade unions were being asked to shoulder too many responsibilities by a state under ferocious external economic pressure. 'Unions are reactive, bargaining organisations, ill-prepared for writing the agenda of government', observed Professor William Brown. 'In attempting to placate for tactical economic reasons a largely unprepared trade union movement, the government did that movement lasting damage.'[23] The social contract showed that the trade unions were unable to reconcile the needs of voluntarism with the obligations of public regulation in a decentralised and fragmented bargaining system, where the national interest dictated the need for pay restraint in a weak economy vulnerable to the pressures of international financial markets. But the period also underlined the lack of concern by employers for the intrusion of public regulation into the conduct of industrial relations. During the early 1970s, companies had displayed no interest in making use of legally enforceable contracts. After 1974 they displayed an equally negative attitude to the modest advances proposed by government to regulate the labour market and strengthen worker and trade union rights. The rapid demise of the radical idea of industrial democracy in the late 1970s underlined the enormous ideological resistance among employers, many trade unions and the state itself to any suggestion of using the law to introduce trade union representation on company boards. The idea was over-ambitious and alien to the voluntarist tradition and it went much further in conception than the more modest steps taken in regulating the labour market through an extension of worker protection. There was no upsurge of popular support from below for such an idea, because it ran counter to the grain of the British industrial relations system despite the idealistic advocacy of workplace change through the enhancement of shop steward power made by Jack Jones. The endless dialectical struggle between the demands of the state on the labour market and the aspirations of the shop floor had detonated a crisis of the entire system for which there seemed to be no way out. The TUC and the Labour Government made efforts to create a new public policy through the so called 'concordat' that laid out hopes for a future of co-ordinated pay bargaining based on the West German model. But it lacked all credibility. Both sides had lost control and authority over a seemingly anarchic labour market. More seriously, it seemed that efforts to underpin and supplement voluntarism by laws to strengthen trade unions and workers had also collapsed in a welter of strife and recrimination. Hopes of emulating the mainland European experience of social regulation faded away. Instead, under

Margaret Thatcher, an unexpected shift was to take place in industrial relations as she sought to destroy over time what was left of the post-war industrial relations settlement with its uneasy interaction between voluntarism and regulation.

The crisis of the British labour market at the end of the 1970s brought about a dramatic increase in levels of worker militancy and strengthened the conviction of most Conservatives that the trade unions had to be marginalised. This was not initially to be done in any crude or radical way but by the slow, incremental use of statutes that sought to avoid any confrontation with the trade unions in a trial of strength. Mrs Thatcher was helped in this project by the growing gap that had opened up inside the trade unions between rank-and-file members, activists and leaders. The crisis of trade union representativeness was first recognised by the support the Conservatives won at the polls in the General Election of 1979 from skilled manual workers in south-eastern England and the west Midlands. Their intense anger at national wage restraint and high marginal rates of income tax made them susceptible to Mrs Thatcher's seductive appeal for a return to 'free' collective bargaining. Moreover, the initial changes in her industrial relations strategy seemed less hostile to trade unions than might have been expected after the excesses of the 'winter of discontent'. Under the direction of One-Nation-Tory Jim Prior as Employment Secretary, the first piece of legislation made only marginal changes in the law to weaken the closed shop, limit the extent of picketing and provide state funds for unions who agreed to ballot their members before calling strikes. 'Our approach is essentially a pragmatic one. We are not in the business of change for change's sake', Prior told the Commons.[24] He emphasised the need for a 'step-by-step' approach designed to shift the supposed balance of workplace power away from trade unions and towards employers. Inevitably Conservatives exaggerated the extent of trade union power at the end of the 1970s. Britain never had a centralised, corporatist industrial relations system. But many union leaders found themselves out of touch with shop-floor opinion as worker loyalties became increasingly hostile to imposed collectivist solutions or wage restraint.

The success of Mrs Thatcher's industrial relations policy stemmed from the fact that it was designed to move with, and not against, the current of the voluntarist tradition of industrial relations. In eight sizeable pieces of legislation, Conservative governments between 1980 and 1993 tamed organised labour through regulations designed to free up the labour market and severely limit the ability of the trade unions to take effective industrial action. Although the laws stopped short of removing all legal immunities from unions in industrial disputes, the Employment Act (1982) overturned the protections provided for trade union financial funds since 1906 in cases of lawful disputes, by making it easier for employers, the state or aggrieved citizens to use the courts against the power of the unions who feared they would be unable to act without endangering their assets.

The Prime Minister drew her intellectual inspiration for radical reform of the trade unions through the use of public regulation from the neo-liberal economic arguments of Professor Friedrich von Hayek. His *Constitution of Liberty*, published in 1960, was highly influential in shaping Mrs Thatcher's attitude to industrial relations and trade union power. In Hayek's opinion, trade unions were 'open enemies' that 'threatened the whole basis of the free society'.[25] The coercive, monopolistic powers of organised labour undermined the effectiveness of the price mechanism in the market, he argued. In Britain, trade union strength stemmed – Hayek believed – from the 'acquisition of privilege' provided for them in the Trade Disputes Act (1906). Without a shred of empirical evidence, Hayek asserted in 1980: 'The unions have turned Britain into a relatively low-wage economy'. He believed the country's economic revival was impossible unless unions were 'deprived of their coercive power'.[26]

The Prime Minister agreed fully with his analysis. She was determined not merely to repeal the social contract legislation of the 1970s but to destroy the post-war industrial relations settlement based on the voluntarist tradition. In part, this was done through the bold assertion of acquisitive individualism. The commitment to sweeping income tax cuts, public spending reductions, profit sharing and employee share ownership and other manifestations of a popular capitalism reflected the government's wish to liberate the labour market from ideas of worker solidarity and equity. Under conditions of 'free' collective bargaining, wage differentials were widened in the name of competition. A heavy price was paid for such change and it came in the form of soaring open unemployment that climbed to over three million by 1985, as well as greater income inequality.

From the mid-1980s onwards the government grew more bold in its avowed intention to tame organised labour in the name of individualism. There was also a noticeable change of emphasis, from the need to tilt the balance of industrial power away from trade unions and towards employers, as ministers began to speak openly about the creation of a 'new' flexible and deregulated labour market in which no obvious public role at all was left for organised labour. The balance-of-power theory was being replaced by a resolute determination to marginalise trade unions in the new world of assertive managerialism. By 1992, a White Paper could openly proclaim the triumph of the individual over the collective, the private over the public interest. 'Successful industrial relations strategies will work with the trends in the labour market, widening individual choice and opportunity, moving away from collectivism and supporting the natural evolution of working arrangements and practices which suit both individual employees and the companies for whom they work', argued the Department of Employment.[27]

It is questionable whether workplace change in Britain during the period was dramatic enough to justify such sweeping rhetoric, even if trade union density and the extent of collective bargaining in the labour market fell sharply. Social-attitude surveys suggested throughout the period that there was a lack of wide popular support for the ideology of Thatcherism and trade unions began to recover their lost popularity as they were seen less as over-mighty subjects and more as underdogs. The assault on tripartite institutions in the labour market was not as total as many expected. The National Economic Development Council was abolished in 1992 as was the Manpower Services Commission whose functions returned to government after 1987, but bodies like ACAS, the CRE and the EOC were allowed to continue. The plethora of organisations established during the social contract period to administer employment law were also saved. A Commissioner for the Rights of Trade Union Members (CROTUM) was established in 1988 to assist aggrieved union members to take legal action against their unions, but its work was limited. In the training area, the familiar ambivalence about the role of the state continued. The Training and Enterprise Councils, formed by the government in 1991, were business-dominated local bodies with the primary function of administering the state's own programmes to deal with training the jobless. But they remained weak, voluntarist organisations and lacked the resources to play the kind of catalytic role Chambers of Commerce performed in Germany. Ministers continued to praise the supposed achievements of Britain's flexible and deregulated labour market based on voluntarist principles. Indeed, they went further in 1993 by scrapping the statutory wages councils that had laid down a minimum pay rate in vulnerable sectors of the economy and then opposed the introduction of a statutory national minimum wage. The victory of individualism and voluntarism without trade unions, however, was not to be total. Indeed, its adverse social consequences in the form of high unemployment and poor training and, above all, its contribution to the spread of a deep sense of insecurity

among workers in the labour market of the 1990s all helped
to encourage a counter-trend in the evolution of public
policy.

Two important developments, in particular, began to modify the individualistic thrust of British industrial relations
strategy, with a noticeable tilt back towards the need for
positive public regulation. After 1985, the social dimension of
the European Community became more of a tangible reality.
Under the enthusiastic presidency of French Socialist Jacques
Delors, a flow of legally enforceable social directives and
proposals poured out of Brussels. They may not have been
as radical in content as UK ministers liked to claim, but they
reflected a growing realisation inside the Brussels-based Commission that the creation of a single EU market could not
be satisfactorily completed without the establishment of a
framework of minimum labour standards to protect and
extend workers' rights. This approach was very much a
reflection of Christian Democratic values although British
Conservatives denounced the resulting social regulation as
having been inspired by the writings of Karl Marx. It
embodied much of the paternalistic ideology that stressed the
concept of the social citizen with responsibilities to the wider
society much more than the self-regarding and acquisitive
individual in the economic free market. Inevitably the sustained pressure from Brussels for comprehensive workplace
legislation clashed with Britain's voluntarist traditions.

But there was also a second and equally important development: the emergence of a radical new attitude inside the
British trade unions themselves to the value of positive law
in reforming industrial relations. All except the most inflexible
of trade union leaders recognised that the Conservatives had
used voluntarism in the 1980s to regulate trade unions in the
name of liberty. Now the trade unions came to accept that
in future they needed the creation of workplace legal rights,
not the restoration of negative immunities, if they had any
hope of surviving and prospering again. At the Trades Union

Congress of 1995 delegates backed a new strategy that called for new positive legal rights of worker representation and union recognition.

The dialectical struggle between regulation and voluntarism in British industrial relations therefore showed no signs of abatement during the 1990s. Indeed, the resurgence of interest in the positive use of regulation in labour market policy, especially as a result of growing European Union influence conflicted with the determination of the Conservatives to carry on making Britain's employment system more flexible. The outcome was an uneasy co-existence, not compromise, a muddled blend of regulation and voluntarism. The British government retreated under pressure from Brussels. It accepted employees were entitled to representation in cases of collective redundancy and transfer of ownership, in an undertaking made after an adverse judgement before the European Court of Justice in Luxembourg. The UK's opt-out from the social chapter of the 1991 Maastricht Treaty failed to thwart the intrusion of the EU's works council directive into the country, as many large, British-owned transnationals decided to comply with the law and establish information and consultation committees for all their employees across Europe. But Britain had still a long way to go before it became a full-blown social-market economy, with a codified system of legal rights and obligations for workers, similar to those that cover most of mainland western Europe. Voluntarism continued to hold its instinctive attractions in the flexible labour market and the extent of trade union conversion to the cause of social regulation to reform industrial relations still had to be tested in practice. It seemed unlikely that there would be any complete repudiation of voluntarism. Shifting involvements between the public and private interest looked set to continue in the British labour market, despite growing convergence with mainland European practice in the twenty-first century.

*　　*　　*

The history of British industrial relations since the end of the Second World War has been concerned with the complex interaction between the voluntarist tradition and the growing pressures from the state for public regulation in the national interest. In 1945, the trade unions and the workers they claimed to represent were strong defenders of the traditional approach of collective bargaining. They continued to insist there should be no legally enforceable collective agreements with employers and demanded the protection of legal immunities provided by Parliament from actions under the common law. Nobody prominent in the Labour movement advocated the introduction of positive legal rights for workers and trade unions as were established in the ruined post-war economies of continental western Europe. Moreover, in such an attitude, the trade unions enjoyed the support of the state which took a benevolent view of their behaviour. Indeed, in the public sector, governments of both main political parties sought to encourage workers to join trade unions while agreeing to avoid any detailed intervention into the workplace relations between companies and their employees. To a surprising extent governments continued to believe employers and trade unions should be left alone to reach voluntary agreements without state intrusion. The management of industrial relations was not even regarded as of vital importance to the wider needs of running a modern economy, vulnerable to severe international pressures from money markets and trading competitors. Of course, there continued to be ill-defined limits to the level of indifference displayed by the state to industrial relations. The detailed legislation covering health and safety in specific industries, for example, indicated an abiding concern at workplace conditions that began with the Factory Acts during the country's first industrial revolution at the beginning of the nineteenth century. Moreover, trade unions – for all their distaste at suggestions of government intrusion into the way they conducted themselves – were at best ambiguous about their attitude to the role of the state in the economy. For most of the century they believed in positive government intervention. In the 1940s, the TUC favoured turning Britain into a virtual state autarchy, with a plethora of controls on prices, profits, dividends and capital flows. Unions backed without question the need to take large tracts of British industry into state ownership. They also favoured the extension of a welfare state funded through general taxation and based on universalist principles of provision. But trade unions insisted that the state should not intrude into the conduct of industrial relations.

However, such an attitude grew increasingly unrealistic. In the late 1940s, under pressure from the Labour Government, the trade unions agreed to swallow national wage restraint to contain costs and help rescue the economy from crisis. They did so reluctantly but only temporarily, as they found it difficult to contain the wage demands of their members at a time when the unexpected arrival of full employment had strengthened the bargaining position of unionised workers in a tight labour market. During the affluent years of the 1950s private concerns predominated over the needs of the public interest as defined by government. Trade unions and workers were considered by opinion formers as obstacles to progress. The economy was said to be stagnating with poor relative productivity, inflationary wage increases, soaring unit labour costs, unofficial strikes and obsolete workplace practices, like demarcation and restrictions on entry to skill grades. By the end of the decade there was a growing chorus of criticism of trade unions. They were said to be too powerful, hostile to technological change, imprisoned in a glorious past. Across the political spectrum calls began for trade union reform through the use of public regulation. But change was slow, uneven and circumspect. Conservative Ministers of Labour continued to back voluntarism in industrial relations and One-Nation concepts. In doing so they reflected the views of their permanent civil servants and many employers. It was not until the early 1960s that public-interest concerns began to modify official attitudes.

That said, the shift from voluntarism to regulation did not initially mean state hostility to the power of trade unions. On the contrary, governments sought to underpin the voluntary approach by trying to introduce some semblance of security and order into the existing industrial relations system. Legislation to require written contracts of employment for workers, to provide statutory redundancy payments, as well as the creation of industrial training boards and industrial tribunals and a tripartite body, the National Economic Development Council, were all seen by their authors as means to introduce over-due and comprehensive minimum standards of civilised behaviour into employer–worker relations. Trade unions favoured such legislative changes and those later, covering such areas as equal pay and sex and racial discrimination, as complements not substitutes for the traditional practices of industrial relations. The public and the private interest were to co-exist, although they were to do so with increasing difficulty.

But international pressures imposed on the British economy during the 1960s and particularly after October 1964, when the incoming Labour government failed to devalue sterling, compelled ministers to accept the need for a statutory prices and incomes policy. This was a direct intervention by government into the processes of collective bargaining in the name of the public interest. In the early 1960s, trade union leaders had supported the idea of a national incomes policy when it was regarded by them as a way to plan the growth of real wages in an economy that the government was expanding through demand management. But after July 1966, an incomes policy was turned by the state into an instrument of deflation. Initially, wage restraint, backed by the threat of penal sanctions, won widespread support among workers and employers, but it soon led to outbursts of workplace unrest, particularly among skilled craftsmen and public sector employees concerned about pay relativities and differentials. Higher levels of income tax on the average and below average wage-earner added to growing discontent and fuelled an acquisitive sectionalism among key groups of workers. The fragmented and unruly informal system of industrial relations – highlighted by the Donovan Commission of 1968 – exacerbated such feelings. Rank-and-file anger among trade union activists took place at a time of change in the leadership of the larger unions. A new generation was emerging, shaped by the left-wing politics of the 1930s which had been dominated by the rise of Fascism, the fatal attractions of Soviet Communism and the miseries of the Great Depression. Many of the new leaders were not corporatists but, on the contrary, were romantic believers in shop-steward power in the working class interest. Syndicalism was to come back into fashion on the industrial left. It brought an ideological edge to the unending sectionalist strife that divided rather than united workers in their endless struggle for higher wages.

During the 1970s, in more difficult circumstances, further government efforts were made to shift the emphasis away from the private to public interest in industrial relations. First, Edward Heath as a radical Conservative went further than any other post-war Prime Minister in trying to construct a social partnership with trade unions and employers in the management of the economy. In the autumn of 1972 he offered the TUC almost co-determination in running government. Union leaders turned him down, preferring Labour and the social contract that they had hammered out together. But public institutions were established, like the Manpower Services Commission, the Health and Safety Commission and, later, the Advisory, Conciliation and Arbitration Service that reflected the strength of voluntary tripartism. With union cooperation, government began to establish a semi-corporatist system in some key areas of economic management. But this tentative development was never to produce the full-blown social-market economy so envied at the time in West Germany and Sweden. An attempt in the late 1970s to introduce industrial democracy into large British companies which would provide by law for direct employee representation on their boards failed, not least because of the serious differences of opinion it aroused among trade unions themselves. Many believed they should stay clear of playing a managerial role and instead defend their autonomy and their freedom as collective bargainers. Under pressure, the instinctive *laissez-faire* assumptions that lay at the root of the country's unique industrial relations remained tenacious. More seriously, further attempts at a national incomes policy once again fell foul of a fragmented and divisive labour market.

But after Mrs Thatcher's victory in May 1979, a new strategy emerged to reform industrial relations. To the delight of many skilled workers, the Conservatives abandoned national incomes policies and accepted 'free' collective bargaining, at least in the private sector. But the new government also abandoned – explicitly after 1985 – any commitment to the maintenance of full employment. Successive ministers legislated changes in industrial-relations law designed to free managers to manage and weaken trade unions and collectivism in the workplace. This involved a dual strategy: the deregulation of the labour market and the re-regulation of industrial relations, both through a highly activist public policy approach. Under Mrs Thatcher's prudent but relentless strategy the state was being used to provide the framework for the creation of a more competitive economy where individual employees were to be encouraged to abandon trade unionism in their best self-interest. At first defensively, but later with triumphalist fervour, the Conservatives sought to move beyond the dialectic of regulation and voluntarism.

By the mid-1990s they could point to what they regarded as a substantial change of attitude among British workers. The number of recorded strikes and days lost because of industrial stoppages fell to their lowest number since official labour statistics were first collected in the early 1890s. Unit labour costs no longer seemed to be a serious problem and productivity improvements across much of industry indicated the introduction of a variety of new workplace practices to replace the old methods that had emphasised demarcation lines and a division of responsibilities. But while the labour market had become more individualistic, more adaptable to personal interests, it was also more insecure and frightening for most workers. Inevitably in the new, abrasive and uncertain conditions, calls began to grow for the return of public regulation to temper the excesses of individualism. The dual pressures coming from the European Union and from trade unions themselves began to lead to the slow but steady emergence of positive legislative measures and proposals to protect workers. Whether this would lead eventually to a new industrial relations settlement based on positive legal rights and obligations remained unclear. But the appearance of a new synthesis in British industrial relations between voluntarism and regulation seemed probable.

CHAPTER 6

'Contract' and 'Citizenship'[1]

Jose Harris

THE RHETORICAL hallmarks of the early years of the welfare state were the replacement of 'charity', 'dependency', 'moralism', and bureaucratic surveillance of private lives by a new ethic of social 'citizenship'. Parliamentary debates on the welfare legislation of 1945–8 paid lavish tribute to the memory of the recently deceased Sidney and Beatrice Webb, who were credited by speakers from all parts of the Labour movement with bringing about the 'break-up' of the coercive, discriminatory and stigmatic Poor Law and replacing it by the new regime of universal social insurance.[2] These tributes put into a nutshell a more general understanding of the social policies of the post-war period that was to dominate political discourse for the next two decades, and remains powerful to the present day. This was an understanding which traced the direct ancestry of social policy from the Poor Law and Victorian philanthropy, via the Webbs, to the Beveridge Report of 1942, and culminated in the Labour social welfare programmes of 1945. It stressed the virtues of 'universality' as opposed to 'selectivity', of social insurance as opposed to Poor Law and public assistance, of 'impersonal' entitlement rather than 'moralistic' discretion, and of benefits paid not on the basis of means-tests and proof of need but as an automatic right of citizenship. In political terms, it identified universal insurance and the expansion of citizen rights with the post-war triumph of Labour – by contrast with the means-tests and discretionary hand-outs imposed by the predominantly Conservative National Government during the inter-war depression. These perspectives dominated the discussion of welfare in the 1940s, they did so again in the Titmuss-inspired debates on universality and selectivity in the late 1950s, and they did so once more in the late 1960s and early 1970s, when orthodox visions of the welfare state were challenged by the proponents of a philosophy of welfare rights.[3] As Peter Baldwin has shown, the 'universalism' of social insurance was widely viewed as the hallmark of a new ethic of 'solidarity and social citizenship', not merely in Britain but in much of post-war Europe.[4]

Yet, as anyone familiar with the more detailed workings of the British welfare state in the twentieth century will be aware, there is much that is odd about this story. As a matter of sheer historical fact, the adoption of Sidney and Beatrice Webb as the founding parents of a non-coercive, morally-neutral system of universal contributory insurance was in the highest degree paradoxical, since – much as they admired the self-governing insurance schemes of the highly-organised skilled trade unions – the Webbs became reluctantly convinced that such schemes were inherently inapplicable to the great unorganised and undisciplined mass of the British people.[5] Moreover, far from approving of the non-coercive and automatic character of national insurance payments, they saw these very qualities as fatally undermining any possibility of re-organising social arrangements on more disciplined, rational, socialist, and indeed 'moral' lines. And although they used the language of 'universal' provision, the Webbs' perception of 'universality' was something very different from that which became popular in the 1940s: it entailed not universal insurance, but provision (and compulsory imposition) of rate-financed social services of all kinds on all persons deemed to be in need of them, 'whether they want them or not' and 'with charge and recovery from all able to pay'.[6]

An even more acute historical problem surrounds the

attitude and role of the Labour Party, since contributory social insurance was by no means the well-honed and hallowed Labour principle that debate of the 1940s and 1950s liked to suggest. On the contrary, Labour had been deeply divided over the insurance principle at the time of the first National Insurance act of 1911 and, more importantly, in the 1930s had fiercely opposed national insurance as a means of meeting mass unemployment, demanding instead a non-contributory, non-contractual, subsistence-level payment for all the unemployed, to be paid for by direct taxation.[7] Labour had also been deeply critical of the working of the 'approved society' system of national health insurance, with its widely varying range of benefits, its segregation of good and bad risks, and its failure to offer any coverage to mothers and children. Similar problems arise at a more theoretical level, since – as many more recent commentators have pointed out – a system of contributory insurance based on paid work and 'interruption of earnings' could never be 'universal' in the way that rhetoric of the 1940s implied, because it necessarily excluded those outside or on the margins of the labour market (mothers, home carers, the long-term sick and disabled). By contrast, it might be argued (and indeed was argued by many nineteenth-century radicals, from Cobbett to Keir Hardie) that – contrary to its reputation for stigma, discretion and selectivity – the English Poor Law had been available for several centuries as a system of relief rooted not in contribution and contract but in mere membership of the community.[8] Despite all the long catalogue of attempts to limit that entitlement – by civic disabilities, less eligibility, settlement laws and workhouse tests – poor relief was, in the last resort, available to all who needed it as a matter of citizen right. An armchair political theorist who analysed the two systems, not as historic institutions but as abstract legal and normative structures, might conclude that, contrary to popular parlance, it was the Poor Law that carried connotations of universality, communitarianism and citizenship, while it was social insurance that entailed exclusion, differentiation and limited contractual rights. How then did it come about that the story of the welfare state in the 1940s came to be constructed by both academics and practitioners of policy in a way almost exactly opposite to that which pure theory might imply?

There are several obvious answers to this question that cannot be discounted. One of the most familiar of these, but perhaps the least illuminating, is that of 'propping-up capitalism': the claim, more common in the 1970s than now, that the Beveridge plan and the post-war Labour government used the cosmetic device of contributory insurance to keep at bay the more radical redistribution of both income and property that full-scale socialism would have required.[9] That both Beveridge and the Attlee government were interested in retaining some degree of private enterprise cannot be doubted; but that this was the main reason for their support for social insurance seems unlikely. Beveridge's scathing attacks on commercial and industrial assurance companies in the plan bearing his name do not sound in the least like the sentiments of one whose main objective was the protection of private capitalism.[10] And the notion that a Labour government which nationalised the steel industry and the voluntary hospitals would have blenched at abolishing contributory social insurance simply out of a lurking tenderness for capitalism seems highly implausible. Moreover, insofar as there *was* opposition to an extension of national insurance in the 1940s, it came overwhelmingly from the inner heartland of private capital.[11] 'Defence of capitalism' cannot therefore furnish us with an adequate explanation of either the political preference for national insurance in the 1940s, or the mythic status acquired by the principle of contributory insurance in subsequent years.

Another explanation is the practical and empirical one: that during the quarter of a century prior to 1945, popular experience of health, unemployment and old-age pensions insurance had, on the whole, been favourable, whereas popular experience of the Poor Law and other tax-financed assistance schemes had been largely negative. Insurance beneficiaries in the 1930s, it might be argued, had drawn their benefits without enquiry into personal means, without penalisation of their savings and without administrative hassle, whereas those dependent on transitional benefit, public assistance and the Poor Law had been subject to degrading inquiries into their private lives, break-up of family networks, 'whispering campaigns' from their neighbours, and enforced attendance at centres for training and 're-moralisation'. Therefore when a Labour government with widespread working-class support came to power in 1945, it was not perhaps surprising that they opted for the former and against the latter system in their legislation for the welfare state. This factor was certainly of great importance, as much contemporary evidence makes clear; debates on wartime and post-war social policy were laden with adverse references, not merely to the household means-test and the stigma of pauperism, but to the distasteful elements of patronage and nosy-parkerdom which clung to the administration of other non-contributory welfare schemes, such as maintenance of 'war widows' and the 'Lloyd George' old-age pensions.[12]

Yet popular rejection of the Poor Law does not tell the whole story, since there were some areas of the Poor Law and its successor institutions which by the 1920s and 30s had gained widespread popular acceptance. Many Labour councils in the 1920s had striven to prove that, within the context of mass democracy, a locally-administered Poor Law *could* be converted into a system of citizen rights.[13] Popular hostility to the introduction of the Unemployment Assistance Board in 1934 had demonstrated that resentment against local public assistance committees was by no means as universal as had sometimes been imagined, and in parliamentary debates on the extension of the UAB in 1940, several prominent Labour speakers (among them Aneurin Bevan) had defended the public assistance committees as much more humane, flexible and sensitive to democratic control than the 'faceless officialdom' of central government.[14] But in any case, as indicated above, Labour's policy for much of the 1930s had been not for a welfare system based on an extended and humanised Poor Law, but for a universal as-of-right communitarian system financed out of centralised direct taxation. Distaste for the Poor Law cannot therefore in itself explain the migration of radical ideas about citizenship and universalism away from communitarian schemes in the direction of contributory national insurance.[15]

Another obvious factor was the issue of gender. As many recent writers have pointed out, the majority of insurance contributors and beneficiaries (with the exception of pensioners) in all advanced welfare societies are male, whereas the majority of the clients of communitarian schemes, whether means-tested or as-of-right, tend to be women and children. The emphasis upon insurance as the normal channel of welfare thus echoes and reinforces, so it is claimed, a predominantly male definition of citizenship. This argument certainly has a strong bearing upon provision of welfare in Britain in the 1940s, since (for all the wartime absorption of women into paid employment) perhaps at no other period of modern British history was there a stronger public perception of highly differentiated male/female, work/household, paternal/maternal roles and functions. Indeed, rapid restoration of these differentiated roles after what was believed to have been the artificial and pathological disruption of wartime was perceived by many in all sectors of society, women as well as men, as part of the long-hoped-for return to peacetime normality.[16] As Susan Pedersen has convincingly argued, the famous lectures of T. H. Marshall, which portrayed the postwar welfare state as embodying a radically new conception of social rights, were implicitly based on the notion that citizenship was vested in employed male heads of household; and the slightly later arguments of Titmuss and Andreski, that social welfare was a reward for mass-participation in the armed forces, pointed, albeit unconsciously, in exactly the same direction.[17]

Yet once again the emphasis on gender does not tell the whole story. Labour's pre-war proposals for tax-financed welfare payments had been overwhelmingly based on a *class* analysis of the structure of national wealth, and on the demand that resources should be recycled from higher to lower income groups. The issue of gender, however important, does not in itself explain how and why the prime emphasis on vertical redistribution came to be obscured. Moreover, discussions on citizenship and social policy in the 1940s were by no means so sensitive to gender as is often supposed. Much wartime discussion of social reform was specifically addressed to the problem of the social, economic and civic status of women, though not always in precisely the terms that a later generation might expect. William Beveridge, Eleanor Rathbone, and bodies like the Family Endowment Society and the National Council of Women viewed women's functions in the home, not as private and politically disabling functions, but as a basis that was equal and in some respects even superior to industrial employment in fostering civic virtue and capacity for public life.[18] When Beveridge started out on the formulation of his famous plan he certainly intended that it should give women in the home equal insurance rights and equal citizenship status with men;[19] although he ultimately failed in this goal, it was not because he discounted women's functions and women's rights, but for other reasons that will be discussed more fully below. Moreover, Beveridge's model of post-war social security was by no means the only one on offer in the early 1940s. The various schemes for a tax-financed citizen wage, regardless of gender or employment status, that were promoted by PEP, the London Women's Parliament, Lady Juliet Rhys Williams and others, all suggest that contemporary thought was by no means so indifferent to the women's question as is sometimes supposed.[20] Gender alone, therefore, cannot fully explain the political and moral ascendancy of contributory national insurance.

Where else then are we to look for an explanation of the peculiar blend of contract and citizenship, principle and rhetoric that surrounded the setting-up of the welfare state? In my view there is no single clue to answering this question; instead there was a range of practical, historical, ideological and normative pressures which intermingled with, and were related to, the popular and gender concerns outlined above. One important factor seems to be that, in spite of the Labour Party's official rejection of insurance in the 1930s, the contributory principle was perhaps never quite so unpopular among the rank and file of likely Labour supporters as the views of Labour's parliamentary leadership might lead one to suppose. This was admitted even in the depths of the depression by so vehement a critic of social insurance as Aneurin Bevan. ('Men now regard it as a great privilege to be employed, and they no longer consider that a hardship is imposed upon them if they are asked to pay 10d a week unemployment premium. They are only too glad to pay it'.[21]) Working-class criticism of the national insurance system focused overwhelmingly on health insurance rather than on unemployment insurance – and consisted, not in rejection of the contributory principle, but in the demand that provision for sick workers and their dependants should be made as generous and comprehensive as provision for the unemployed.[22] In 1942, the leaders of the Trades Union Congress not merely strongly endorsed the Beveridge Plan, but submitted in advance of the Plan independent evidence to Beveridge demanding a comprehensive national insurance scheme in many respects identical to that which Beveridge was eventually to adopt.[23] Moreover, the doyen of Labour intellectuals, Harold Laski, had long argued not merely that social insurance was functionally indispensable, but that it was a central feature of any socialist reconstruction of the national community.[24] The massive support for Beveridge among Labour constituency associations, with only a small minority standing out for the much more redistributive Labour programme of the 1930s, is a pointer in the same direction. The findings of the Nuffield College Reconstruction Survey seemed similarly to confirm Beveridge's belief that 'benefits in return for contributions, rather than free allowances from the State, is what the people of Britain desire'.[25] Moreover, among Labour M.P.s who were returned to Westminster in 1945, many had had experience of contributory insurance administration, as members of local insurance committees, trade union administrators, or officials of approved societies. Nearly two hundred of them were said to have given election pledges to support Beveridge's partial retention of the approved society system; and there was clearly much disappointment on the Labour backbenches at the leadership's decision that approved societies should be totally abolished. Among those who spoke on the subject in parliamentary debates on the National Insurance bill, there was widespread support for the insurance principle and some expression of regret that rates of benefit could not immediately be higher, but very little reference to, or apparent awareness of, the fact that large sectors of the population would be partially or wholly left outside.[26]

A second crucial factor was the question of costs and public finance. The whole wartime debate on the reconstruction of social security took place within the context of profound anxiety on all sides about anticipated scarcity of post-war resources: a fact which right from the start appears to have ruled out of the arena of practical discussion any serious consideration of proposals based on the Labour Party's pre-war ideal of a tax-financed benefit payable without means-tests.[27] Except in the one area of family allowances, discussion about abolition of poverty after 1939 was almost entirely conducted in terms of contractual social insurance *versus* means-tested public assistance, rather than social insurance *versus* tax-financed benefits payable as a citizen right.[28]

Beveridge himself was under constant pressure from both the Treasury and the Cabinet Office to pare down his social security budget to an economically defensible minimum, in the light of the expected post-war economic crisis; the Beveridge Plan laid great emphasis on the claim that unified state insurance would be extraordinarily cheap to administer, by comparison both with quasi-private social insurance run by approved societies and with public schemes that involved means-tests and personal enquiry. But Beveridge was an enthusiast for national insurance in any case; the argument from cheapness and financial scarcity was of even greater significance in pushing people who were intrinsically sceptical of the insurance principle into the contributory insurance camp. J. M. Keynes, for example, suggested in private that social insurance was little more than an elaborate fiction that merely replicated other, more equitable forms of direct taxation. But it was nevertheless a very convenient fiction, in that it was a relatively painless tax, it forced employers to make some contribution to public welfare and it helped to restrain public expenditure by discouraging the view that the state had a 'bottomless purse'.[29] Even James Meade, severest critic among young Whitehall radicals of what he saw as the wasteful and regressive character of contributory insurance, nevertheless admitted that the very high levels of wartime and post-war taxation made the prospect of transferring social security costs to general taxation in the highest degree unlikely.[30] There was also the argument, particularly popular in the Economic Section of the Cabinet Office, that adjustments in flat-rate benefits and contributions would constitute a much simpler means of stabilising post-war employment levels than more wide-ranging fiscal management.[31] And, finally, there was the issue of inflation. From 1940 onwards much of the search for new income-maintenance devices was driven by the fear that high wartime demand would fuel wage-inflation,[32] a fear that was no less acute during the severe labour shortages at the end of the war. Political enthusiasm for insurance was closely linked to the belief that – in a period of prolonged fiscal and monetary crisis – insurance (even when compulsory) would reinforce the ethic and practice of saving, whereas benefits paid for out of taxation would reinforce demands for higher pay.[33]

Such functional and utilitarian arguments undoubtedly helped to buttress and popularise social insurance in an adverse economic climate. Yet there were other influences of a less tangible and measurable kind that also wove themselves into the social security debate. One of these was the specific character of the debate on citizenship, which took on a new lease of life from the circumstances of fighting a 'people's war', and deserves much more detailed historical scrutiny than it has so far received.[34] In the early 1940s there were several models of citizenship competing in the ideological arena, but all of them had in common the fact that they tended to cut across and diminish the centrality of arguments based on social and economic class. Within the Labour Party, social policy theorists did not cease to discuss poverty and inequality in terms of class, but there was nevertheless a marked shift of emphasis away from problems peculiar to the poor towards concern with all forms of economic insecurity across the social spectrum. In the debate on the introduction of national insurance, Clement Attlee claimed it as a positive virtue that Labour's social legislation was 'designed not for one class but for all' and that it was 'not directed to the mitigation of one special hardship, such as sickness, old age, or unemployment, but simply to loss of income wherever it should occur'.[35] Universal contributory insurance fitted much more harmoniously into such a vision of common citizen experience and shared economic problems than vertical redistribution between taxpayers and non-taxpayers, rich and poor (particularly in a period in which it was widely assumed that wide economic differences were in any case being whittled away by controls over profits and investment and by steeply progressive taxation).[36]

A comparable, though more complex and ambiguous, vision of citizenship can be found in the writings of Beveridge. Beveridge's support for insurance was deeply embedded in a more general political philosophy that was not peculiar to Beveridge himself but was widely pervasive in Whitehall and in many wider areas of public life throughout the early and mid-twentieth century. This philosophy had its roots in certain features of nineteenth-century liberalism, but it was not, as is sometimes supposed, simply one of sustaining or adapting market economics. It consisted rather of an ancient theory of citizenship, within which citizenship was earned or acquired by means of some kind of moral or behavioural entitlement, rather than merely as a passive birthright open to all comers. As Quentin Skinner has recently argued, the classical view of citizenship as a bundle of 'duties' (as opposed to the democratic emphasis on 'rights') survived until well into the nineteenth century; and I would like to suggest that it survived well into the twentieth century too, and was of particular salience in discussions of social policy.[37] Often reference to this question was somewhat oblique because, particularly after 1918, policy-makers and administrators were uneasily conscious of the new political culture of encircling mass democracy.[38] But the persistence of, and attachment to, this older idea of citizenship can be perceived in many spheres. It can be found most clearly in the view that full citizen rights should be attached to some kind of tangible foothold in the body politic – a foothold originally linked to ownership of property and capacity to bear arms, but gradually extended to include payment of rates and taxes, headship of a household, tenured employment, and all other forms of economic independence (such independence being deemed the indispensable guarantor of freedom from undue influence or corruption). By contrast 'dependence', in any form, disabled its victim from full citizenship by turning him or her into the client of a patron – be the patron a great landlord, a capricious employer, the local parish, the head of a household, or the administrative organs of a benevolent state.

Such ideas had clearly exercised a powerful influence on the history of the constitution, but they were no less ubiquitous, if less explicitly spelt out, in the history of social welfare. They were evident in the disqualification of paupers from voting rights (not repealed until 1918), and in the exclusion of public assistance beneficiaries from standing for election to all forms of local government (not repealed until 1946). They can be seen in the recurrent anxiety of the early twentieth-century Treasury to make the scope of taxation coterminous with the franchise and in the efforts of Edwardian reformers to use social-welfare schemes to foster the growth of representation and self-government. In the social-welfare literature of the 1920s, the themes of poverty and unemployment were closely intertwined with, and often secondary to, the theme of instructing the new mass electorate on its duties as well as its rights.[39] Beveridge, in the 1930 edition of *Unemployment: a Problem of Industry*, had specifically linked the theme of contributory insurance to the advance of civic freedom, whereas non-contributory public assistance was associated with a semi-feudal dependence and servility.[40] In other words, contribution based on employment was both the sign and the substance of full citizenship, as public service based on property had been in ages long gone by. The deliberations of the Royal Commission on Unemployment Insurance in 1932–3 suggested that such a theory still had a powerful resonance in many quarters, even in an era of mass unemployment. The war of 1939–45 not merely restored the prospect of work for all, but also re-legitimised the language of ancient constitutional and 'Anglo-Saxon' freedoms – themes which fed powerfully into the vision of the 'British community' and the 'British race' set out in the Beveridge Plan.[41] Echoes of such connections abound, not merely in the writings of Beveridge, but in wider administrative and parliamentary discussions of the insurance principle between 1942 and 1948.[42]

As Barbara Wootton succinctly put it, 'universal' insurance 'offered a way round this deserving and undeserving business ... we are all, so to speak, made "deserving" by Act of Parliament'.[43]

This vision of contributory insurance as a sort of modernist embodiment of antique civic virtue explains something of its vogue among administrators and Whitehall intellectuals of the Beveridge stamp, but more remains to be said about its wider popularity. This can also be, at least partially, explained in subjective and ideological terms. A great deal has been written over the past forty years about the impact of mass unemployment and total war on the transition to 'collectivism': about the wartime shift to fiscal and economic management, the expansion in social services and public ownership, and the change in popular expectations of government that led inexorably to the Labour victory of 1945. Even historians who have been sceptical about the degree of those changes have nevertheless seen the Second World War as a watershed in the growth of 'positive liberty' and the interventionist role of the state. What is often overlooked however is widespread evidence of sentiments of the opposite kind: of continuing scepticism of state authority, dislike of personal contact with officialdom and tenacious attachments to old notions of privacy and personal liberty – all of which were not weakened but reinforced by the experience of mass mobilisation. These attitudes manifested themselves in many different ways, ranging from public opinion surveys to popular humour, and were often expressed by the self-same people who were pressing most strongly for measures of redistributive social policy. They were evident, for example, in the numerous surveys of opinion about the future of the social services, which revealed again and again that people were hoping for more social security and better health services – but that at the same time they were strongly opposed to the growth of bureaucracy, and to all forms of official interference in private lives.[44] The dilemma which these attitudes posed was clearly spelt out in wartime discussions of full employment, when, for example, representatives of the trades unions expressed their total hostility to all forms of post-war price and wage control, except through the agency of free collective bargaining, and to all forms of compulsory re-training and direction of labour, except in respect of a minuscule minority of habitual vagrants and tramps.[45]

Such attitudes were closely linked to widespread popular resentment of officialdom and they also go some way towards explaining the perhaps surprising lack of electoral interest in, or enthusiasm for, Labour's pre-war proposals for a universal welfare system financed out of direct taxation. The latter was not of course supposed to be linked to a means-test or other official enquiry; but there appears to have been widespread scepticism about whether a universal non-contributory system *could*, in practice, be operated without disciplinary constraints. In 1932, Beatrice Webb had carefully spelt out to the Royal Commission on Unemployment Insurance her views on the administrative regulations under which a non-contractual 'Universal Subsistence Allowance' would be put into effect. It would, she explained, be essential for labour exchanges to have 'the means of *ordering* men and women to put in full-time attendance *somewhere*'. For younger men and women there would be 'a prescribed attendance for a *Health Course* giving a varied day at Swedish Drill and other appropriate exercises, varied by lectures, etc'. All benefit-drawers would take part in daily physical exercise, and in 'Fatigue parties in which all would serve in turn, to do all the necessary cleaning, cooking, serving, etc'. Any who refused would be 'struck off subsistence for wantonly throwing up their job', or 'offered admission to one or other type of Occupation Centre': 'a hundred years of experience teaches us that the "economy" of unconditional Outdoor Relief is delusive, because the number of claimants quickly increases, in such a way as to transcend all limits to the total cost'.[46] Such a vision of social security appears to have had little popular appeal even in the depths of a world depression and mass unemployment. It was even less appealing a decade later to a workforce struggling under the impact of rationing, defence regulations, and wholesale military and industrial conscription.[47] It was perhaps therefore unsurprising that, for all the levelling rhetoric of the war, public opinion responded so enthusiastically to the more prosaic promises of contributory social insurance. At the end of the day, maybe the debaters of 1946 were right after all: the Webbs, with their stark and lucid vision of the real issues at stake in the moral economy of welfare, had served the cause of limited reform, pragmatic compromise and tenacious private libertarianism only too well.

None of these factors in itself provides an adequate theoretical rationale of the contributory insurance principle, but together they give some idea of the complex cultural and historical context in which the curious harnessing of insurance to the moral rhetoric of 'universalism' came about. Contributory insurance became the financial keystone of the post-war welfare state, not because, as Beveridge had claimed, interruption of earnings was the major cause of poverty, but because insurance fitted in with current perceptions of fiscal reality and with current evaluations of virtue, citizenship, gender, personal freedom, and the nature of the state. It was a package that was to prove extraordinarily tenacious. Even Richard Titmuss – who fiercely criticised Beveridge for muddling the issues of 'contract' and 'citizenship' and conflating two principles that were mutually contradictory[48] – nevertheless ended up by endorsing and even reinforcing that contradiction: like the Beveridge Plan, Titmuss's national superannuation scheme of the late 1950s aimed simultaneously *both* to cover everyone as a matter of universal entitlement *and* to reward people according to what they had paid. To make these points is not to suggest that, from some ahistorical vantage-point, the emphasis upon contributory insurance was somehow misconceived and mistaken. On the contrary, all social welfare schemes are part of a specific historical environment: from the historian's point of view they are neither right nor wrong, but simply periscopes into the mind, morality and power structures of a given period. Our job is not to rewind or re-write the policies and political theories of past times, but to draw out the large elements of culture, convention, compromise and rhetoric in what are often seen as 'scientific' policies or models of abstract justice.

CHAPTER 7

Social Policy

Chris Pierson

THERE IS perhaps no area of Britain's post-war experience in which the apparent contrast between attitudes in the 1940s and the 1990s is so acute as in the field of social policy. For many, the forging of the welfare state in the years immediately following the Second World War, in line with the vision of the messianic Beveridge Report and under the purposeful direction of Clement Attlee's Labour Government, was central to the creation of a new and, upon some accounts, socialist Britain. Building upon a sense of communal purpose and governmental competence generated by the experience of total war, social provision 'from cradle to grave' was to be part of a new order from which the poverty, mass unemployment and urban squalor of the 1930s would be expunged. Experience proved a little less heroic than this. Nonetheless, implementation of the Beveridge-inspired social policy agenda in the aftermath of war might still be seen as the partial basis for a new political consensus in which left and right, capital and labour, Labour and Conservative, agreed about the fundamentals of social, political and economic life. In social policy, this meant agreement about the public provision of core social services (including health, education and pensions) and about the diversion of an increment from an expanding economy to fund the extension of these state-delivered services. So central was social policy to this post-war agreement that some commentators simply call it 'the welfare state consensus'.[1]

In these accounts, the quarter century that followed the end of the war is set in the sharpest possible contrast to the experience of the last twenty years. The election of the first Thatcher government in 1979 is often seen as the symbolic moment at which the post-war welfare state consensus was abandoned, heralding a period of intensified political polarisation in which the Conservatives sought, in the end successfully, to abandon the centrist ground of the post-war years. Abandoning the ambitions of both Labour and Conservative governments of the 1950s and 1960s, Margaret Thatcher's first administration explicitly jettisoned the governmental commitment to sustain full employment, celebrated the virtues of private rather than public provision and set itself to reduce the burden of social expenditure which, it argued, had seriously eroded those economic incentives which alone made sustained economic growth possible. Following the Thatcherite lead, public opinion was slowly weaned off its growing dependence on the state and a popular base of political support was constructed around the common-sense logic of self-help and reward for personal endeavour. In some versions of this story, what is emerging in the Britain of the 1990s is a 'new consensus', built around the policy successes of the Thatcher era and driven by the imperatives of a global economy. These changes have obliged 'New Labour' to join the Conservative Party in embracing the merits of a free-market economy with minimal state intervention. Just as the Conservative Party found itself in the post-war period drawn onto Labour's terrain, so is it argued now that Labour's only chance of electoral success lies in embracing the anti-welfarist agenda of its political opponents.

Of course, such a gloss on post-war experience is not wholly mistaken. Clearly, both public sentiment and governing opinion are decidedly different from 1945. So too are the welfare state's institutional structures, its funding arrangements and, perhaps most consequentially, the structure of its constituent population. But, in fact, accounts of changing ideas about the welfare state – perhaps even these changing ideas themselves – are strongly parasitic upon a very familiar but nonetheless seriously flawed account of the post-war social policy experience. It is with redressing this account, and relocating the place of changing ideas within it, that this chapter is principally concerned.

'IN THE BEGINNING, THERE WAS BEVERIDGE...'

Casting his long and rather imperious shadow across half a century of social policy debate in Britain is the imposing figure of William Beveridge, a man who still occupies a unique place in the iconography of the British welfare state. The long-popular story is one in which Beveridge, the lifelong liberal reformer, was charged in 1941 with preparing a report in which he would tidy up the administrative loose ends of the hotchpotch of social legislation that had grown up, in a more or less *ad hoc* way, in pre-war Britain. From this rather unpromising remit, Beveridge is seen to have fashioned an agenda which allowed him to present a 'revolutionary' blueprint for an encompassing system of social insurance in the post-war world. Through a mixture of adept politicking, brilliant PR and lucky timing, Beveridge was able to channel a flood tide of popular acclaim behind his proposals and browbeat a reluctant wartime coalition (led unusually, in this instance, from the rear by Winston Churchill) into committing itself to implementation of the broad lines of his proposals at the war's end. The Labour government, swept into office in 1945 on a wave of reforming zeal, became the instrument through which the Beveridgian blueprint was realised in the 'Five Shining Years' from 1945 to 1950.[2] What he offered was a uniquely British blend of innovation and continuity, in his own words, 'a British revolution'.[3] In their dizzier moments, some commentators were even persuaded to see

Beveridge as a kind of pragmatic socialist (though again of a peculiarly British kind).

Fifty years on, Beveridge's stature is curiously undiminished. Every major piece of government legislation and every serious-minded proposal of the opposition parties pays due homage to the great inheritance from Beveridge. Labour and Conservative have each been happy to claim him as their own, (a little more the collectivist in Labour's view, rather more of an individualist for the Tories), thus conveniently glossing over his membership of the Liberal Party. Although the reputation of both the post-war Labour government and the wartime coalition have now been subject to the most thoroughgoing revision at the hands of right-wing historians, Beveridge remains a central figure. In Correlli Barnett's acerbic *Audit of War*, Beveridge ranks high indeed in the pantheon of late Victorian liberal-minded, elitist do-gooders responsible for Britain's post-war decline.[4] Whether as the 'People's William' or the Number One 'New Jerusalemist', Beveridge has been afforded centre stage in the fashioning of post-war Britain in general and its welfare state in particular.

Crucial as the role of Beveridge was, it will not quite bear the weight of all this responsibility. If his report was something more than a tidying up of pre-war arrangements, it was also something less than 'a social revolution'. Folklore has it that the British welfare state was sprung, pristine but fully-formed, from the capacious mind of the great reformer. It was Beveridge's genius to encapsulate the wartime spirit of community and solidarity and to harness it to a practical programme for collective provision once the war was over, guaranteeing the British citizen social security 'from the cradle to the grave'. But this gloss is misleading. Much recent historical scholarship has been concerned to show just how much the welfare state after 1945 owed not only to the innovating Liberal Administration of 1906–11, but also to Conservative state interventions in the late nineteenth century and between the wars. Similarly, the fount of post-war reform has been relocated (rather less romantically) in the widely perceived threat of a commonly uncertain future or even in the pressure of a trades union movement strengthened by the experience of wartime full employment.[5] Certainly, the financial consequences of implementing the Report made some members of the Coalition Cabinet – above all the Chancellor Kingsley Wood – uneasy. But Beveridge was far from proposing to write a blank cheque upon the largesse of the state. He repeatedly stressed the centrality of the contributory and insurance principles to his plans. The levels of benefits, which he envisaged would secure subsistence, were set extremely low. Non means-tested pensions were to be phased in over a twenty-year period to allow for the build up of contributions. Family allowances for the first child were abandoned in the final Report in order to save the Treasury about £100 million per annum.[6] The nature and levels of provision were designed not to 'stifle incentive, opportunity, responsibility: in establishing a national minimum, [the State] should leave room and encouragement for voluntary action by each individual to provide more than that minimum for himself and his family'.[7] As Addison has noted, what was really radical about Beveridge's Report were the assumptions he made about other areas of government policy in the post-war period: most notably, the commitment to support full employment and to introduce a National Health Service.[8]

Despite the comparative modesty of Beveridge's proposals, in the austere climate of post-war Britain they were never fully implemented. The two elements of the adequacy principle (that benefits 'be sufficient without further resources to provide the minimum income needed for subsistence' and that they 'continue indefinitely without means test, so long as the need continues') were never satisfied.[9] Although eliminating the means test was a central ambition of Beveridge's Report, (and explains, in part, its extraordinary popular acclaim), the role of means-tested benefits has actually expanded in the subsequent fifty years. Claimants of means-tested Income

Support (and its precursors) rose from about 2 per cent of the population in 1948 to 10 per cent in 1993.[10] Beveridge's cautious approach to phasing-in the contributory retirement pension proved politically unsustainable and pensions were paid 'in full' from 1948, but at a rate which was acknowledged to fall beneath subsistence levels. Although the pension grew relative to average (disposable) incomes up until 1983, it has now fallen in relative terms so that by 1993 it was worth about 15 per cent of average gross male earnings. This relative decline in the value of the statutory pension looks almost certain to continue.[11]

Thus at its very inception we can see in prospect several of the most salient features of British social policy throughout the post-war period. Of these, the most important have been the dual concern with costs and political feasibility. At times these twin imperatives have coincided, on other occasions they have pulled in opposing directions. But in whatever combination, they have been responsible for many of the most acute anomalies and irrationalities of the post-war welfare state. We can also see in this period the formative mythologisation of Beveridge's legacy. For some, he offered the safety net that lay beneath an extensive apparatus of voluntary and private provision, for others he foreshadowed a network of universal provision for all life's contingencies which would make private provision increasingly irrelevant. It was this ambivalence that allowed a broad (but far from universal) swathe of political opinion to welcome the report. Fifty years on, the historians' verdict is not so kind. Rodney Lowe, no knee-jerk critic of the welfare state, characterises Beveridge's social policy heritage in the following terms:

Far from being a revolutionary and logical document – as it was popularly portrayed in the 1940s – the Beveridge Report was conservative, illogical and ultimately impractical. Its objectives at the time appeared visionary [but it was] inherently conservative in its retention of the insurance principle, its limitation of the state's responsibility to the provision of a subsistence-level benefit and its emphasis on voluntary insurance.[12]

Beveridge's report also helped to underwrite three further peculiarities of post-war British sentiment about the welfare state. First, there was the supposition that the welfare state was in some sense a uniquely British achievement. It has taken twenty-five years of comparative studies of social policy elsewhere in the world to begin to persuade even quite informed opinion that these things have been done differently, and sometimes rather better, in other places. Secondly, it helped to set the terms for an increasingly fruitless debate about 'universalism' and 'targeting', giving universalism a particular cachet in a system which could never deliver it. Thirdly, and perhaps inadvertently, it opened up that space between the rhetoric of the welfare state (both for and against) and the reality of social policy practice which has remained a characteristic of British discussions right down to our own time.

THE COMING OF CONSENSUS

It is also to this formative time around the end of the war that many have looked for the roots of that ideological consensus which was said to have lifted the welfare state 'above party politics' for the best part of thirty years. In fact, the commitment to a 'comprehensive' welfare state was just one (very important) foundation of the newly consensual terrain of post-war British politics. The other elements were a commitment to broadly Keynesian economic policies designed to secure full (male) employment and economic growth, a mixed and managed economy with elements of both public and private ownership, and a broad-based agreement between right and left, and between capital and labour, over these basic social institutions (a mixed-market economy and a welfare state) and the accommodation of their (legitimately) competing interests through elite-level negotiation.[13] For many commentators in the 1950s and 1960s, the coming of this consensus politics heralded 'an irreversible change'. Within the sphere of social policy, Tom Marshall argued in 1965 that there was now 'little difference of opinion as to the services that must be provided, and it is generally agreed that, whoever provides them, the overall responsibility for the welfare of the citizens must remain with the state'.[14] Still more confidently, Charles Schottland proclaimed that 'whatever its beginnings, the welfare state is here to stay. Even its opponents argue only about its extension'.[15] Looking back from the much more troubled perspective of the 1980s, Ramesh Mishra comments that 'state commitment to maintaining full employment, providing a range of basic services for all citizens, and preventing or relieving poverty seemed so integral to post-war society as to be almost irreversible'.[16]

This sense of a shared and irreversible commitment to the new terrain of the welfare state was further entrenched by the collective common sense of the flowering sub-discipline of social administration. Under the aegis of Richard Titmuss at the London School of Economics, social administration turned out a wealth of policies and policy-makers whose agenda was to improve the delivery of a range of social services, the purpose and nature of which seemed uncontroversial. Tom Marshall's famous 1949 lectures on 'Citizenship and Social Class' set the Beveridge reforms in a suitably grand pageant of British history, with well-developed social rights (embracing 'the right to share to the full in the social heritage and to live the life of a civilised being according to the standards prevailing in the society') as the pinnacle of a centuries' long expansion of British citizenship.[17] Writing at the end of this epoch, David Donnison captured the essentials of this reforming mind-set:

'Social' policies were regarded as dealing with the redistribution of the fruits of economic growth, the management
of its human effects, and the compensation of those who
suffered from them . . . the people who constitute the broad
middle ground of the electorate . . . could gradually be
induced to give general support to these ideas and the
programmes which follow from them . . . government and
its social services, accountable to this central consensus,
were the natural vehicles of progress. Equalising policies
could be carried forward by the public services, propelled
by engines of economic growth which would produce the
resources to create a juster society without anyone suffering on the way.[18]

At one level the consensus was real enough. Most of the
immediate post-war social policy initiatives had been
developed under the wartime Coalition government (whatever the internal differences within that government had been).
The Beveridge Report had been (more or less reluctantly)
endorsed and the Family Allowance Act passed before the
advent of the Labour Government. Butler's Education Act,
which was to set the framework for education in the post-war
world, had been passed in 1944, as had the White Paper on
Employment, which opened with the declaration that 'the
Government accept as one of their primary aims and responsibilities the maintenance of a high and stable level of employment'.[19] The National Insurance Bill – through which the
Labour Government sought to enact Beveridge's proposals –
excited very little Parliamentary opposition. The creation of the
NHS faced rather sterner resistance, above all from the medical
profession, but also from critics within the Conservative Party.
Although, fifty years on, the Labour Party continues to make
political capital from the Tories' initial hesitation in supporting
the NHS, the Conservatives were astute enough to swing their
unequivocal support behind the service once its enormous electoral popularity had been established.

For some, the acid test of consensus came with the return of a Conservative government in 1951. In the welfare arena at least, there was considerable continuity in the early 1950s. Indeed, in the first decade after the war, when housing was an especially pressing issue, it seemed as if the competition between Labour and Conservative focused principally upon who could build the most new homes.[20] Perhaps the Conservatives were a little more conscious of questions of cost, but it was Labour that had made the highly symbolic (and hotly-contested) decision to introduce user charges in the health service.

Yet recent scholarship suggests that the ubiquity of consensus in the 'Butskellite' years may well have been exaggerated. Certainly the electoral campaign of 1945, with Churchill's notorious 'Gestapo' claim and Labour's radical plans for widespread nationalisation, did not present itself to contemporaries as especially consensual. The creation of the National Health Service was, as we have seen, no straightforward affair and Peter Taylor-Gooby has argued that the apparent commonalities of policy direction through the 1950s concealed quite divergent understandings of the appropriate bases of the welfare state.[21] The 'little local difficulty' that Macmillan experienced in 1958, when the Treasury team under Peter Thorneycroft resigned over the Cabinet's unwillingness to back cuts in social expenditure, indicated the conviction of some Conservatives even in the 1950s that the costs of the welfare state were growing too fast. In a recent reappraisal, Ben Pimlott writes of 'the myth of consensus', whilst, from (what was) the centre-right, Timothy Raison quotes Lord Fraser of Kilmorack to a similar effect: 'To say ... that the situation after 1945 amounted to a "consensus" is a myth of more recent origin. No one thought that at the time'.[22]

Rodney Lowe offers a nicely balanced judgement:

The period from 1945 to 1975 has been conventionally portrayed as one of political consensus. This is justified in relation to the basic framework of welfare policy, where there was a continuing all-party commitment to the mixed economy, the maintenance of full employment and a minimum standard of social security. However there was bitter animosity between the two major parties ... as well as fundamental differences in their underlying philosophies. Labour's priority was to engineer a more equal society through greater state intervention and, if necessary, higher taxation, the Conservatives were willing only to accept that degree of intervention and taxation which was compatible with market efficiency and personal initiative.[23]

In reality, the two parties were pursuing rather different agenda through what we have already seen was the quite ambivalent logic of the Beveridge settlement. Both were constrained by electoral imperatives, (the Conservatives by the popularity of the welfare state, Labour by a resistance to ever higher rates of taxation). Both parties and their several governments were the beneficiaries of an unprecedented period of sustained economic growth and near-full employment, (just as both faced the problem of a long-term comparative decline in Britain's economic performance). The politics of consensus is almost always a positive-sum game. In this period, consensus – or at least the steady growth of social spending under all governments – was, above all, a product of economic growth. Agreement rested upon the capacity to generate a growing economic surplus with which to satisfy simultaneously a multiplicity of disparate claims. The ending of this epoch of consensus had little to do with changing ideas, (whatever the subsequent rationalisations). It was primarily the product of a changing external environment which turned games of rather inefficient positive-sum into pure loss.

THIRTY WASTED YEARS?

With the benefit of perfect hindsight, it has become the habit for some to write off the years between the end of the Second World War and the late 1970s as a rather shabby interlude in the continuing story of Britain's comparative economic decline. The welfare state, after its admittedly rather 'heroic' phase in the late 1940s, had settled into a routinised pattern of incremental growth and institutional torpor. It had become the object of official complacency and increasingly the feeding ground for a set of vested (and often well-organised) producer interests. Critics from both the right (Hayek, Powell, the early IEA) and the left (Abel-Smith, Townsend, Titmuss) had apparently come and gone with comparatively little effect upon the opinion of either government or public.

In fact, the existence of these critics gives the lie to the view that nothing of much interest was said about the welfare state between the implementation of Beveridge and the rise of Thatcher. Indeed, 'the Jewel in the Crown' of the new welfare system, the NHS, whilst enjoying unparalleled and virtually uninterrupted public esteem, has been under financial duress and official review almost constantly since its founding in 1948. Although studies of the welfare state have tended to concentrate upon certain decisive episodes of profound legislative and administrative innovation, (1906–11, 1945–8, the period after 1987), it is a characteristic of welfare state development that many of the most profound changes can only be observed in the *longue durée*. The basis for entitlement of many benefits, plus the inexorable logic of demography, mean that any legislative reorganisation is characteristically followed by a slow but sustained increase in citizens with a quasi-legal title to what is, in sum, a significant part of society's productive output. So it was that the legislative innovations made before the First World War only had their cumulative political, fiscal and financial consequences in the two decades between the wars.

In this way, a period of comparative social policy inactivity may nonetheless be a time of profound change in the structure of the welfare state – in the number of its beneficiaries, in the size and distribution of its costs and even in its public esteem. Thus in the period between 1945 and the mid-1970s, the proportion of GDP spent on the main welfare services rose from just 5 per cent to around 20 per cent.[24] The proportion of the population above pensionable age moved towards one sixth. Expenditure on the NHS rose from about £500 million in 1951 to £5596 million by 1975.[25] In a pattern that replicated international experience, the terms and conditions under which benefits were granted tended to be 'liberalised', with growing numbers of groups given claimant status, qualifying criteria more loosely interpreted and benefit levels increased in line with the growing levels of affluence in the wider national community. As critics on the right were swiftest (but not quite alone) in pointing out, these changes not only massively increased levels of state expenditure (and the corresponding need for tax revenue), they also generated massive new lobbies of political interest (of both producers and consumers). Both the producers of welfare services and their clients had an active interest in seeing the size and resources of the public sector expand, as they did consistently if at times a little erratically throughout the twenty five years following the war.

'THE WELFARE STATE IN CRISIS': A LONG CHAPTER IN THE HISTORY OF IDEAS

Amongst those who have seen a decisive shift in the politics of welfare after 1975, changing ideas are often given a quite central place. Certainly, in the 'quality' press, the idea of 'the welfare state in crisis' was the stuff of a thousand hand-wringing leaders. But initially, the crisis tended to be seen in terms of a short- or medium-term problem of costs in a context of recession brought on by the first oil-price rise of 1973. It was critics from the New Right (and, ironically, the New Left) who first identified the problems of the mid-1970s as an expression of the contradictory underpinning structure of entire post-war welfare-state order.[26] Of course, a libertarian critique of the welfare state settlement had always been available, but it had not commanded much support in the political mainstream since the accession of Macmillan in 1957. Since that time, its critics now argued, the welfare state had become a part of that unthinking (and debilitating) social-democratic consensus which it was the historic task of the emergent New Right to break. In the most heroic version of this story, a small number of leading Conservative politicians (most significantly Keith Joseph and, subsequently, Margaret Thatcher), disillusioned at the fall of the Heath government, were won over to the cause of the neo-liberal free marketeers by the sheer clarity and force of their intellectual argument. Armed with this intellectual (and moral) conviction, they set about an ideological transformation of the Conservative party, carrying it away from the pale pink 'me-too-ism' of the post-war years, towards distinctive New Right terrain. Upon this account, the newly ideological Conservative party was able to tap into a growing (if inarticulate) strain of popular disenchantment (not least amongst skilled manual workers) about the state of the welfare state and thus to fashion the historic victory of May 1979.

Certainly, as an account of the politics of party support, this story has a number of bald electoral facts on its side, and the revisionist story that now sees the passage from Callaghan to Thatcher as one of seamless continuity is surely mistaken. Yet it is not really clear that changing perceptions of the welfare state in either governing or public opinion had quite so much to do with this political about-turn and, as is now widely recognised, the rhetorical claims about transforming the welfare state, which helped to drive forward the Conservative juggernaut, were actually rather poorly vindicated by political practice.

At the elite level, probably the most important ideological change of the early-to-mid 1970s was the collapsing faith in the characteristic claims of Keynesianism, (often set alongside Beveridge's reforms as the other and more important half of the post-war settlement). Of course, there is considerable doubt about whether any phase in Britain's post-war economic policy should really be called 'Keynesian'. Andrew Gamble's judgement is that 'Keynesianism when it was tried was not needed and when it was needed was not tried'.[27] However, there is some reason to think that it was in this period that governing opinion increasingly deserted what it had long taken to be its commitment to a Keynesian policy. In so far as there was a kind of Keynesianism to be abandoned, the decisive move, as has been frequently observed, came before the election of Mrs Thatcher in 1979. Indeed, the symbolic moment of change is often identified with Jim Callaghan speaking at the Labour Party Conference in 1976; instructively, the key passage in the Prime Minister's speech referred not to a change in the external economic environment but rather to a transformation in governing beliefs. ('We used to think that you could just spend your way out of recession [but] the option no longer exists'). Abandoning the commitment to full employment meant abandoning one of the core supporting elements in the Beveridgean welfare state. With the policy shift after 1976 (and the imposition of cash limits) sentiment drifted away from the egalitarian revisionism of the post-war period (in which public services were to be part of a gradualist strategy of equality) towards the more residualist aspiration of 'protecting the weakest in hard times'. In the great public services (such as health and education) the watchword was affordability; in terms of income maintenance and cash transfers, the ideology, at least, was to concentrate resources where they were most needed.

To this extent, when Mrs Thatcher came to power in 1979

she was pushing at a door that was already half open. She was able to take up with vigour and conviction an attitude to public spending which Labour had found itself forced (rather shamefacedly) to adopt. With a renewed enthusiasm after 1979, the emphasis was upon reforming the supply side of the economy, reducing marginal tax rates, reshaping the labour market and controlling the welfare budget. But whilst the private sector was lionised by Mrs Thatcher, and a programme of privatisation of public corporations, income tax cuts and labour market reforms vigorously pressed throughout the 1980s, for the best part of a decade the public provision of welfare remained curiously untransformed. To understand this stasis, we must consider the climate of opinion about welfare amongst a wider and voting public.

In turning to these mass attitudes, we find that the pattern of public opinion, measured by any index other than the willingness to vote for the Conservative Party, is much more ambivalent than a straightforward shift from state and collectivism to market and individualism would suggest. Some critics have argued that the working class was never strongly attached to ideas of welfare rights and social citizenship and trace out 'the long hostility of working people to what is perceived as dependency on public provision'.[28] Others detect, in the 1979 election, the eleventh-hour recognition amongst just enough of the British electorate of 'the incoherence of the providential idea of government in a free society'.[29] It is certainly true that the idea of income maintenance as an aspect of social citizenship has never been strongly entrenched in British popular opinion (in part because it was never really embedded in political practice). It is also true that in the circumstances of the late 1970s it was possible to mount an anti-welfare campaign by tapping into deep-seated resentment of 'something-for-nothing' welfare beneficiaries, to especial effect when it could be suggested that those in receipt of the state's generosity were largely 'outsiders'.[30] But this is a very ancient theme, with the distinction between the 'deserving' and the 'undeserving' poor, hostility to 'shirkers', 'scroungers' and 'fiddlers', and the stigma attaching to 'the dole', 'national assistance' or being 'on the social' having roots which long pre-date Beveridge and even Lloyd George.

In fact, it is ambivalence rather than outright hostility which most characteristically marks out popular attitudes to the welfare state. Taylor-Gooby's several surveys found consistent evidence of differential attitudes to benefits targeted upon minorities (above all, lone-parent benefits and unemployment benefits) which elicited considerable hostility alongside substantial endorsements of the mainstream (and most expensive) forms of public provision in health, education and old-age pensions.[31] Indeed, even with questions that control for tax-blindness (that is, using prompts which explicitly state that an increase in social spending will mean raising taxes), a large and growing majority expressed support for increased social expenditure throughout the 1980s. Such results meet with some scepticism amongst those who believe that respondents will express what are perceived to be positive views when these are cost-free, but in the privacy of the polling booth express a preference (however misplaced) for the party they believe will cut social expenditure. In itself, this is not a watertight response. Electoral surveys tend to show that Labour's social policies have been preferred by many voters, but that this preference has been trumped by a belief in the Conservative's greater capacity to manage the economy successfully. The public also appears (quite understandably) to be much less concerned than political parties about questions of public or private provision. Voters, it seems, are inclined to support those elements of public provision that they believe will favour them and disavow those which they believe will not. Questions of market or state, individualism or collectivism come some way down their list of priorities.

It is this which, at least in part, explains the peculiar record of Conservative governments on the welfare state over the past seventeen years. Committed to the retrenchment of public expenditure, the first Thatcher Administration (1979–83) saw social expenditure rise by 10 per cent, increasing as a proportion of GDP from 21.7 per cent to 23.6 per cent. Of course, this was not because the Thatcher government had 'gone soft' on welfare but because running a welfare state with mass unemployment is (as Beveridge had warned) extremely expensive. Social expenditure fell in the second half of the 1980s (as the economy expanded and unemployment fell) but in the recession of the early 1990s it grew as a proportion of GDP by 5 per cent from 21.4 per cent to 26.4 per cent.[32] The level of social spending as a proportion of overall national production and the overall levels of taxation needed to sustain it were little different in 1995 from what they had been in 1979.[33] The greatest retrenchment – and the greatest increase in disciplinary administration (the obverse of social citizenship) – tended to be focused upon those who were most dependent upon the state for income maintenance. According to one conservative estimate, 'the number of individuals in poor households rose from 5.1 million [in 1979] . . . to 9.4 million in 1985'.[34] Income inequality became more pronounced, especially after 1985, when benefits came to do rather less work in counteracting the inequalities of original (market-generated) incomes.

Still more instructive is the record of housing finance under recent administrations. One of the most successful policies of the 1980s (in terms of meeting its ambitions and realising an electoral dividend) was the promotion of owner-occupation through the sale of public sector housing. Between 1970 and 1990, levels of owner-occupation rose from 55.3 per cent of households to 67.6 per cent. One of the themes attending this movement was that of greater self-reliance within a 'property-owning democracy' and certainly the government was able to cut its housing budget in half during the 1980s. Yet the withdrawal of funds to local authority housing was probably matched by the increasing costs of housing benefit (an element of the social security budget) and by tax expenditure on income tax relief on mortgages (which amounted to nearly £8 billion in 1990/1). One form of disbursement (spending on public housing) was deemed to be public expenditure, the other (subsidising private housing through tax expenditures) was not. On the back of this accounting distinction, a contrast was drawn between a debilitating and dependency-creating subsidy of public sector homes on the one hand and the state's support for the home owner's self-reliance on the other. This captures a more general problem with the classification of social policy efforts. Policy on housing tenure may have looked like a major shift away from 'the welfare state' but the net costs to the public exchequer were probably little changed. Defining activities and expenditures into (or out of) 'the welfare state' may make them subject to a particular political interpretation – but it does not change their costs.

This problem of the politically consequential business of defining where the limits of public welfare lie often makes it quite difficult to see what is really going on. In the run-up to the 1979 election, one set of images associated with welfare – as producer-controlled, dependency-generating and wasteful, feather-bedding the indolent at the cost of the industrious, sponsoring the morally subversive at the expense of 'ordinary families' – was used to mobilise support against Labour and the 'post-war consensus'. At the same time, the provision of the great public services and many of those who delivered them, above all in the NHS, remained popular. The expectation was that, stripped of the inefficient, the inessential and the undeserving, there would be more public welfare to go around. The popular aspiration was not really for less but for more public welfare – but delivered in ways which were less wasteful and more sensitive to the requirements of the final consumer. The more ideologically-driven (and perhaps consistent) right wished to see a more systematic abandonment of the welfare state in favour of market mechanisms (in education and health care, for example). But those who had to gather up the votes were much more mindful of what a less ideologically-minded (and perhaps somewhat inconsistent) electorate wanted: ideally, more for less; at the very least, more for the same.

This points us towards a continuing ambiguity in public thinking about welfare. It is really not very clear what people think the welfare state is. Given its catch-all character and powerful, if imprecise, normative overtones, this is hardly surprising. When people associate the welfare state with the apparatus of social security and/or income maintenance, they may be driven by imperatives of adequacy for deserving cases (targeting and minimising costs), though there will always be few political prizes for calling old age pensioners a drain on the nation's reserves. When they are thinking principally of the NHS, they may wish to see the optimal affordable provision for all citizens (universalism often combined with considerable 'cost-blindness'). Popular sentiment probably still tends to think of welfare states as redistributing downwards (to the variously conceived 'poor', 'dependent', 'disadvantaged' or 'less privileged'), yet there is substantial evidence that, in practice, the welfare state redistributes across the individual life-cycle or even upwards.[35] One of the reasons Conservative administrations have found it so difficult to constrain social expenditure in recent years is that, in the face of certain rhetorical claims about the welfare state and its redistributive consequences, many of the advantages of public spending flow to their own natural supporters, making further retrenchment difficult. Given the structure of public opinion, it may be easier politically to redistribute the burden of welfare services by changing the taxation regime (from direct to indirect), restructuring the services internally or changing the charging regime than by seeking to transfer services directly into the private sector. It is this logic that has shaped the actual pattern of welfare state reform under Conservative administrations since 1987.

BRINGING THE MARKET TO THE STATE

It seems clear that the original and 'authentic' aspiration of the New Right is to bring the state to market. Ideally, neo-liberals would wish to see welfare provision transferred from public administration to private markets. The state's role should be confined to the legal regulation of these privately-provided services and (perhaps) the sponsorship of those unable to fend for themselves. This has not generally accorded with British experience. Despite some inducements to encourage private provision through the 1980s, health care and education, at least, are services which are still met for most families through the state. In pensions, the state is still a major provider, though it is clear that private and occupational pensions will have to carry much more of the weight of income maintenance in the future. When wholesale reform of the welfare state did finally get started under the third Thatcher Administration, the central premise was this: to bring the market to the state. In this most recent period of reform, the general strategy has not been to privatise the welfare state (though significant areas of welfare provision have, of course, been 'contracted out'). Rather, it has been to introduce market-like structures within the public sector. The promise has been that choice, competition and the power of the consumer can all work their magic without a transfer of ownership into the private sector. On the one hand, the government's pursuit of such a strategy (generally without any piloting of the reforms) shows its deep-seated conviction that market solutions will work. Less obviously, it may also point towards at least a residual feeling in British public opinion that for commercial interests to profit from the pro-vision of welfare services (especially health care and the residential care of the elderly-infirm) is improper.

At the most generic level, the strategy of reform for the public services – sometimes referred to as 'the new public management' – has sought to introduce private sector management, organisation and labour market practices into the public sector in the expectation that the service can thus be made to deliver the sorts of service and efficiency that it is supposed the private sector (and its competitive environment) has already realised. More specifically, and most clearly in the areas of health and education, there has been an aspiration to introduce 'internal markets' within the domain of public provision. In these reforms, public funding has been retained but steps have been taken to divide the purchasers from the providers of services. The intention is that individual units (schools, colleges or health care trusts) should compete for consumers of their services. The purchasers of these services (parents, patients or their surrogates) should be able to move their custom between providers with relative ease. Greater information (examination results, waiting list times, proportion of successful procedures, prices) should make it possible for consumers to make effective choices. With resources broadly following consumer choices, competition should encourage efficiency and reward the more successful producers.

Although the techniques of the new public management have also been applied within the Department of Social Security (the single largest area of government administration), the idea of the 'internal market' has rather less purchase in the field of income maintenance. Here, the policy changes of the last decade have been less innovative and more incremental. Although the government has sought 'value for money', its overwhelming concern has been to constrain absolute levels of spending. This is unsurprising. The social security budget constitutes the single largest items of social expenditure, projected at £99 billion for 1997/8, nearly one-third of all public spending.[36] The vast bulk of this money goes on benefits and pensions and is widely regarded as 'consumption' expenditure, contrasting with what is seen as an element of 'investment' in health and education spending. An increasingly important secondary theme has been the impact of benefit levels and entitlements upon the labour market. A continuing ambition of Conservative governments has been to create greater labour market flexibility, not least by making it more attractive to be in low-paid work than in receipt of unemployment benefit or income support (a rather ancient principle which can be retraced at least to the Poor Law Amendment Act of 1834). The carrot has been some form of income supplement for families with a low-waged breadwinner, while the sticks have been a repeated tightening of entitlement to state support and constraint upon the level of improvement of benefit rates. Most recently, this tightening of terms and conditions has included the replacement of unemployment benefits and income support by a more stringently administered Job Seeker's Allowance and closer medical supervision of entitlement to Invalidity Benefit. In 1993, the DSS was able to isolate its 'strategic priorities' in these terms:[37]

- focus benefits on the most needy
- minimise disincentive effects
- simplify the benefit system
- ensure that the system adapts to the differing needs of people it is intended to benefit
- bear down on abuse and fraud
- encourage personal responsibility

It is clear that the climate of opinion within which social policy operates now is profoundly different from that in 1945. Indeed, so much has changed, both within the economy and in our political culture very broadly conceived, that we now occupy a world of ideas which is qualitatively different from that of early post-war Britain. The notion of a public service, for example, has been comprehensively eroded both by the technical arguments of public-choice theory and by a more general scepticism about everyone's stated good intentions. One way or another, permanent mass unemployment has become an accepted commonplace in a way that would have been unthinkable as little as twenty years ago. It is clear, as well, that there has been some movement in popular sentiment from collectivism to individualism and that public expectations about the respective capacity of markets or states to deliver satisfactory outcomes have shifted decisively in favour of the former.

Yet generalisations of this kind can be misleading. Faith in the capacity of state and public solutions was close to an historical peak at the start of our period and was always countermanded by a powerful and longstanding sense that market disciplines should prevail. The welfare state has always serviced individual aspirations and has never been a straightforwardly 'collectivist' institution. Hostility towards the public support of the able-bodied poor and concern about the costs of welfare provision are not products of the political changes of the past twenty-five years but very ancient themes of public policy, (a good deal older than the welfare state itself). Certainly, we should be extremely cautious about attributing the causes of social and political change in recent years to the power of new (or revived) ideas. We know that the ideas of dead economists do have very material effects in the political practice of the present but we also know that the mediation of ideas and practices is extremely complex, perhaps impenetrably so. In fact, systematic sets of ideas about public policy are often read retrospectively into the process through which busy politicians and policy-makers 'puzzle' their way (largely by trial and error) to new solutions in the face of new problems. As Michael Mann observed twenty-five years ago, most people, most of the time, do not carry systematic ideologies around in their heads.[38] In the light of these observations, I think we can be reasonably confident in saying that, although both ideas and practices have changed, the history of social policy in the post-war period is not primarily one of changing ideas shaping a changing political practice.

Certainly, we can reject that story which begins (for good or ill) with the ideas in the Beveridge Report as the founding charter of a radically new post-war system based on social security and social citizenship, proceeds through a period of ideological agreement in the 1950s and 1960s through to a crisis of faith in this established order in the 1970s, issuing in the radical shift rightwards consummated under Mrs Thatcher and thence to a new post-Thatcherite social policy consensus grounded on a new (and much more right-of-centre) terrain. In essence, the original settlement was never so comprehensive or coherent and the similar policy outcomes of the 1950s and 1960s were more a reflection of confronting the same needs in the same circumstances and with similar resources than the expression of a shared commitment to a particular consensual ideology of welfare. What divided Mrs Thatcher from her social-democratic predecessors in Britain (and her contemporaries abroad) was, above all, her enthusiasm for a set of policy responses to a changing global economic environment which most governments found themselves (to varying degrees, according to local circumstance) driven to adopt. And whilst her New-Right agenda was fairly systematically pursued in some areas (trade union reform, for example), in social policy the record was patchy and inconsistent. Growth in the social budget has been reined in, (though it is still subject to substantial cyclical variation), and there has been some success in lowering citizens' long-term welfare expectations. But the real driving force of social policy has been a complex mixture of social, demographic and economic change which has left social-policy makers struggling to keep up. The transfer of spending from public to private sector that a consistent neo-liberalism ought to bring has yet to be realised, and if internal-market reforms deliver in the way that their advocates suggest, there may be decreasing incentives to shift the provision of health and education into the private sector. There are elements of a new consensus in some policy areas (in the massively important and expensive area of retirement pensions, for example). But these are much more the product of financial and demographic imperatives or of changing external parameters (acting within the ubiquitous framework of a market economy) than of a new sympathy for personal responsibility. It is not a new belief that pensioners are becoming 'spongers' which fuels the general sympathy for greater personal pension provision (still heavily underwritten by the state) but an expectation that without change, the state's existing pay-as-you-go system will come under unsustainable financial strain at some time in the next century.

Social policy (not just in Britain but throughout the developed world) is likely to continue to experience profound change in the coming decade. The new policies will continue to deploy a managerialist lexicon of customers, markets, contracts and accountability which is largely absent from social-policy discussions of the early post-war period. But we should also expect that this process of reform will be driven not so much by the logic of new ideas as by the evolving parameters of economic and demographic constraint.

CHAPTER 8

Social Democracy

Raymond Plant

T HE AIM of this chapter is to analyse the rhetoric and
indeed the reality of reaction to British social democracy.
In order to give some specificity to my argument I shall concentrate on the writings of C. A. R Crosland, whose book,
The Future of Socialism (1956), provided the most articulate
synthesis of social democratic thought in the post-war period
and provided both a political analysis and strategy which
inspired many, not only of his own generation but also the
one that followed him. Equality was at the heart of Crosland's
view of social democracy (or democratic socialism) and in
his writings he developed a reasonably clear view about the
kind of equality he thought was appropriate for a modern
democratic society with a mixed economy, together with an
account of the social policies which he thought would
enhance this version of equality. This was coupled with a view
of the most appropriate strategy for achieving this outcome, a
strategy which relied heavily on the assumption of incremental economic growth and Keynesian techniques of economic
management. Although this chapter will concentrate on Crosland, I think that it is perfectly reasonable to take his work
as paradigmatic of the mid-century stance of British social
democracy: therefore an exploration of the nature of the reaction to this has a much greater salience than would normally
apply to a discussion of the work of one political thinker.

While there is no doubt about the historical and contextual

importance of the Croslandite position, since the mid-1970s (and more particularly since 1979) the advent of a Conservative government committed to a much more neo-liberal agenda in both economics and social policy has comprehensively undermined this approach to social democracy and I shall try in this chapter to explore why this is so. I do not believe that a Croslandite strategy can be revived in anything like the form in which he presented it. Despite the fact that Tony Crosland was my own chief inspiration in politics I do not think that the task of social democrats can be confined to some kind of updating of his views – a much more comprehensive rethinking is required by those who want to call themselves social democrats. I console myself with the belief that Crosland would have been one of the first to recognise this. In an early unpublished letter to his close Oxford friend Philip Williams, Crosland expressed the wish to perform the role of a revisionist in the tradition of Bernstein (who had revised the socialist project in *Evolutionary Socialism* against the background of what Bernstein took to be the defects in Marxism). As a committed revisionist seeking always to make values relevant to modern circumstances, I believe that Crosland himself would have recognised the need to revise his own version of social democracy in the light of the major changes in politics, economics and social policy that have taken place in the twenty years since his own premature death.

I shall try first of all to outline Crosland's own view of the nature of equality as the fundamental social democratic value and then go on to consider his view of how this might be achieved as a political, economic and social strategy. I shall identify those aspects of his thesis which seem to have been so comprehensively undermined and conclude with an assessment of the present position of social democracy and the tasks facing a reformulation of the social democratic project in the very different circumstances which we now face.

The fact that Crosland put the pursuit of greater social equality (and thus the pursuit of greater social justice) at the heart of the social democratic project is itself of fundamental significance for understanding the nature of his own Left revisionism. Social democracy was to be understood in terms of the pursuit of social values such as equality and was not to be identified with a doctrine about the ownership of the means of production. This allowed him to both differentiate his position from Marxism, while at the same time putting his own thought within the revisionist tradition in left-wing thought. I suspect that Crosland might well have agreed with Hayek's view that both social democrats and Marxist socialists agree at least to some degree about ends – that is to say they both wish to see a just society in which there is a just distribution of resources and opportunities. There is, however, a fundamental disagreement about means, a disagreement which is really very profound. Marx himself bitterly criticised social democracy in its German, Lasallian form in *The Critique of the Gotha Programme*, in which he argued on the basis of his analysis of politics and economics that it was impossible to produce a fundamental change in the distribution of resources within a capitalist society by political means. If there is private ownership of the means of production, then the distribution of resources in society will reflect this unequal distribution of ownership. Social democrats are too confident and naive about politics. There can be no political strategy to counter the maldistribution of economic outcomes in capitalist society because at bottom, politics is inert in the face of the power of those who own the means of production. Social democrats are interested in symptoms and not causes. The unjust outcomes of capitalist markets are caused by injustice in the ownership of the means of production and unjust outcomes can only be tackled by changing the unjust causes of those outcomes – namely by a fundamental change in the ownership of the means of production, and a consequent change in the relations of production.

Bernstein, the first great revisionist, argued that Marx's

economic analysis, and its political consequences, were fundamentally flawed and that it was possible to pursue the ideal of a just society via political means. Crosland stood firmly within this tradition, following a three-track argument: firstly, Marx's account of capitalism was mistaken, or at least it did not apply to capitalism in the modern world; secondly, there was a need for a corresponding emphasis on a political strategy for achieving a more just society in terms of one that was more equal; and thirdly, as is obvious from this trenchant view, that the project of democratic socialism (or social democracy) could be understood in terms of values such as social justice and equality, rather than a revolutionary emphasis on expropriating those who own the means of production.

Crosland argued in the early part of *The Future of Socialism* that capitalism in the post-war world was fundamentally different from the economic system which Marx had confronted. This was so for a number of reasons which I shall just identify, rather than discuss in detail. Capitalism had changed first of all because ownership of the means of production had been dispersed and continues to be so – we do not confront a number of individual owners of capital who form an homogeneous class with common economic and political interests, as Marx had assumed. Indeed, the 1945 Labour government had taken into public ownership those means of production which bore most directly on the infrastructure of the economy, a settlement which Crosland welcomed and showed no signs of wanting to change. Because of the dispersal of ownership and the common ownership of central industries, the question of management was now much more important than ownership – how to ensure that the management of private industry with a dispersed ownership could become more socially responsible and incorporate some sense of the public interest. This was much more important in this context than further acts of nationalisation. Secondly, greater democratisation in British society had put severe constraints on the power of private ownership in the modern economy. Not only did dispersed ownership mean that there was no capitalist class with a common interest, but the growth of democracy (again a change from Marx's time) was a major countervailing power to the interests of private owners. This was backed up with the view that trades unions now had a central role in politics and economics and again acted as a strong countervailing role in society to that of private owners. Thirdly, Keynesian economic techniques meant that government was able to manage the general macroeconomic climate within which firms operated and the idea that capitalists (even assuming that we were still in a situation of non-dispersed ownership) could pursue an economic agenda which did not take account of government managed macroeconomic conditions was false. Keynesian economic management implied, to a degree, the relative autonomy of politics, in that it could no longer be seen as an arena of class interest. Governments, using Keynesian techniques, could pursue macroeconomic policies that would serve its view of the public interest, and which would in turn be shaped by its political values. Equally, class relations had changed: there had not been a polarisation of classes, nor had there been the immiseration of the proletariat (a view of Marx which was central to Bernstein's revisionism, which Crosland self-consciously followed). Finally, the growth of the welfare state and welfare rights after the reforms of the 1945 Labour government meant that in terms of health, education and welfare, citizens were no longer subject to the vagaries of the market but had a stake in society mediated not only by non-capitalist institutions but also based on the principle of recognising need, a profoundly anti-capitalist notion.

All of these meant that for Crosland, we were no longer living in the kind of capitalism which Marx had confronted. This allowed socialism to be seen in value terms because capitalism had been reshaped by the economic and political forces outlined above, and Marx's critique of the politics of social democracy looked threadbare in the light of this.

Nevertheless, Crosland did want to be seen as a revisionist, updating the idea of what a just society might mean and how it might be achieved. At the time that he was writing, and particularly later in the 1960s, the main challenge to the coherence of the social democratic project seemed to come from a revitalised form of humanistic Marxism rather than a reassertion of classical liberalism (which Crosland, no doubt, would have regarded as having been consigned to the lumber room of history). This is not because political opponents on the right would have been happy to be described as social democrats, but they were certainly not at that time in possession of an alternative paradigm of politics and economics. Indeed, those vestiges of updated classical liberalism – for example the writings of Hayek and Friedman and the assiduous pamphlet writing going on at the Institute of Economic Affairs – just seemed eccentric. So in mid-century it did look as though the social democrats had perhaps the most coherent political and economic paradigm. It was not really effectively challenged on the Left from a Marxist perspective and the potential for revitalised neo-liberalism looked minimal. Yet today it is precisely the challenge of rampant economic liberalism that social democracy of the Croslandite sort has to face, and in order to explain this challenge we need to look more closely at Crosland's own political values and political strategy.

In his last book *Socialism Now,* Crosland described his own view of equality as being more or less the same as that developed with great philosophical force by John Rawls in *A Theory of Justice*. It seems clear from unpublished correspondence with Professor I. D. M. Little concerning the proofs of *Socialism Now* that Crosland had read Rawls's book and he took from Rawls the phrase 'democratic equality' to describe the nature of his own commitment, as set out nearly twenty years previously, in *The Future of Socialism*. Crosland's view of equality, like Rawls's democratic equality, lies on a spectrum between equality of opportunity and equality of outcome. While Crosland recognises and welcomes the gains which greater equality of opportunity has secured, he makes it clear that he does not think that it is a sufficiently rich conception of equality for a recognisably social democratic commitment. It is not, in his own words, 'enough'.

It is not enough for two main reasons, both of which he shares with Rawls. First of all, equality of opportunity does not pay sufficient attention to starting points and unequal endowments. Family background and genetic legacy make an enormous difference to starting points and are morally arbitrary, in that those who benefit from a regime of equal opportunity will be those with fortunate backgrounds and genetic endowments, but an individual bears little or no responsibility for these. Thus a regime of equal opportunity alone may be unjust in its outcomes, since it will offer greater rewards to people who bear little personal responsibility for their success. In Crosland's view, there is certainly a case for income inequality and those positions which carry differential rewards should be subject to the fairest competition under equality of opportunity, but two conditions are important. The first is that differential rewards should not be seen as a matter of personal desert for the reason given above – namely that those who are successful in the competition can bear only small personal responsibility for their position at the starting gate (which is influenced by family, environmental and genetic factors that successful individuals cannot claim credit for). This undermines the idea that what income inequality there should be is to be justified by desert. It is rather to be justified by the rent of ability criterion – that higher rewards will motivate and mobilise people with talent to use their talents to the benefit of the community as a whole. In this sense, Crosland's view of equality of opportunity is close to Rawls's 'difference' principle. The second point, which is closer to social policy and bears on Crosland's commitment to comprehensive education, is that we have to be concerned with starting points and use education to compensate, so far as possible, for negative features in family and environmental background, so that the starting point in the competition for differentially high rewards is fairer.

From these points, it should be obvious that Crosland is also a critic of strict equality of outcome. Everyone benefits from a system in which talent is mobilised for the public good, and if talent will only be mobilised by differences in income, then it is rational to do that. The point however, to reiterate it again, is that such rewards are not based upon the principle of desert but on the principle of rent of ability.

Crosland is not a philosopher and he does not attempt a full philosophical defence of his views, but there is nevertheless a philosophical issue at the heart of this position that has important consequences for political strategy. Although by the time he wrote *Socialism Now* he may have regarded Rawls as having provided the best philosophical setting for his own conception of democratic equality, when he wrote *The Future of Socialism* he took a rather more conventional view – namely that moral outlook was a matter of personal commitment and emotional predilection. He seems to have been influenced by the emotive theory of ethics propounded by A. J. Ayer in *Language Truth and Logic*, that we cannot give philosophical foundations for our value commitments. Crosland seems to take the same view of his own commitment to equality in *The Future of Socialism*. This means that he was dedicated to a view of political values which would always be underdetermined by empirical argument. This meant that there could be no decisive arguments for a particular set of political values, including his own. Given that he wanted to pursue an egalitarian strategy, he had to accept that this was a personal preference and this had an important bearing on the nature of his political strategy. People's value preferences had to be taken as given and ultimately incorrigible, and there was a very definite limit to what argument might do to shake this.

This poses particular problems for an egalitarian, in that

it may well be that, by and large, people's preferences are not of an egalitarian kind (or not sufficiently so to support a direct egalitarian strategy). To put the point crudely, how, in a democratic society, does an egalitarian get people to vote for the degree of taxation necessary to pay for those forms of public provision which will compensate for the effects of poverty, poor schooling and limited health provision and which, taken together, would compensate for inequality of starting point? One needs to convince the better off to pay more tax by changing their values – but Crosland's ethical non-cognitivism puts severe limits on this. That is to say, an egalitarian strategy can only be pursued by creating egalitarian citizens – what might be called a bottom-up strategy – which would be to put into doubt Crosland's own view of the limitations of argument in morals. The alternative is to look for a more indirect strategy, which might create a more egalitarian outcome without having to create shared egalitarian values. Crosland opts for the second course. Before going on to say something about this, it is perhaps worth alluding to an important distinction between 'moral' and 'mechanical' reformers in politics, a distinction that the historian Peter Clarke propounded in his seminal work, *Liberals and Social Democrats*. Moral reformers are essentially bottom-up reformers. Values can only be effective in politics when they are widely shared, and the task of the moral reformer is to take the long view and try to transform the values by which people live in the direction that he wants to see. The mechanical reformer is a top-down reformer, who believes that there might political, social and economic strategies available which would produce the desired results, without necessarily having to transform the underlying moral culture of citizens. As I shall try to show below, in Clarke's sense, Crosland is a mechanical reformer. The cost of mechanical reform though can be very high and, I would argue, the Croslandite position has borne this cost: if one attempts to pursue a political strategy that does not draw deeply on values held by the population at large, it may well collapse very quickly once it is challenged by a belief system which is more confident about its salience to the values of the society in which the reform is sought. It is really quite amazing that a political settlement so influenced by social democracy could have collapsed as quickly and as comprehensively as it did after 1979, and one of the explanations of this may well be that it was a form of mechanical or indirect politics. In so far as a Croslandite strategy assumed that one could produce a social democratic society shaped by egalitarian outcomes of his preferred sort, without creating a more social democratic and egalitarian culture, this rapid demise may well be partly explained by the fact that it was a mechanical rather than a moral reform which actually was anchored in only a rather shallow way in the culture of society, and one whose general weakness was exposed by a neo-liberalism confident and direct about its moral force. I shall go on to examine the onslaught of the neo-liberals on the moral assumptions of social democracy shortly, but before doing so I need to say something about Crosland's mechanical reform strategy.

The role of public expenditure on health, education, social security and welfare was central to Crosland's egalitarian strategy. This was partly due to his conception of equality, which meant that the state had a role in compensating for unmerited and undeserved social disadvantage, though he eschewed expounding an explicit strategy for redistributing income and wealth. This was, I think, for a number of reasons: direct redistribution would actually have limited effects, in the sense that the amount to be redistributed, given the levels of taxation which might be acceptable, would make only a limited difference to the worst off and that it would not tackle family-cultural disadvantage, which could only be addressed through state-provided services (particularly in education). In addition, while public provision would differentially help the worst off, it was nevertheless something in which all might share and would make the more egalitarian effects of public expenditure more acceptable than direct redistribution. Finally, and this takes us back to the issue of mechanical reform, direct redistribution through the tax system, which would require an explicit appeal to citizens to make substantial numbers of themselves worse off, would raise the question of the general salience of egalitarian values. High levels of public expenditure to finance high quality public provision was therefore central to Crosland's egalitarianism. This was, in his view, to be financed by economic growth. Economic growth allows indirect levelling up rather than levelling down – a point which he is perhaps most explicit about in his Fabian Pamphlet *Social Democracy In Europe*. Here he argues that growth will produce a fiscal dividend for government to invest in public services which will have an egalitarian effect (at least in terms of social if not income equality) and will allow the absolute position of the better off to be sustained while incrementally improving the relative position of the worst off. Economic growth and its fiscal dividend for public provision was therefore critical for Crosland's indirect or mechanical strategy. It meant that the absolute position of the better off would not have to be challenged directly through redistributive taxation but would allow an incremental advance in social equality by improving the relative position of the worst off. Thus greater social equality could be produced by Keynesian economic techniques to produce incremental growth that would avoid a direct challenge to substantial numbers of citizens who may not share egalitarian values but who would also benefit from increased public provision. In some ways, the Croslandite dilemma here became obvious in John Smith's 1992 shadow budget, when tax rises for the better off were presaged as part of a commitment to securing improvements in the position of the worst off in a situation in which incremental economic growth could not be relied upon to take up the slack. The reaction to that exercise perhaps showed that egalitarian sentiments were not as widely shared as was hoped and that little explicit attempt had been made in the run up to that shadow budget to put the case explicitly for the moral underpinning of the strategy adopted.

I want to turn now to the neo-liberal critique of the social democratic commitment to greater social equality and social justice, since this is the greatest challenge that a revitalised form of social democracy will have to face. It is a rhetoric of reaction with a vengeance, because against the background of a rather timid moral case for social democracy, the neo-liberal critique had developed a great deal of moral force and political acumen.

I shall deal first of all with the critique of social justice generally, of which a commitment to greater social equality would be a part. As I have argued, social justice in the sense of a more egalitarian society was Crosland's – and indeed social democracy's – core value and therefore the neo-liberal critique of this has the greatest salience. Hayek particularly, and the neo-liberals generally, regard social justice as both a moral and political illusion. It is a moral illusion for several reasons. The first, and most fundamental one, is that those who believe in social justice are concerned that a free market economy left to its own devices will produce unjust outcomes, in that the gap between rich and poor will increase, which will in turn lead to a decline in social equality generally. The neo-liberal, however, wants to concentrate initially on the claim that free markets can produce injustice, a claim that he would vehemently deny. The reasoning here is as follows. Injustice can only result from intentional action. This is why we do not regard the havoc wrought by the weather as an injustice. If my field of corn is destroyed by the rain and yours is not, I have suffered a misfortune, but not an injustice, since it was an impersonal and not an intentional act which produced the outcome. Similarly if I am born with a genetic handicap that, too, is a misfortune. In a market, millions of people buy and sell for countless particular reasons, but the outcome of all that buying and selling, the so-called distribution of income and wealth, is an unintended and unforeseen consequence of all those individual acts of free exchange. As Sir Keith Joseph argued in his book, *Equality*, we do not regard it as the duty of the state to remove people from the wheel of fortune, whereas we might all agree that it is the duty of the state to rectify injustice. Unintended outcomes in the marketplace are misfortunes that the state has no general duty to relieve, and therefore the idea of social justice has no moral purchase. We have no collective responsibility to compensate for the inequality which results from the operation of a free market. Thus the central value which animates social democracy is illusory.

The second argument against the salience of a concern with inequality is again due to Hayek and relates in some ways to Crosland's havering about the basis of the moral case for social justice. Social justice is a very general notion and if it is to have any purchase it needs to be made more specific. The trouble is that the attempt to specify social justice into a distributive rule shows its moral fragility. There are many different possible distributive rules, each of which, given the appropriate arguments, could be regarded as plausible principles of distribution. We could distribute according to need, according to equality, according to merit or desert, according to prior entitlement (for example by regarding existing property rights and the resources attached to those as being just), according to the marginal product of labour (which some economists would regard as being instantiated in a free market economy) and so on. There are people who would leap to the defence of each of these distributive principles and yet the principles would lead to radically different distributions of resources. Hayek's point is that attachment to one or other of these competing principles is a matter of subjective preference. In a morally subjective society we can neither claim objectivity for our particular distributive principles, nor can we reach inter-subjective agreement over them. In some ways this corresponds to Crosland's implicit non-cognitivism in ethics but whereas this leads to what I have called Crosland's indirect or mechanical strategy, Hayek draws a much more radical conclusion, namely that with a clash of subjective opinions about the meaning of social justice in a free society we should abandon the search for a just society, which the earlier argument shows has no moral purchase in any case.

The neo-liberals attack the philosophical basis of egalitarian social justice in another way too, which concentrates on the link between equality specifically, or social justice more generally, to individual liberty. This link between equality and liberty does not loom very large in Crosland but it has had salience for the social democratic project in that the link between social justice and liberty was a theme of such Idealists and New Liberals as Haldane, Hobhouse, Wallace, Ritchie and Tawney, who influenced the Labour Party in earlier generations. The argument here is about what has come to be called positive liberty. The idea is that freedom is not to be understood just in terms of being free from interference, as in classical liberalism, but is also concerned with the possession of resources and opportunities. This raises the question of the just distribution of resources and opportunities and connects with egalitarianism in the following way: given that we believe in the equal liberty of citizens in a free and liberal society, we should be concerned not only with equal freedom from interference, but also with the most equal distribution of resources and opportunities we can get, as part of what equal freedom means.

This argument is decisively rejected by the neo-liberals because in their view it confuses freedom and ability. Once the ideas of being free to do something and the ability to do something are assimilated, then it opens the way for the social justice/equality argument. Neo-liberals such as Hayek argue that this assimilation is fundamentally mistaken, in that no one is able to do all that they are free to do. I am currently free to do everything that no one is intentionally preventing me from doing and this is an indefinitely large class of things. No one, however rich and energetic, is able to do all that they are free to do and this then shows that freedom and ability are quite different. The political inference in all of this is well drawn by Sir Keith Joseph when he argues in *Equality* that poverty is not unfreedom. Poverty, or lack of resources, has nothing to do with freedom since freedom and ability are quite different. We can, on the neo-liberal view, have a free society against the background of substantial inequality as the result of the market since freedom is about mutual non-interference and not about the possession of resources and opportunities.

Leaving aside the cogency of these arguments, one cannot help but be led to the judgement that there has been a massive moral failing among social democrats in not working out the proper moral basis of their political position. This in turn has practical political implications. The first and most general one is that social democrats seemed to be bereft of argument in the face of this philosophically sophisticated neo-liberal onslaught and this led very much to the sense that social democrats had lost the battle for ideas to the neo-liberals over what is central to them – namely the meaning of social justice and the salience of distributive politics. There are other more direct political costs too of a failure to work out a moral basis for social justice, consequences which neo-liberals make much of.

The first of these is that if we have distributive politics which are not guided by a clear moral case for a particular form of distribution we shall face anarchic politics. The social democratic state is committed to distributive politics without having (as indeed it cannot have, according to the neo-liberal view) clear principles of distribution. So the state will be committed to distributive politics but will be so committed in a way that is without criteria. This means that individuals and groups will expect to receive from the state what, from their subjective point of view (and there is no other from a neo-liberal stance), they regard as their just share. The real danger is that, far from a commitment to social justice being a noble political ideal, it in fact licenses a particularly grinding zero-sum game in which coalitions of interest groups try to secure from government what they take to be their just share of resources. In the view of the neo-liberals one would not have to look very deeply into the politics of Britain in the 1970s to see the truth of this, particularly during periods when incomes policies or the social contract were in operation. Again, without a clear and specific moral vision, social democracy can quite easily fall foul of the neo-liberal critique and, more importantly, fall into the type of politics which the neo-liberals stigmatise and which has little to do with social justice and much more to do with the power of strong coalitions of interest groups.

The second practical political effect of pursuing the social democratic project for the neo-liberal is that a liberal society should be characterised by the rule of law and a prevention of the operation of arbitrary power. The neo-liberal view is that it is perfectly possible to draw up rules of law governing mutual non-interference or negative liberty, but it is not possible to do so in respect of resource distribution. This is so for two reasons. The first follows from what has gone before, namely that the idea of social justice is too vague to underpin distributive rules. Secondly the needs of individuals and groups who are recipients of government resources will vary in a way that mutual non-interference does not. Hence, according to this view, it is not possible to draw up rules of law to govern the distribution of resources. This then means that the public officials in bureaucracies who distribute resources have to act in arbitrary and discretionary ways. This is not the result of bad faith but is intrinsic to the situation in which they find themselves. On this view, therefore, the social democratic principles not only undermine the rule of law, they increase the size and professional power of bureaucracies.

This leads to a further point. The neo-liberal assumes, I

should have thought correctly, that social democrats take a rather high-minded, public service approach to the bureaucracies charged with public provision of resources in the interests of social justice. The neo-liberal challenges this view by arguing that bureaucrats like everyone else are engaged in utility maximising behaviour, but they do this outside the disciplines of the market and without the challenge of bankruptcy. Given such utility maximising behaviour, it is in the interests of public servants to see their services grow, their sphere of responsibility increase, their incomes grow and to seek ways to keep accountability – either to government or to the 'customer' – at arm's length. Public officials are neither like Plato's Guardians, nor Hegel's Universal Class, seeking in a disinterested way to pursue the public interest. Like everyone else, their behaviour is to be understood in utility maximising ways. So a further charge against Croslandite social democracy is that it involves a commitment to large-scale public services in the interests of social justice, without paying attention to the culture of bureaucracy in the public services.

I want, for the moment, to leave the directly moral argument, although there are some further points to be made, and concentrate on the nature of public provision. Crosland argued strongly for a large public sector as a vehicle for greater social equality. The neo-liberals reject this on two grounds. The first is one that is shared by some thinkers on the Left, namely that public expenditure does not create greater social equality because it differentially benefits the middle classes. This is not to say, from the perspective of those on the left who are tempted by this argument, that the poorest groups in society have not benefited, but rather, it is not a vehicle of equality. The argument here is that studies of public provision and the use made of such provision show that they differentially benefit the better off. Some cases of this are clear, for example public investment in universities and the payment of tuition fees by the state; but it is also found particularly in health and some social benefits. From this view, therefore, Crosland's indirect approach to social equality through a public expenditure is flawed as a strategy for equality. The Right draw the conclusion from this that the welfare state, as broadly conceived, should not be seen as an instrument of social justice and social equality, but should be reduced to a safety net for those who cannot provide for themselves; the Left often draw the conclusion that if one is looking for equality it should be via the direct redistribution of resources rather than being mediated via public services.

The second reason why the neo-liberal Right reject the public provision strategy for equality is that it leads to what has come to be called the culture of dependency. This is the view that instead of creating a more socially equal, independent and robust citizenship, the public expenditure strategy has in fact created a culture of dependency, particularly among the young, the unemployed, single mothers and so on. Instead of being robust citizens, they are dependent upon a state giro cheque. This view has also gained ground on the Left in recent years with 'welfare-into-work' policies, in an attempt to use policy as an incentive to get particularly the young unemployed into either work or training. Indeed, the Labour Party's current policy is to reduce the benefits going to the 18–25 year old group if a job or training is refused. Again, with this view the drive for greater social equality via the welfare state has created moral hazard and the opposite effects from those intended by social democrat thinkers and policy makers.

I now want to come back to a final tranche of moral argument between the social democrat and the neo-liberal which draws, to some extent, on the preceding point. The public expenditure/public provision strategy of Croslandite social democracy has created a set of entitlements to welfare, or what we might call a new set of social rights to health education and welfare to go alongside civil and political rights.

This theme does not loom at all large in Crosland but it has been influential in social democratic thought and has its roots in the impact of Marshall's writings on citizenship and social class. The neo-liberals are critical of this approach too, and again it is difficult not to think that there has been a failure among social democrats to think through its agenda properly. On the neo-liberal view it is a dangerous illusion for social democrats to foster the idea that there are social rights of citizenship as part of equal citizenship and this is because there cannot be enforceable rights to scarce resources. If people come to think that they have these rights as part of the status of citizenship, it is going to create a climate of deep resentment and distrust in public institutions when in individual cases it becomes clear that what they thought was a right is unenforceable either because of an absolute scarcity of resources in the area to which the right is being asserted, or because of the effect of other spending decisions in that area. So, for example, it is dangerous to develop the belief that there is a right to health care, because as a number of cases in recent years have shown, when treatment has been denied as the result of scarce resources and individuals have gone to court on the assumption that they had a right to health care, judges have thrown out the case. Even if social democrats do not explicitly argue for an explicit right to particular forms of public provision, the centrality of public provision for their strategy naturally gives rise to a sense that there is such an entitlement among the public at large and this is a dangerous illusion and will lead to a loss of confidence in public authorities. In the neo liberal view, rights are best reserved for the civil and political realm.

So the neo-liberals have engaged in the rhetoric of reaction with gusto and force and this has shown up weakness, partly in the hold of social democratic ideas among citizens and partly the extent to which the social democrats, perhaps largely because they seemed to have the hegemony over ideas in political economy in the 1950s and 1960s, failed to attend to the moral and political case they were presenting in the light of fundamentally changed circumstances. This has been exacerbated by the fact that the social democratic value system and political strategy depended very largely upon Keynesian economic assumptions which came under great pressure from the mid-1970s onwards with the growth of monetarism and supply-side economics, changes which have been accelerated by the growth of the global economy. In the neo-liberal view, the concern with equality and relative positions in the economy has become a dangerous distraction in a globally competitive market in which we are competing against states with low labour costs and very little internal concern with increasing social equality. This has led the neo-liberals to reverse most of the mid-century social democratic assumptions. Equality is a bad thing because it is a distraction from the real needs of the British economy, as I have said, and because incentives are necessary in order to provide individuals with the motivation to act as entrepreneurs and to take risks. So far as the poor is concerned there is a very clear reversal of the Croslandite strategy which was a concern with the relative position of the worst off while seeking to maintain the absolute position of the better off. On the issue of poverty, the Conservative government's view, which was made clear when John Moore (now Lord Moore) was Social Security Secretary, is that what should matter to the poor is not their relative position *vis-à-vis* the better off, but rather their own absolute position; that is, as a poor person am I better off this year than I was last year irrespective of whether inequality (which is a good thing for incentive purposes) has increased? In this view, the absolute position of the poor will be made better by the trickle-down effect of the market economy rather than by state action and certainly better than state action to improve the relative position of the poor.

Similarly, we should abandon the idea that the welfare state should be seen as a vehicle of social justice and greater equality, not just because it has not been very good at it but because it is a misconceived enterprise. The welfare state should be seen ultimately as a safety net, moving to a position over time when individuals will have incentives to move out of the welfare state for their health and social security. In the neo-liberal view, welfare bureaucracies should be constrained not by a sanctimonious public service ethic, but by either removing certain services from the state altogether and taking them to market, such as mortgage insurance for the unemployed; or by introducing internal or quasi-market mechanisms, as in the Health Service; or by surrogate markets or market substitutes as in education; and in all areas of the remaining public sector by introducing the constraints of the citizen's charter to make welfare bureaucracies more accountable to the recipients of the services. This will ideally produce, in turn, a reversal of what seemed to be an inexorable growth in the size of government and in the rate of taxation under social democratic policies. I have tried to show how the social democratic agenda has wilted under this onslaught and there is no countervailing social democratic paradigm fully developed at the moment which has the coherence of the Croslandite agenda of the 1950s and 1960s.

This does not mean that such an agenda cannot be created, but it is a painstaking task and I doubt whether it will reach the kind of coherence and synthesis that Crosland managed in the 1950s, partly because he wrote during a period in which there was a widely accepted economic paradigm – namely Keynesianism – which played a critical role in his overall vision, and partly because within the other social sciences on which he drew there was much more agreement then than there is now. In the so-called post-modern world, it is very difficult to produce a work of synthesis which links together a political vision, political economy and sociological research in the way that Crosland did. So the revision of revisionist social democracy has to be a slow, careful enterprise that is probably beyond the reach of one person. In what remains of this chapter however, I shall try to reinstate something of the moral basis for social democracy which I have been very critical of Crosland for neglecting, and in order to do this, I shall start with the core value of social justice, an issue which clearly separates the social democrat from the neo-liberal.

Firstly, I think the neo-liberal is wrong in believing that social justice has no salience because economic outcomes are unintended and that injustice arises only as the result of intentional action. This is mistaken because injustice can occur as the result of foreseeable consequences of actions, whether or not these consequences were intended. If this were not so there would, for example, be no such crime as manslaughter. If the consequences of the extension of markets are foreseeable, then we can be taken to be collectively responsible for those consequences. It would be a very strange thing if neo-liberals thought that the outcomes of markets were not foreseeable, since part of their whole strategy has been to argue for their extension because of the supposed benefits that will accrue. We can therefore take ourselves to be collectively responsible for the foreseeable outcomes of markets and thus social justice, as a form of such collective responsibility for those who have been disadvantaged by market outcomes, is a salient moral concept.

This point needs to be attached to a second argument. We do not, I think, generally believe that the question of whether something has produced an injustice or not is settled by the question of whether the action was intended. John Rawls argues, correctly in my view, that the question of justice and injustice is raised by the nature of our response to an action as much by the intentional or otherwise nature of its cause. Take the following simple case. A child is blown over by the wind (an unintended force) and is lying face down in a gutter full of water. Unless I, as the only person present, can save the child from death by plucking it out of the gutter at no similar risk to myself, the child will die. Do we really believe that I have not committed an injustice if I fail to do so since the child was placed in that position by an impersonal force. I hardly think so. This example by analogy, I think goes to show that if we can compensate people for the foreseeable, even if unintended, consequences of markets and can do so without putting ourselves into poverty, then we have an obligation to do so. These two arguments taken together I believe justify the continuing political salience of social justice.

I also think that Hayek's attempt to block the claims of social justice in respect of liberty are also mistaken. Hayek argues that freedom and ability are two different things and therefore that resources have nothing to do with liberty, they are indeed categorically different. The conclusion being drawn from this is that in protecting equal freedom the state needs only to be concerned with mutual coercion and not with resources. There are three good reasons for doubting this argument.

The first is as follows: given that the neo-liberal believes only in negative liberty, or freedom from coercion and interference, then what answer can be given to the question, why is liberty in this sense valuable? Why should I want to be free from coercion? The only plausible answer the neo-liberal could give would be to argue that if I am free from coercion then I shall be able to live a life shaped by my own purposes and interests and not those of others. But note that the worth of liberty, or the value of liberty, is linked to an account of ability – it is what I am then able to do that makes liberty valuable. So, at the very worst, ability is part of what makes liberty valuable to us. However, the argument can be built on further, namely by saying that in a free society in which individuals are supposed to enjoy equal liberties, they could also be seen to have a claim to as equal a value of liberty as can be secured without mutual impoverishment, and this would link an egalitarian concern with liberty and its value.

Secondly, if liberty and ability are categorically different, some surprising results follow. If I asked, 'Were people free to fly in 1066?', the obvious answer would be that the question does not make sense since no one was able to fly. In order to be free or unfree to do X, there must be a generalised capacity to do X. We then can determine whether person A is free or unfree to do something in the light of this general capacity or ability. If this is so, freedom and ability are not categorically different and one cannot use this supposed difference to block the resource implications of liberty.

Thirdly, if liberty is negative – that is, to do with the absence of coercion – then the question of whether one society is more free than another will depend on the number of coercive rules in one society rather than another. Hence, to take an example from Charles Taylor, it might be thought that Albania under Communist rule was a freer society that Britain was since, there were very few cars and therefore few traffic laws and little by way of financial transaction and thus of laws governing such transactions. Hence, a negative view of liberty makes it hard to avoid the conclusion that resolving the question of whether we were freer than the Albanians is simply a matter of counting up the number of laws. Since Albania was a relatively simple society it might well have had fewer laws and thus be a freer society. No one should be convinced by this and the reason why not is because we think that we are not coerced in relation to the more important things that we are able to do, like criticise the government or emigrate. That is to say an account in which human abilities are taken to be important is central to the judgement about whether or not we are a free society.

Given this link between freedom and ability and the linked view that we must have some conception of what the important human abilities are in relation to the defence of the idea that we are a free society, then this can give rise to social justice considerations – namely whether people have equal access to those resources that bear most directly upon those abilities which are central to the judgement that we are a free society.

So I believe that it is perfectly possible to block this part of the neo-liberal's critique of social democracy's concern with social justice, democratic equality and liberty. This is very important because, as I have tried to show, these values are at the heart of the social democratic political project. Of course this leaves one central element of Hayek and the neo-liberal's critique untouched, namely whether there can be agreement about social justice in a liberal society marked as it is by value subjectivism. I do not think that there can be an *a priori* answer to this question. The first stage is to reinstate the salience of social justice and this I have done. After that I think that one needs to turn to a number of subsidiary points, some of which are implicitly recognised by neo-liberal thinkers, although they often fail to see the force of them. First of all, the neo-liberals' commitment to a residual welfare state based on the recognition of basic needs that an individual cannot meet out of his or her own resources. This concession seems to imply that we do have a common and well understood conception of basic needs and the recognition of them generates a moral obligation on the part of society to justify the taxation to meet this residual welfare state. Now if we were so far gone in moral pluralism, what could possibly be the moral rationale for this? So it seems that the neo-liberal is prepared to concede a need-oriented principle and the justice of the moral claim to which the recognition of need gives rise. However, the neo-liberal wants to differentiate this from a commitment to social justice, but this dichotomy cannot, I believe be maintained. It assumes that the needs to be met in the welfare state in its residual form are clear and self specifying, so that it will not expand and become more like a welfare state oriented towards social justice, but this defies all experience and indeed undercuts their own view about the expansionary powers of welfare bureaucrats who will build up need in the interests of their own utility maximising motivation (which I discussed earlier). Additionally, how is it that we can recognise these needs if all values are subjective in a way that blocks social justice but allows not just the recognition of need but also the recognition of a taxation-based moral obligation to meet it? Finally, a commitment to a needs-based residual welfare state is a commitment to a distributive principle – namely we should distribute resources to meet basic needs when the individual is not in a position to meet them. This is some way from the richness of social justice within social democracy but nevertheless it is hardly a strong basis on which to block all other forms of distributive politics.

The more egalitarian Croslandite/Rawlsian version of social justice can of course be justified in the immensely complicated way that Rawls's great work attempts, but within the culture of British society and much more modestly in terms of ambition, one could, I think, argue the following case drawing upon an idea of citizenship and the points about freedom and ability made earlier. Both neo-liberals and social democrats seem to have common ground in terms of seeing the value of equal citizenship in a free and liberal society. The neo-liberal wants to restrict this to civil and political rights, the social democrat wants, for reasons of social justice, to extend it to access to resources. If one accepts my criticisms of the neo-liberal view (that ability and freedom are categorically distinct), then one can have general concern about the level of resources which the exercise of free citizenship involves. The Croslandite view of democratic equality then comes into play in the following respect. If we believe in the equality of freedom of all citizens in a liberal society then we have to be concerned about whether freedom has equal value for them; that is to say, do they have the resources necessary to exercise this citizenship when such resources are concerned with what might be called, following Rawls, primary goods – those goods which are necessary conditions for pursuing others, such as education, health and social security? From the Croslandite point of view, which I think is eminently defensible, the argument would go like this: we have no antecedent reason in a free society for one citizen to have more goods than another (particularly when allied to Crosland's idea that desert is dubious, given family background and so forth); that is to say, there is a *prima facie* case for equality of condition. But knowing that economic performance depends upon differential salaries paid as a rent of ability in the interests of all citizens, then inequality is justified when it is in the common interest. So, in the argument for equal citizenship in a free society, it would be rational to move from an equal distribution of resources, if doing so furthers the economic well being of all, and assuming that the competition for differentially high rewards is open to the fairest degree of equality of opportunity that we can manage. This latter point in turn means reinstating the idea that the education of the most deprived, so that they can effectively compete, as a condition of citizenship under a regime of democratic equality.

So I believe that it is perfectly possible in these neo-liberal times to justify in moral terms a concern with both social justice and within that, equality. It would also be a mistake to say that we cannot afford it and compare ourselves with emerging East Asian economies. Obviously this is a large and important point but two quick responses are in order. Equality of opportunity is in everyone's interest in that we have no antecedent reason for believing that talent is not widely spread and we should take every opportunity for expanding the range of talent in our own economic self-interest. Secondly, the East Asian economies have shown that good economic performance is not incompatible with social cohesion. Obviously what social cohesion demands differs across societies. In our sort of society, almost whether we like it or not, social cohesion is not likely to be maintained in a situation of vastly increased inequality and denial of opportunity.

My final point in this attempt to reinstate the moral vision of social democracy has to do with social rights, which as we have seen, the neo-liberals reject. Their rejection is not well thought through. It depends upon the following linked ideas:

there can be no rights to scarce resources; there can be no rules of law which can govern the allocation of resources; in the absence of rules of law resources will be allocated in arbitrary ways. From this view, we should link rights only to those in the civil and political sphere, and equality should range only over such rights. Before moving to a criticism of this view, I want to make a central philosophical point. A right is, I believe, conceptually or logically tied to the idea of enforceability. We have all sorts of interests, needs, desires and preferences but only some of these are regarded as rights and they are viewed as such because they are important enough to be enforced. That is to say, we can only really think about rights in relation to enforceability. The neo-liberal wants to restrict rights to the civil and political realm, but as rights these have enforceability conditions attached to them. That is to say, in order to enforce rights, for example, to mutual non-interference we need the police, the courts, prisons and so on, and we also need public provision of things that enhance freedom from assault like, for example, street lighting. These are not contingent or detachable aspects of rights but are part of their logically implied enforceability conditions. Such conditions imply quite large scale public expenditure and this in turn implies that in particular cases the resources may be in scarce supply. Take, for example, the police. The Chief Constable does not have unlimited resources and so long as he does not have a settled policy of not pursuing certain types of crime he has to have discretion about which crimes will be pursued and with what resources. How is this different from a consultant deciding that against the background of scarce resources it is not cost effective to treat a particular patient? Discretion is central to the role of the chief constable as the holder of scarce resources as it is for the consultant. Now the neo-liberal is in a very paradoxical position. The rule of law and civil rights are central to his vision of a *Rechtsstaat*, and following from this he has argued that a welfare state is morally inadmissable (other than in its residual form) since resource allocation cannot be brought within the rule of law. However, this applies to the enforceability conditions of civil rights too such as the police. The enforceability conditions of the rule of law cannot be brought within the rule of law. This is not a very satisfactory position to be in but seems to be a clear consequence of the supposed rigour of their own critique of the social democrat. Either one has to say that rights and the rule of law do not mean very much or one has to say that in the protection of all sorts of rights which take up scarce resources discretion is central. The latter point is surely the most plausible and indeed the social democrat will be on stronger ground here in that the social democrat will want to see an institutional setting which requires those who are exercising discretion to do so only in relation to a conception of a broadly just general allocation of resources to different areas: to put the point crudely, that the chief constable is not giving disproportionate resources to policing in rich areas. That is to say that all rights involve distributive questions and the neo-liberal attempt to put distributive questions off the agenda of politics is simple minded.

I have tried in these last few pages to counter one aspect of the rhetoric of reaction against social democracy by trying to provide some case for its moral vision and the political salience of that vision. That is not to say that I believe that Croslandite social democracy can be revived *in toto*. We do not have to assume that public provision is the only way of addressing social disadvantage, we do have to look at dependency and find ways of countering that by welfare into work approaches. Our other central objective should be to look at political institutions and their effectiveness. It is odd to reflect on the fact that social democracy, which of all political ideologies probably demands most from government, has been content until recently to accept the institutions of power as they stood, as though the only problem that social democrats had was summoning up the appropriate level of political will. We can no longer believe that, and political reform as well as moral vision, economic ideas and social policy will have to be woven together if the neo-liberal rhetoric of reaction is to be defeated in the long term.

CHAPTER 9

Culture

The Problem With Being Public

Geoff Mulgan

MUCH modern writing about culture and society assumes that the public realm is one of virtue. It is associated with civic activism and being outward looking and alive. It may be subject to disappointment and re-evaluation but it has a moral dignity that private life and private ambition lack. We share this assumption with a long tradition that dates back to classical Greece and Rome, and which was brought back into the West's frame of reference in the eighteenth century. But what happens if the public realm is not in fact one in which the public feels completely at home; what if it is coloured by class, by hierarchy and by the imposition of values and ideas?

This has, perhaps, been the central unanswered question of the social-democratic years after 1945. It was taken for granted by many that the public sphere would naturally be an inclusive one: that into the world of public enterprises, public health services, public libraries and public transport, all would be welcomed equally.

In many areas this was indeed true. The public services catered for an overwhelming majority. Even in the 1990s, public secondary education was provided for 93 per cent of pupils, public health services for 100 per cent (with only

15–16 per cent supplementing them with private health cover), public transport too for well over 80 per cent at some point in each week.

It could, of course, be demonstrated that the beneficiaries were skewed. Analysts like Julian Le Grand demonstrated how the middle classes managed to benefit disproportionately from the welfare state. Others, like Albert Hirschman, could demonstrate that there were overriding cycles of dissatisfaction with public and private provision, both generally and within specific services (for example the cycles in schooling might not coincide precisely with those in transport). But such arguments didn't disprove the basic equation of publicness and inclusion.

One field however stands out as an exception, as a field where the rhetoric of public action was almost wholly at odds with the everyday reality. This was the field of culture and the arts. To its protagonists, including such almost sanctified figures as Jennie Lee, Minister for the Arts in the 1960s, the story was one of the creation of a virtuous public realm to replace the particularist, aristocratic and unequal production and distribution of the past.

But in reality, despite tangential successes like the Open University (which demonstrated that tertiary education could be genuinely open), the consistent theme about Britain's cultural policy not only since 1945, but probably long before, has been its exclusivity: the overwhelming skew of funding to the pleasures of the elite, to London and to traditional art forms, and the deep hostility to any kind of democratisation.

Yet for those who ruled in the 1940s, the outlook was remarkably different. Their hope was that the same principles of enlightened leadership by government that were then fashionable could be applied to culture as to every other sphere of governance. As the state took over the patronage role once performed by the rich, and as it, in a new guise, continued the very ancient role of state largesse in culture, the whole field of creativity could be brought into the twentieth century. There could be a steady expansion of production, planned by benign boards acting at arm's length from government, and a fairer distribution of its benefits. Moreover, in the realm of culture there was also an added benefit: by introducing the public to the best of culture they could be inculcated with the civilised (and democratic) values that Britain was meant to be defending during the Second World War, values that were embodied in the nation's culture and traditions, in museums and stately homes, concerts of Elgar and performances of Shakespeare. In other words democracy, high culture and the nation were a unity.

This approach has recently been given a sophisticated theoretical analysis in Ernest Gellner's study of nations and nationalism. For him the high culture of the metropolitan elites, together with compulsory education, is what makes nations cohere, and what provides the appropriate workforce for the industrial age. In his scheme, such high culture is counterposed to the pre-modern culture of the folk dance, myth and music. But in Britain high culture was counterposed to something quite different: a fairly vibrant and even quite industrialised popular culture, organised around the pub, the musical hall, printed ballads and even the popular press.

These were the main targets for the pioneers of public policy. For them the goal was to wean the public away from the pub and later Hollywood films, from cheap detective fiction and popular songs. Although there had been various agencies responsible for arts in the past, the progenitor of modern arts policy was the Council for the Encouragement of Music and the Arts. This was set up in 1939, originally to encourage amateur music, drama and painting, through grants to bodies like the Music Travellers which energetically toured Britain setting up music groups.[1]

But CEMA soon turned away from the amateurs and became instead a sponsoring body for professionals, one that was given a progressive sheen by the belief that high culture

– plays, operas, classical music – could be taken to deprived areas to widen horizons and cultivate souls.

In itself, CEMA was not an organisation of great significance. But it turned out to be the embryo of something altogether grander. The midwife was CEMA's second chairman, John Maynard Keynes. His role in arts policy was not quite in the same league as his economic role (at just the same time) in Bretton Woods, but it was in many ways closer to the concerns of his class and milieu, and indeed to his philosophical outlook. For Keynes was essentially an optimistic believer that growth would indirectly lead to happiness and fulfilment (ultimately, he wrote in one essay, 'we will turn away from growth and work to the higher pursuits'). In the meantime, however, arts policy was a more direct tool for bringing people into contact with the finer things in life. State intervention was justified to keep the debilitating effects of commerce at bay, although in time, as audiences' tastes improved, he believed that even the high arts would become self-financing.

Keynes' great institutional achievement was to persuade the government to turn CEMA into the Arts Council of Great Britain, which in 1945 was given a royal charter, a council of the great and good, and a budget. Ever since then the arts council has been the agent of state policy in the arts: arm's length (like the BBC, its model), nominally independent, and essentially bipartisan.

As in so many other areas, the mid-1940s saw a crystallisation of policy approaches which subsequently survived for half a century. Four set the tone and priorities of the new institution. One was the commitment to a few centres of excellence or, as they put it 'powerhouses': key art galleries, theatres, orchestras and opera houses. These were predominantly in London and there was an implicit and sometimes explicit belief in 'trickle down', that somehow 'good' art in these centres would trickle out to the wider public. The second theme was a hostility to popular and modern culture and an overwhelming emphasis on pre-twentieth-century forms, such as unamplified music, theatre, painting and sculpture, rather than film, publishing, video and electronic music – the twentieth-century forms that even in the 1940s already dominated cultural consumption. The third was a working assumption that the Council should use the traditional techniques of aristocratic patronage, in the form of grants, rather than the modern techniques being used by other agencies. In other words, the Council eschewed investment, equity and loans in favour of direct subsidy. Fourth there was an assertion, again at various times more or less explicit, that arts policy and high arts were somehow the vessels of the spiritual heart of the nation. Matthew Arnold's hope that culture might fill the space vacated by the receding tide of religion became a defining part of the rhetoric. It was a view given perfect expression by Sir John Tooley, administrator of the Royal Opera House, when in the early 1980s he claimed that arts cuts would mean 'spiritual bankruptcy for the country'.[2]

These ideas institutionalised what was already a long tradition of the role of culture, that dates back to the creation of the British Museum and the 1845 Libraries Act, both of which sought to establish an alternative to the pub, and new, healthier pursuits for working-class weekends. As a result, the rhetoric after the 1940s turned out to be an interesting mix of the 'progressive' and the 'reactionary', two words whose meaning becomes even more ambiguous than usual in this context. There was a left-wing belief in a fairer distribution of goods (in this case high art) combined with a traditionalist fear of the damaging threat of popular, and above all *American*, culture which would corrode people's sense of nation and their moral fibres. The policy was also a hybrid of traditions of aristocratic patronage, of art for art's sake, and of the social principles of the welfare state based on bureaucracy and rational principles of assessment and distribution.[3]

This rhetorical ambiguity made life difficult for those who

actually had to implement and justify policies. Whereas policies in health or education could be given practical and common sense justifications (a healthier or more employable population), it was very hard to make explicit or straightforward justifications for spending on art. Instead, in a tradition which remains to this day, the explanations by successive arts ministers and chairmen of the arts council have been, almost without exception, ambiguous, flowery, anxious about avoiding any too rational or clear-cut justifications such as employment, or audience numbers, and even anxious about asserting too strongly their capacity to make aesthetic judgements. Indeed until quite recently there was deep hostility to any transparent criteria for assessing the success or otherwise of policies.[4]

It could be, and often is, argued that the use of terms like 'progressive' and 'reactionary', and the application of distributional principles to art, is misleading. According to this view, the arts are 'existence goods': the majority of taxpayers are willing to finance them even if they do not benefit directly. For them the key is to know that they exist.

Similar arguments can be made in relation to universities or remote forests. For example, obscure research into archaeology or philosophy cannot be justified in terms of interests or consumption. They can be described as public goods only in the vaguest way. But two characteristics mark out the arts from these. Most funding is not for 'art for art's sake' but rather for the provision of rather specialised services to very clearly defined audiences: the opera audience is one example. Very little, by contrast, is spent on bursaries or sponsorship of new plays or musical compositions.

Secondly there is also little evidence that the high arts are existence goods in the sense that the public wishes them to exist. Instead, most evidence suggests that it has only been their obscurity, and the relatively small sums of money involved, that has kept the arts from the same scrutiny that has been applied to other areas of spending. Certainly the experience of allocating National Lottery funds has dramatically heightened public awareness of spending decisions and confirmed the public's opposition to most of them.

One might have expected the Labour Party to address such issues head on. It might also have been expected to propose a more inclusive approach, rather than simply filling the role of elite patronage that was previously filled by wealthy philanthropists. Instead there was very little original thinking and Labour skewed the Arts Council very much towards elite concerns. In 1948, for example, more than 15 per cent of the whole arts budget went to a single institution, the Royal Opera House. None was directed to popular forms of culture. Nor has much changed in more recent administrations. In each government since 1945, intimate links have continued to exist between Labour's leadership and the opera. The last Labour Arts Minister, for example, had been director of Covent Garden for 15 years and of Sadlers Wells for 12. Even now, one of Labour's leading spokespeople, and the Chair of Labour's policy think tank, is also a trustee of Covent Garden.

What lay behind these attitudes? The answer may lie in the fact that culture was seen as an alternative to everyday life, not as part of it, as an alternative to working class traditions, not as an aspect of them. As a result, where the redistributive state was meant to take from the rich and give to the poor in arts it did the opposite, using general taxation to subsidise the leisure pursuits of the relatively prosperous. Every survey showed a great skew towards privilege. For example in 1979 the Writers and Arts Council showed that of those receiving literary bursaries, 42 per cent lived in Greater London and 63 per cent went to Oxbridge. A similar story has been told by every survey of theatre and opera, or of attendance at galleries and museums. London still receives more than three times as much per capita as any other region.

That the arts could retain their funding despite this highly regressive character confirms a rather more general point about the professions in Britain post-1945, for the arts were in a sense the purest of the professions, a profession for profession's sake, engaged in art for art's sake. Those engaged in classical music or the theatre were in many ways very different from doctors and teachers, although their trade unions fought successful battles to win them parallel rights of job security. But they shared with the other post-war British professions an inherited capital of political strength which meant that their virtues were rarely questioned.

In part this was a matter of deference: of that cultural lack of confidence that so marked the first Labour administrations. There may have been the occasional sally from an Ivan Illich or from community activists but, by and large, the professional middle class was not attacked during the period of social-democratic hegemony between 1945 and 1979. Working-class Labour was generally deferential, while middle-class Labour was, most of the time, part of the professions – those of law, the universities and teaching. As a consequence, it could be argued that it enjoyed its most benign moments in that period after 1945, protected by a new umbrella of well-being, guaranteed by state salaries and by a political deal that enabled the professional middle classes simultaneously to present themselves as guardians of the newly enfranchised working class, as partners in progress and as defenders of traditional values.

The combination of social-democratic hegemony and a legacy of deference (which remained strong not only for the GP, whose surgery was the practical hub of many communities, but perhaps even more so for the teacher) rendered the professions free from the need to justify themselves.

The 1980s brought this period to an abrupt end. For the Thatcherites, the professions were no longer benign public servants but rather self-interested monopolists, carving out their share of taxpayers' money, resistant to competition or to scrutiny. Instead of deserving trust, for a protected domain in which their judgement was allowed to be sovereign, they were subjected to audits, oversight and demands that they justify themselves. This was as true for the theatre director as it was for the lecturer.

For the professionals, this assault was experienced as something deeply disorienting, almost as a crime against nature. It offended against the principle of trust that underpins the role of the professional. The unease was probably deepest amongst those groups, like the universities and those in social work, which had least day-to-day contact with the ordinary general public.[5] It forced them for the first time in living memory to justify themselves, and revealed in some cases just how threadbare those justifications were, and how dependent on the assertion of authority.

The subsidised arts, by dint of the relatively narrow base of users, were one of the more vulnerable groups, and many experienced the 1980s as a succession of horrific attacks. This was certainly true not only of the more radical community arts groups, whose funding was often chopped for overtly ideological reasons, but also of those like Baroness Warnock, who viewed Thatcher and Thatcherism as 'low', ignorant and philistine.

But despite the shift to business sponsorship and a new language of marketing and efficiency, what is striking is how well arts budgets stood up, how well, like other parts of the middle-class welfare state, they survived the talk of retrenchment. Indeed, contrary to rhetoric, public arts funding continued to increase in real terms throughout most of the Thatcher period.

But Thatcherism was no more able to modernise arts policy than social democracy. Instead, under the aegis of traditionalists like Lord Rees-Mogg, it remained very much in tune with the characteristics defined in the 1940s. Sponsorship was given more encouragement, as was professional arts management. But otherwise the focus on the elite, pre-twentieth-century forms and the use of grant aid remained intact and unquestioned.

In this way the deficiencies of an earlier period were carried on into the 1980s and 1990s. For by ignoring the dynamics of modern culture, of how it works in an age of mechanical reproduction and electronic transmission, cultural policy had only a marginal impact on culture. One early consequence was the inability to respond to the demise of theatre. At the end of the First World War there were 206 towns with at least one playhouse, and many had more – Liverpool had twelve, Newcastle and Manchester eight each. Today, unsubsidised theatre barely exists outside of a few seaside resorts, and although the West End has never been more commercially successful, substantial public subsidy goes to support organisations like the Royal Shakespeare Company.

Much the same story was then repeated with cinema, which had been responsible, with television, for displacing the theatre. Having dominated cultural consumption amongst all age groups, it shrank rapidly after the 1950s, and turned into a minority pursuits for teenagers and twenty-somethings. Yet during this period, public policy was at best confused and at worst impotent as various tax incentive schemes, the Eady Levy (a levy on every cinema ticket sold, some of which was re-directed into the British film industry) and later the funding of specialist independent regional cinemas, had little or no impact on audiences.

More recently, the local culture of civic halls, baths, gardens and theatres, which reflected the municipal role in culture (always much more significant in terms of spending than central government) has been steadily bypassed by the commercial culture of the shopping centre and the multi-screen cinema. In the 1940s, watching the band on a Sunday afternoon was seen as a defence against commercial degradation (and for local government, bandstand concerts were the most popular form of expenditure, followed by indoor art exhibitions). But in retrospect it turned out to be a defence that was easily bypassed, like so much of the confident civic architecture of the nineteenth century. The public simply voted with their feet, while sections of the young went even further, making civic monuments and spaces their first target for vandalism.[6]

In each case, the problem with cultural policy was that it came to be much more about preservation and heritage than about influencing real life. Indeed, it sometimes seemed as if a preservation society was trying to protect some marvellous antique while all around it was being carved up by a greedy developer to whom the preservers turned a blind eye.

The story was not wholly different in broadcasting, although there, the pressures towards some public accountability were much greater and forced its managers to define a more convincing notion of what the public meant. In its early days the BBC was unapologetically patrician. Its role was to present the best of high culture: if some of the public could not keep up then this was inevitable (although as Reith put it, the BBC's role was to 'lead, not follow, but . . . it must not lead at so great a distance as to shake off pursuit'). The BBC also set itself an explicit role of improvement: in A. J. P. Taylor's words, to use 'the brute force of monopoly to stamp Christian morality on the British people'. Nor was the task just one of distributing high art. The BBC also acted to define and police standards of speech and behaviour, waging war on the messy vowels and dropped consonants of the English regions (and of most Londoners). As late as 1981 a BBC booklet recommended forms of speech 'of the person born and brought up in one of the Home Counties, educated at one of the established Southern universities and not so set in his ways that all linguistic change is regarded as unacceptable'.

This attitude, not surprisingly, made the BBC, vehemently opposed to any new broadcasting. Reith famously described commercial broadcasting as akin to the introduction of 'dog racing, smallpox and bubonic plague'.[7] The left agreed, and ever since has opposed every single measure to expand broadcasting, from commercial television and radio to satellite, and from cable to community radio. Indeed in broadcasting, as in other fields, the public was defined extremely narrowly, to include only those engaged in activities directly owned and overseen by national government. When ITV was being debated in the 1950s, the result was an intriguing pattern of coalitions: in favour was an odd alignment that ranged from Conservatives to A. J. P. Taylor and Canon Collins, against were the BBC, the Labour Party, the TUC and the liberal establishment.

When ITV did come on air, the BBC was shocked. As the critic Peter Black put it, 'once they had the choice the working class audience left the BBC at a pace that suggested ill-will was more deeply entrenched than good'. An institution that had seen itself as the embodiment of an elevated notion of the public was treated instead as not only class biased but also as politically slanted (the public has always viewed the BBC as more pro-Conservative than commercial broadcasters, despite the attempts by the Conservatives in the 1980s to paint the BBC as a hotbed of leftism).

Fortunately this pressure of disappearing viewers had positive effects. It forced the BBC to be popular. A decade later, the huge success of pirate radio stations like Radio Caroline achieved the same effect, with the establishment of Radio 1 (and the co-option of many of the illegal stations' DJs). Audience pressure cajoled it into finding new formats, like *Z Cars* for example, which spoke in the vernacular, and *That was the Week that Was*, which replaced pompous deference with irreverence.

For the BBC, the pressure of ratings, and the direct political pressure of having to justify a licence fee, has helped it steadily evolve, not too far behind public values. It has had to develop popular genres of entertainment, soap operas and dramas, game shows and documentaries. As a result, its notion of the public could never become too abstract, too distant from the reality.

In this sense, it has had a huge advantage over those other

professions which received their funding direct from the state, from pooled taxes, a funding model that never required them to answer to the public. This direct connection to the public also gave the BBC greater resilience. It enabled it to make its case directly to viewers, as it did through special programmes in the late 1980s and early 1990s. And it kept it protected from cultural attack over shocking or outrageous broadcasts.

It would be wrong to portray the BBC as wholly insulated from political pressures. During the 1980s it was consistently attacked by government ministers and the Conservative Party. Highly political appointments were made to the board of governors to drive an internal reform process. And many of the internal reforms led to what staff described as 'a climate of fear'. But nevertheless, it is equally striking that through all of this, the BBC has survived intact as a vertically and horizontally integrated monolith, with very little legislative imposition or weakening.

Others were not so fortunate. For example the Tate Gallery made itself a marvellous target for ridicule when it put a pile of bricks on display (although subsequently it became hugely successful at attracting large crowds). Even more pertinent was the experience of local authorities which funded gay and lesbian theatre workshops and were then pilloried in the national press. Yet throughout this period of cultural warfare between an often populist government and what it portrayed as out-of-touch elitists, cultural institutions like the BBC survived intact, and indeed survived Margaret Thatcher's period in office as the only major public service which had not been subjected to legislation to restructure it according to new principles (the only reforms, such as producer choice, were almost entirely internally driven).

But the real comment on post-war cultural policy has been not what it did, but what it didn't do. The elite view was that, in Lord Goodman's words, 'a dose of culture could turn hooligans into citizens'. But in practice, for most people culture did not come from the Arts Council and the opera houses. Nor did it even always come from the BBC. Instead it often came closer to home. For example, in the 1990s 1.8 million people are involved in amateur music and drama, 3.7 million practise photography, 3 million textile crafts and 1.8 million painting and drawing, part of a larger tradition of vibrant self-organisation which has been viewed with suspicion not only by the professionals who helped turn CEMA away from the amateurs, but also by the producerist left, whose trade unions, such as the Musicians Union and Equity, have long dominated Labour Party policy.

Nor did the state institutions mean much for the pop groups like the Beatles and Rolling Stones, which swept the world in the 1960s, laying the foundations for the UK to have a world market share of between 15 and 25 per cent during the 1970s and 1980s, something it has in almost no other industry. The Beatles may have been given honours by Harold Wilson, Bob Geldof may have been knighted by Margaret Thatcher (and Cliff Richard by John Major) but even today, popular music remains largely invisible around the institutions of official culture, whether those promoting Britain abroad (like the British Council) or those (like the various Tourist Boards) promoting it here. The state may have played an indirect role in the rise of rock and pop through the arts schools, and later the DSS, but it did so by mistake.

Later, the generation of artists and musicians who came of age in the 1980s and 1990s were equally distant from government, and equally unlikely to believe that the public realm of culture had room for them. Instead, for most, the priority was not to become dependent on subsidy but rather to enter the market-place and succeed in it. The dividing line between commerce (bad) and public sector (good) made little sense to those who perceived themselves to be on the margins. This was certainly as true of the black and Asian music, film and writing groups, of feminist publishers, independent music labels and impresarios, as it was of the multiplying radio stations in the 1980s (like Kiss and Dread Broadcasting

Company) that paved the way for official licences in the 1990s. In each of these cases the key divide was not between the public and the private. It was, instead, between a sphere of independent production and what was seen as a tightly controlled, class-based, sphere of public funding, organically linked through boards of the great and the good to the elites of London.

In recent years, some concessions have been made. Funding bodies have acknowledged the twentieth century art forms (even though it took the best part of a century for film to be accepted). There is some support for the more experimental work in fields like video and audio. Official documents have even used the term 'the cultural industries', acknowledging that the majority of cultural work and distribution takes place within competitive industries rather than within the welfare umbrella of state subsidy. The problem however is that these newer currents are incompatible with what has gone before: with the focus on subsidy, with the pre-twentieth century forms and the language of excellence. If the old justifications (which boiled down to faith in the authority of a few decision makers on funding) no longer hold, then the question moves on to what should replace them: a purely industrial concern for national competitive advantage, job creation, urban regeneration, or ethnic pluralism?

This question is difficult to answer for one particular reason. The loss of aesthetic authority by an elite which was once proud of its convictions and taste is emblematic of a wider decline in deference and authority. In the 1940s, few questioned that public resources should be devoted to the culture of the ruling class, and in particular to the opera. But over time, a respect for authority rooted only in tradition has waned. A nation in decline, that talks endlessly about decline, inevitably sees the authority of its ruling institutions decline too. In this context it has always been very hard for the official culture to decide which sides to take – for example whether to side with those opposing modernity, Larkin and

Amis, later Lindsay Anderson and John Taverner – or whether to keep going with modernists, the avant-garde which had almost lost the power to shock after seventy years.[8] Should it back the 'angry young men' (and women) of each generation? Should it be subversive, supporting the radical playwrights like Trevor Griffiths and Howard Brenton (who depended ironically almost entirely on state largesse even as they denounced the state)? Should it support artists like Francis Bacon (or Damien Hirst) because they are good according to their peers, because they are popular, or simply because they have something to say and only time will tell whether it has any innate virtue? And if there isn't a clear view of good and bad, of useful and useless, what is left to justify it? Perhaps nothing, as the early 1990s National Arts and Media strategy (a report produced by a widely based committee) suggested in its sad meanderings in search of coherence.

Many other countries share these problems. But none so acutely. In America, there is still, at least, the tradition of schemes like Roosevelt's Federal Writers Project and the Federal Arts Project, which provided work for many artists, some very interesting oral history and folklore, and played a genuine social role in job creation as well as a cultural one. In the USA, if there is conflict, it is far more likely to take the form of a Christian backlash against the cosmopolitan depravity of a Robert Mapplethorpe than anything else.[9] Meanwhile, in many other European countries there are at least self-confident states which can follow France in the mobilisation of almost any kind of culture as self-aggrandisement for the nation and government, which are treated as synonymous.

In Britain, by contrast, culture is a place of conflict. It has been said that nothing so divides the nation as music. It could equally well be said that culture was the graveyard not only for Conservatives (made fun of by the joyful nihilism of popular culture – and indeed some would argue that John Major as well as the Liberal leader David Steel were destroyed more by *Spitting Image's* puppet versions than by anything else) and of progressives (after all the Beatles sang 'You say you want a revolution' in opposition to the activists, and fifteen years later it was the Sex Pistol's *God Save the Queen* more than the political correctness of 'Rock against Racism', which captured the spirit of the time).

For the same reason, culture has always been oddly distant from politics, not fitting easily into those narratives which suggest that there was a coherent spirit of each age. The 1980s, for example, saw a more creative boom in radical culture of all kinds than almost any other decade. Playwrights, poets, rock musicians and novelists all drew on the experience of rule by Margaret Thatcher to produce their most angry, committed work, all without any discernible influence on the nation's mood beyond the fairly small audiences that enthusiastically welcomed being told that they were living in a corrupt, secretive, quasi-fascist state. Nor were the late 1940s, seen then and now as a halcyon period of socialist construction, mirrored in much of an outpouring of utopian, inspirational art. Instead, by a nice irony, the works of fiction from late 1940s Britain that are probably best remembered around the world are the final, dystopian novels of George Orwell, and today's writers look back less at the heroic collectivism and more – through the work of people like Carolyn Steedman, Elizabeth Wilson and Jerry White – at the liberation achieved through the growth of cheap fashions, make-up and small amounts of additional discretionary spending.

This sort of liberation, everyday, prosaic, about fun and pleasure and intimate passions, has always been looked down on by elite culture. It achieved its influence not through the state, but through the market – through Hollywood cinema, cheap magazines, Sky Television and the *Sun*, through zoot suits and mohicans, Northern Soul and rave. And for this very reason, it subtly called into question the social-democratic project which took its culture from the elite and became its most ardent defender, usually against both the interests and the arguments of its working class supporters.

In this respect Britain went a different route from Continental socialists. In Italy and France, Germany and Scandinavia, the post-1945 left was often in the forefront of culture, actively supported by its parties, which organised comprehensive political cultures embracing festivals, poetry reading, public subsidy for working-class literature. In Britain, by contrast, a distinctively social-democratic culture never emerged, perhaps a reflection of the roots of the Labour Party in the workplace, not in the pleasures of the evening or weekend. Only belatedly, under the more radical local authorities of the 1980s, and particularly the Greater London Council, did a more pluralistic and modern political culture briefly emerge: a rainbow coalition manifest in big popular music festivals, multi-culturalism and subsidies for community-based arts projects.

The lack of an organic link between the social-democratic project and a live culture also had one other effect. It linked social democracy to tradition, and to the traditionalism of an elite that had become doubtful of the virtues of modernity. J. B. Priestley even went so far as to write that the modern world 'is alien to the English temperament'. Perhaps this is why the Conservative government in 1992 chose to dub its ministry of culture the 'Department of Heritage', despite offering no very clear guidelines as to what that might mean. This attachment to the past may also explain why one of the major recent arguments in the high arts has been about preserving for Britain Antonio Canova's 'The Three Graces', a very minor example of neo-classical sculpture.

There was nothing inevitable about the failure of the social democrats to develop an authentic popular tradition. Indeed, at times, more populist instincts seemed to strike chords. For example, the Festival of Britain attracted crowds in excess of 150,000 on some days, to be denounced by the Conservatives as a 'monumental piece of imbecility and iniquity', and countered two years later when substantial sums were spent to celebrate the Coronation. But in practice, the cultural vision was deficient, never distinctive and never linked to the full power and diversity of popular culture.

As a result, in culture more than anywhere else, the social-democratic rhetoric was in time unravelled, as it transpired that public service was *for* the public, not *of* the public, for professionals not amateurs or volunteers and for balance and sobriety, not pleasure and risk.

CHAPTER 10

The European Question

Rules, National Modernisation and the ambiguities of *Primat der Innenpolitik*

Jim Bulpitt

> The language of greatness was one which everybody could
> understand and which made the practice of mass democratic
> politics, once so feared, really rather easy; the language of
> national modernisation, in contrast, strained not only
> people's intellects, but undermined the unity of the people
> under its accustomed leaders.[1]

THE SUBJECT of this chapter, Britain and Europe since
1945, is huge, complex and contentious.[2] Hence, no consensus exists as to how it should be tackled, even less what
conclusions should be drawn. In these circumstances, the best
that can be done, once narrative history is rejected as the
appropriate mode of discourse, is to be open about possible
sources of bias and attempt to produce a parsimonious, plausible, fruitful polemic.

Narrative history has been ditched because its method, best
summed up by the words, 'Once upon a Time', is long-
winded, peculiarly unable to confront the problems of macro
analysis, and overall, yields few benefits. Moreover, its oper-

ational assumption, that 'the facts speak for themselves', is simply not true. The bias will come from this writer's adherence to the intellectual case for Euro-scepticism, a case which is not a cover for principled opposition to European Union and not the same as the arguments employed by the various Euro-sceptic groups in Britain.[3] Producing a parsimonious, plausible and fruitful polemic is a difficult exercise. Accounts of Britain's relationship with the process of western European integration are plentiful. Most, however, merely recycle the relatively small amount of information on the subject, or round up the usual suspects. Not surprisingly, most come to the same conclusions: Britain missed the 'bus' of European integration in the 1950s, mounted a delayed bid for membership of the E.E.C. in 1961 to bolster its ailing economy and remaining Great Power ambitions and, once membership was achieved in 1973, suffered from a continual inability, or unwillingness, to play the Euro-game. Britain, in other words, was/is an 'awkward', or 'semi-detached' partner in the great Euro-enterprise.[4] Hence Europe, since 1945, represents one of the most significant British *foreign policy* failures.

The line pursued here is somewhat different. Its prime focus is on a problem older – and wider – than Britain's relations with the European Community. It is concerned to examine the relations, or interconnections, between the domestic management of the British polity and external affairs. In this scenario Europe assumed the rôle, for some considerable time, of just another method of resolving the governing-Britain problem, just another external zimmerframe for its hard-pressed governors, just another attempt to construct an easy modernisation strategy by stressing the language of national greatness. In this sense, Europe reflected that old British concern to subordinate foreign policy to domestic objectives, for *Primat der Innenpolitik*. The crunch came after the mid-1980s, when the British political elite was suddenly confronted with two awkward messages. Europe was not just another game but, perhaps, 'end-game': there was nowhere else to go, no other zimmerframe was in sight. Equally embarrassing, the process of European integration increasingly revealed, on the domestic front, a basic and long-concealed ambiguity in the primacy of domestic political statecraft, an ambiguity which threatened both the public's reception of the issue and party political unity, particularly in the Conservative Party. The consequence was that Europe could no longer be presented as a foreign policy adventure, like 'exporting is fun': rather, it went to the roots of how Britain was to be governed in the future and, even though most Euro-enthusiasts have sought to downplay this, of the nature of democracy in Britain.

The agenda for discussion runs as follows. First, some key problems of analysis are considered. Secondly, the nature of the governing Britain problem and the role of external affairs in resolving that problem before 1960 are examined. Thirdly, Britain's relations with the various manifestations of European integration are considered in the period 1961 to 1995.

PROBLEMS AND ASSUMPTIONS

A macro survey of a complex, contested subject demands that some attention be paid to the major analytical problems encountered and the assumptions made to confront those problems. Five problems will receive some brief attention.

The Concepts Jungle

Public debate concerning Britain's appropriate response to the process of European integration has persisted for some thirty years, albeit with a decidedly spasmodic rhythm. Its principal themes – sovereignty, interdependence, federalism and interests – have never changed. These are the concepts which dominate the contested intellectual, or ideas, domain of the debate. Let me parody their employment by the opposing camps.

The Euro-enthusiasts suggest that in an increasingly inter-dependent world, old-fashioned ideas of sovereign nation-states must be replaced by new notions of sovereignty-sharing within regional politico-economic blocs, such as the European Union. For Euro-enthusiasts, size does matter. Britain, so it is argued, is simply too small and too fragile economically to survive, let alone prosper, outside the European Union. There is simply no alternative (TINA). Moreover, Britain must be at the heart or centre of Europe in order to structure its politics to benefit Britain's interests. The best outcome is a federal, non-centralised Europe operating on the basis of the subsidiarity principle (bringing decisions down to the lowest possible level) alongside a beefed-up European Parliament to insert more democratic procedures and popular represen-tation into the workings of Community-wide institutions. Their opponents (a very varied bunch) largely react to these visions. They emphasise that state sovereignty is still impor-tant and that even in an interdependent world Britain can, and should, maintain control over key policy areas. Federal-ism they regard as an exercise in centralisation, and subsidiar-ity as something which the European Commission and Court conveniently forget in their actions and judgements. More-over, Europe is composed of too many starkly different inter-ests to produce a viable democracy. What is required is an insertion of democracy into the Euro-debate in Britain, namely a referendum, a referendum which (wrongly?) they think they will win.

What is wrong with all this? At this stage in the discussion, let us consider the three concepts of federalism, interdepen-dence and sovereignty. Federalism is a word devoid of any generally accepted meaning.[5] It seems to suggest a nice *via media* between too centralised unitary systems and too decentralised confederations. In fact, there are a variety of federal models, a variety of unitary models and too few confederations in the world to draw any useful conclusions. Perceptions of federalism depend on the status quo. If the move to federalism comes from a centralised empire or system of gross internal colonialism, then federalism can be viewed as providing the benefits of decentralisation. If, however, the move is from a 'normal', established nation-state, then it might appear to be a move towards centralisation. In all circumstances it will depend on the nature of political power in the old and new units; constitutional blue-prints have only a marginal impact. It is difficult not to conclude that individuals and groups use the word 'federal' when, and in ways, that suit them. Pretty much the same applies to 'subsidiarity' which has received far less attention if only because it is such a new, and untried, concept.[6]

Interdependence and sovereignty can be considered together. Interdependence between states – their increasing sensitivity to, and penetration by, external forces – is the development which supposedly renders claims to sovereignty unreal. It is a basic tenet of the Euro-enthusiast case that interdependence is a part of the new world order and sovereignty a part of the old. The problem is that sovereignty, other than as a convenient legal faction, has no history, whereas interdependence has a very long one.[7] The global interpenetration of agricultural, manufacturing and finance capital has existed for several centuries. The British, above all, should recognise this if only because in the eighteenth and nineteenth centuries it was their capital which was orchestrating the penetration. Even the problems posed by the international currency markets are not new, as most members of the 1931 Labour Government realised only too well. Hence, any differences between interdependence in times past and present are best viewed as those of degree, not of kind.

Both sides, it is clear, employ concepts which at best are ambiguous and, at worst, should have been jettisoned ages ago. As the more positive side, it is the Euro-enthusiasts' case which suffers most. It is not only the concepts they use which are interesting but those they sideline, particularly power, autonomy and democracy. We should not be too surprised at this development. It simply highlights the well-known point that concepts (and ideas) are rarely neutral. In debates like this they are simply used as weapons to control, rather than to illuminate, the subject.

Understanding the European Union.

What happens when we shift the level of analysis from Britain and Europe to the workings of the Union or Community itself? We need to make this shift because how the Union works, or is supposed to work, is a major item in the debate. The authorised answer to this question remains that developed in the 1950s and 1960s, namely neo-functionalism. The central themes of this theory are that greater Community integration is both beneficial and inevitable. Beneficial, because all member states are advantaged, inevitable because of the powerful integration momentum provided by policy and political spill-overs, notably economic policy and the operations of the Commission and Court of Justice. Neo-functionalism is often criticised on both theoretical and empirical grounds.[8] Nevertheless, until the 1990s, its general messages were largely unchallenged. This is surprising because neo-functionalism is not so much a theory of how the Community operates as part of a political strategy to ensure that integration takes place. There are, however, other ways of viewing this matter. One is to argue that the Community is, and always will be, an intergovernmental organisation, designed to rescue the nation state from its economic weakness. Another stresses that it an institution designed to maintain peace in western Europe. Yes another views the Community as an ideological conspiracy favouring Euro-federalism.[9]

What is missing from these perspectives is some recognition that the Community is not an association of equal states that have joined together to provide themselves with policy benefits. It is more plausible to understand it as a power system in which (a) two states, France and Germany, when acting in combination, have considerable influence, (b) four states, Ireland, Greece, Spain and Portugal, are so heavily dependent on Community funds that their votes are usually available to any grouping which promises to continue or improve their 'pensions', (c) two other states, Belgium and Italy, usually support federal-type schemes because of the extreme fragility of their domestic politics, and (d) one state, or statelet, Luxembourg, exists simply to provide the Community with key personnel in crises and further the 'ever closer Union' objective. The point can be put in two other ways. If, as is often suggested, Euro-politics is a matter of coalition building at the centre, then this particular configuration of forces will make life difficult for any member state doubtful about the principle, or pace, of integration. Alternatively, up to the mid-1990s at least, no permanent coalition of member states had emerged to rival the Franco–German axis and its satellites.

It is often suggested, by both Euro-enthusiasts and sceptics, that the Community is an attempt to reduce the role of the nation state. One group applauds this, the other denounces it. The problem is that the Community, as it has operated up to now, resembles an old-fashioned power play by diplomatic means. It is not so much a community as a two-state hegemonic alliance (France and Germany), an alliance which appeals to the integration nostrums of European Christian (that is Catholic) Democracy when convenient. The problem for Britain is that in the 1990s that set of ideas became more and more convenient for these players, especially Germany under Helmut Kohl's leadership.

The Calculation of Advantage

Outside the restricted world of academic and quality media comment, few people are interested in the concepts, theories and process of European integration. What concerns most people are the outcomes of the whole business – is it in

Britain's interests to participate in a Euro-Union? Or, more crudely (and intelligently), 'What's in it for me?'

Euro-enthusiasts and Euro-phobes have no doubts about the outcomes. A representative text in terms of such certainty runs as follows: 'The real choice now is between a full commitment to European Union or an increasingly dispiriting and almost certainly bitter irrelevance on the margins of Europe.'[10] Statements like this, or similar ones expressing opposing views, conveniently push to one side the problems encountered when attempting to calculate the advantages and disadvantages of Britain's membership of a more integrated Union.

First, Britain, even more the United Kingdom, may be an inappropriate unit for calculation. Some people in Northern Ireland, Scotland, and Wales, may employ different formulae to assess the issue, formulae which grant more significance to their past and present relations with England (or, in the case of Northern Ireland, with the Republic) than with Europe. For 'Ulster Loyalists' Europe may be a device for weakening ties with England. For some groups in Wales, and above all Scotland, it provides a beneficial exit option from the Union with England. Alternatively, those in England who support the Union may see Europe as a danger to its continued existence. It follows that most discussions of Britain and Europe are really directed at the English. This one certainly is. I do not presume to talk for the Welsh, Scots and Northern Irish.

Secondly, the advantages and disadvantages of territorial Unions have to be assessed in terms of the common conceptual currency of such calculations, namely interests. But 'interests' are a notoriously soft currency in which to deal. The obvious question is can they be calculated objectively, or do we rely on subjective perceptions? Is there any single English interest, or do we need to deconstruct it into region, class or occupational function? The usual response to these questions from Euro-enthusiasts is to say that 'on balance', Britain or

England, will gain. This, however, doesn't get us very far. It also suggests that some will be losers, though for how long is not certain. Time, therefore, becomes an essential part of the calculation. Time, in the sense that the detailed blueprint for Euro-Union, particularly EMU, has still to be decided in the future. Time, in the sense that territorial Unions which emphasise economic advantage seem to take a long time to repair initial relative economic backwardness. Have the Old South, the Mezzogiorno or Scotland, for example, actually gained from their membership of economic and monetary Unions called, respectively, the United States, Italy and Britain? They are certainly better off, but have they overcome the initial advantage of the core regions? Would they have reaped even greater advantages on their own, with their own governments and currency? Scotland is a superb illustration of how difficult and contentious such calculations become. Perhaps in England we ought to pay more attention to the debates in Scotland on these matters in 1707 and in the 1990s. They may have something to teach us.[11]

The issue of advantage is a 'Leap in the Dark'. Couched in the usual positive terms – more Euro-integration will, or will not, yield more benefits – the whole exercise becomes mere speculation. There are simply too many interests involved, and the future politics of benefits distribution too complex and uncertain for these sums to be nicely calculated. We cannot even say with any accuracy that Britain has gained (or lost) from its Community membership up to now. Just what the course of events would have been after 1973 without membership is one of the great counterfactuals of modern British politics. Many Euro-enthusiasts recognise this problem. So, increasingly, they have shifted the argument from the positive to the negative mode. In other words, the calculation of advantage becomes 'there is no alternative for Britain'. Whether 'Britain' likes it or not, there can be no viable existence outside a Euro-Union: nobody else wants us and the country is too small and too inefficient to survive on its own. In debating terms this is a clever move. It fits the depression culture of the 1990s. It grants Euro-Union the force of inevitability. Above all, it highlights a major weakness of the British Euro-sceptics, namely, their unwillingness to do anything other than respond to the arguments of their opponents. Nevertheless, the problem remains. Who knows how much of Britain would prosper outside (and that can signify many things) a more integrated Euro-Union? Only one thing is clear: this particular aspect of the Euro-debate has never assumed any prominence. It is, however, crucial to any understanding of the advantage issue.

Principal Actor Designation

In the present context this is a crucial issue. Only if we are explicit about 'Who Governs Britain?' can we deal effectively with the related question of 'Whose behaviour towards Europe are we considering?' As indicated above, there is little point in discussing Britain's, or even England's, relations with Europe. On the other hand, the disadvantages of moving to the other end of the methodological spectrum and concentrating on key individuals – the 'Great Person' approach – are also pretty obvious. The story then degenerates into an itemisation of the preferences and prejudices of important people. Equally significant, such an approach obstructs inter-temporal and inter-spatial analysis.

Ideally, the choice of principal actor needs to satisfy a number of initial assumptions. Analytically we seek a unitary (united), rational-capable actor, in constant contact with, and having a significant impact on, the 'high politics' of both governing Britain and relations with Europe. The particular form of rationality assumed will be a very weak form, namely bounded rationality or 'satisficing' – the pursuit of self-interest allowing for constraints of time, knowledge and calculating skills.[12] The awkward point, however, is that these conditions exclude most of the popular actor options, such as the state, the ruling class, the political elite and senior ranks of the civil service. There is, of course, the Cabinet, or Cabinets. But they are too large to be especially united or rational. Increasingly they function as meetings of departmental heads most of whom are not constant players in the 'high politics' of governing Britain and relations with Europe. This is clearly a problem and the response to it may be regarded as unsatisfactory. The only actor unit which fulfils the conditions laid down above is variously labelled the 'Inner Cabinet', the 'Prime Ministerial clique' model, or the unit which best catches the style of British governing, 'the Court' – that is, the Prime Minister and key ministerial and political 'friends'. This, therefore, is our designated principal actor. One important outcome is that most of the analysis below will be dealing with Conservative leaders in office, or a series of Conservative 'Courts'.

Rationality in Context: Statecraft

Question: what do 'Courts' do when they govern Britain? The answer comes in two forms, both conditioned by the rationality assumption adopted above. In the first instance that assumption leads to the rejection of several popular ways of explaining the governing process. One of these is to regard policies as the primary function of government. Policies, however, are only one dimension of the process. In a broader sense, governing is often viewed as characterised by a number of alternative styles, namely either 'muddling through', or populism (that is responding to public opinion), or pluralism (responding to interest group pressures), or, what can be called, idealism (the pursuit of ideas or doctrines). The rationality assumption means that all these styles must be rejected simply because they exclude the essence of rationality, namely the purposive pursuit of self-interest, as the 'main bias' of governing.

So, what counts as rational behaviour by the 'Court' in

Britain? Answering this question requires us initially to put rationality in the context of the British structure of politics over the last seventy-odd years. This, it can be argued, has been marked by the following features. First, a lethal electoral system based on single member constituencies and simple majorities. Secondly, the persistence of a predominantly adversarial two-party system. Thirdly, the fact that both the major parties, Conservative and Labour, have been dominated by temporary professional parliamentary leaders, that is persons who, for the duration of their leadership, give up most of their time and ambitions to managing their parties. Fourthly, the absence in Britain of any significant degree of institutional pluralism. In combination, these structural characteristics of modern British politics have produced party elites with common, initial, subsistence-level objectives, namely winning national office, avoiding too many problems while there and getting re-elected. Any other objectives are jam on the bread. The logic behind these objectives is crude but real. The electoral system provides few guarantees of certain office. The adversarial party system normally excludes coalitions, and professional politicians must win office to justify their commitment. The absence of other significant centres of institutional power means that only national office is worth gaining: losing office – elections – means the political wilderness.

The outcome is that British governing is one long electoral campaign, albeit with different phases of intensity. In these circumstances, rational politicians in office will pursue governing strategies and employ supportive manipulative techniques to ensure, as far as possible, that they achieve their crude, subsistence-level objectives. In combination, these governing objectives, strategies and manipulative mechanisms can be labelled 'Court statecraft'.[13] Statecraft is the rational pursuit of Court interests within the British structure of politics. Statecraft, then, is what the game of governing Britain is about: not all Courts will play this game equally well, but they will all be forced to play the same game. The consequences for the analysis of the Britain-and-Europe issue are threefold. Courts will put their own perceived interests first and hope they can be presented as the country's interests. The playing field for this game will be party politics in Parliament. Extra parliamentary actors, such as party conferences and the public, will only be called on to play a role when they can no longer be avoided, or when they can grant some support to Court objectives. It follows, finally, that if this is the way Courts behave, our assessment of their behaviour must take account of this. Of course, we can assess them with respect to other criteria – the consistency, coherence, and plausible nature of their arguments, the extent to which they protect and promote the general interest (whatever that is) and the degree to which they respond to public opinion. We should never forget, however, that within the British structure of politics, politicians in office (and opposition) will do what they have got to do. They will play 'dirty pool' to protect and advance their own interests.

In this situation, politicians in the Court will rarely be able to afford the luxury of treating ideas too seriously as ideas. On most occasions, ideas will form part of the manipulative mechanisms of British governing. As such, they will be variously employed as weapons of attack, defence, praise or denigration. More generally, they will be used to control what is and what is not regarded as 'common-sense' on any particular issue.

A more positive role will be played by the rules underlying the policy preferences of the governing strategy.[14] These will be particularly important in economic and foreign policy. Rules can have either an 'externalist' or 'domesticist' bias. For example, the rules associated with economic policy may stress either exchange rate stability (externalist) or domestic monetary indicators and targets (domesticist). Although in both cases the ultimate objective will be competent management of the economy, their motives and impact can differ significantly. Similarly, foreign policy can be run on the basis of an externalist or domesticist bias. Externalist rules for foreign policy suggest that this activity will be insulated from, or assume primacy over, short term domestic political objectives. Domesticist rules will amount to *Primat der Innenpolitik*. It is at this point we can see why Europe poses so many problems for domestic political management. On the one hand, Euro-Union threatens both the distinction between externalist and domesticist economic rules and the distinction between domestic and foreign policy. On the other hand, it promises to relieve British governors of the burdens associated with managing the rules, and therefore, of the wider polity or estate management. In short, Europe promises to either traumatise or anaesthetise the governing Britain problem. Put another way, it offers the 'final solution' or the ultimate zimmerframe.

L'ANCIEN RÉGIME

We need a temporal base point. In other words, we need to consider the governing Britain problem and the preoccupations and responses of politicians in office to that problem during the *ancien régime*, the period before the emergence of European integration as a serious issue in British politics. Such an exercise will enable us more easily to trace continuities and change over time. It will also explain why, from the late 1940s, most British politicians regarded Europe as a problem rather than an opportunity.

In the form which it was to be sustained for some seventy years, the governing Britain problem emerged in 1918. At its heart was the new, mass electoral democracy resulting from the provisions of the Representation of the People Act.[15] That provided the main domestic political context within which party leaders' preoccupations and responses to other components of the problem – an uncompetitive economy, the new political significance of the labour movement, bourgeois irritation with that new significance and the gap between the country's external commitments and the resources it was prepared to devote to them – had to be worked out. An important link between these components and the extensions of the franchise was the fear of inflation, something which could destroy stability in both domestic and external affairs. No politician articulated his general awareness of the governing Britain problem better than Baldwin. In a speech at Manchester in 1923, for example, he claimed that 'the times are new and strange and extraordinarily difficult': the Great War had destroyed old certainties, compressed half a century of political evolution into just four years, and nurtured new ambitions and demands in the electorate. Moreover, the 1918 Act had 'created millions of untrained and inexperienced voters ... with no party traditions, all alike affected by the ruthlessness that was in the atmosphere.'[16]

Baldwin played an important role in bringing to an end the first statecraft response to the governing Britain problem, namely the Lloyd George Coalition of National Unity of 1918 to 1922.[17] Essentially, this Coalition had been a response based on a cross-party formula – anti-socialism – and the presumed abilities of one man, Lloyd George, to appeal to all classes, confront effectively the principal post-war problems and, more generally, manage the necessary national modernisation strategy. It collapsed because 'sound chaps' came to the conclusion that the Coalition was not the right vehicle to achieve these aims. It was unsound on inflation, too adventurous in foreign policy, associated with sleaze in public life and, above all, threatened to undermine 'the unity of the people under its accustomed leaders'. The new statecraft which took its place aimed to avoid these mistakes by returning to the stability and soundness associated with the two-party system (which meant sidelining the Liberal Party). The new statecraft was to prove a very flexible friend in both the domestic and external arenas. It was called the Treasury View.[18]

Approaching the Treasury View in this way calls for several preliminary comments. First, the Treasury View did not emerge out of nowhere in 1922. In its modern guise, that is the perceived necessity to have some sort of 'macro' economic strategy, it was born during the great inflation of 1919–20. Secondly, for a long time after 1945 the Treasury View was held responsible for just about all the ills of the inter-war period, especially unemployment and appeasement. Thanks to the PRO mafia, that is no longer the case. Finally, the Treasury View was not simply a doctrine supported and pushed by senior civil servants in that department. It represented the overwhelming statecraft consensus of almost all sections of the political elite in the inter-war period.

In terms of governing objectives, the Treasury View is best seen as a domesticist strategy, one supporting prudence, flexibility and national modernisation. It was concerned to maintain political tranquillity at home and eschew external adventures, and adventurers, abroad. It wanted to avoid hassle and to sustain as much relative autonomy for political leaders in office as possible. In short it was essentially a limited liability statecraft on both the domestic and external fronts. If these objectives were achieved, then leading politicians in office could develop a governing competence which, in turn, could help them stay in business. The code, or strategy, underlying its policy output prioritised domestic macroeconomic management, particularly the constant necessity to combat inflation threats (even in the midst of a World Depression). It argued that only by defeating inflation would Britain increase its share of world trade and, hence, improve employment prospects. What we would now call supply-side measures were perceived as necessary, but always subordinate to the anti-inflation policy. It was recognised that in a mass electoral democracy, and the British structure of politics, control of inflation would always be a fragile thing. What was required was a set of economic rules devised to restrict the discretion of politicians, especially in terms of public works, public spending and public borrowing. The best rule was the 'knave proof' Gold Standard. If you couldn't have that then other domesticist rules were required which would depoliticise economic management, sustain an austerity culture and accept the importance of maintaining foreign confidence in sterling. Foreign policy was subordinated to these domestic management concerns. Hence the commitment to the 'Ten Years' Rule' in the 1920s and appeasement in the 1930s, both of which were designed to make the Foreign Office, and the armed services, take the strain of the limited liability strategy. Despite concern for the markets' confidence in sterling, the role of foreign policy in this statecraft reveals its essentially domesticist bias. Britain was to maintain its Great Power status, but on the cheap, at least until the economy had returned to 'normalcy'.

One seemingly reasonable response to the argument above is 'So, what?' Why bother with the detritus of the inter-war period? After all, everything changed after 1940 and 1945. But did it? And, if it didn't, what messages does this send us about the Britain and Europe issue?

The following points are relevant. First, we should not forget that in the late 1930s the National Government was popular and regarded as a success. Without 'Mr Hitler', Neville Chamberlain would undoubtedly have won the General Election of 1940. And victory would have been deserved since none of his opponents had anything serious to offer in terms of either domestic or foreign policy, apart that is from vague talk about public works and alliances with the United States or the Soviet Union.

Secondly, British perceptions of the War were determined by the events of 1940 and 1941. These were the Churchill gang's Parliamentary coup of May 1940, the fall of France the following month, and the Battle of Britain later in the year. 1941 saw the German attack on the Soviet Union, the belated entry of the United States into the War after Pearl Harbor, and Hitler's curious, yet enormously important decision, to declare war on America. The events of 1941 determined that Germany and Japan would lose the war and Britain would be on the winning side. The events of 1940 suggested that the French could not be trusted and that Britain could 'stand alone'. The short-term consequence of all this was a reaffirmation of Britishness and the British 'way' of doing things. Far from creating a radical, 'all-change' culture, the War gave Britain the opportunity to carry on regardless, sustaining a culture of continuity.

But what about '1945', the 'Attlee consensus', and the 'new Conservatism' of the 1950s? What about 'Butskellism' and the 'post-war consensus'? What about 'nationalisation' and the 'welfare state'? These social democratic post-war slogans were undoubtedly important in terms of party rhetoric, and were enormously assisted, it should be noted, by the reluctance of the Conservative victors of the 1940 coup to find anything good to say about the National Governments. They ignore, however, too many awkward points. Nationalisation, that is public corporations, was not new, nor did it have a radical impact on the British political economy. Similar comments could be made about the welfare state. Indeed, for the most part, there was no welfare state, merely a mass of unconnected agencies delivering bits and pieces of welfare provision at the local level. As regards post-war economic policy, account must be taken of the structural constraints on all British governments – their fragile debtor position, the costs of reconstruction, and the limits imposed by the Bretton Woods system of fixed, but adjustable, exchange rates linked to the dollar. The result was that until the end of the 1950s, all governments pursued what amounted to another prudent domesticist national modernisation strategy, allied to a constant preoccupation with inflation, sterling and the necessity to maintain foreign confidence. This was pretty much the same situation as the 1930s, although no one dared mention it.[19] There was, of course, one big difference: the absence of mass unemployment. However, that can be explained either by the post-war world boom and the benefits of American economic hegemony, or it cannot be explained at all.[20]

External affairs after 1945 were dominated by the Cold War, NATO membership and the special relationship with the United States. All this looks very different from the pre-war world. Chamberlain would never have accepted the special relationship and, on the surface, the resources Britain committed to its NATO and East of Suez roles seems to deny any adherence to the primacy of domestic politics.[21] Yet the special relationship and the concentration on military–security issues undoubtedly eased Britain's adjustment to the new superpower hegemony. In that sense, there was an important connection to domestic politics. Moreover, until the late 1950s, all British governments sought to use their colonies and the Commonwealth to support the national modernisation strategy – as had been done in the 1930s.[22] What the Cold War and the special relationship contributed to the continuity between pre-war and post-war was essentially a two-fold negative. They provided a comfortable, interesting, even exciting, framework for British politicians in office. There was never any need to rethink British foreign policy, and any other framework seemed dull and unworthy of the skills acquired over the years. They also served to reinforce the traditional British limited liability approach to Europe and the process of European integration. Consider, for example, the following: 'Our policy should be to assist Europe to recover as far as we can ... But the concept must be one of limited liability. In no circumstances must we assist them beyond the point at which the assistance leaves us too weak to be a worthwhile ally for USA ... in the last resort we cannot rely on European countries.'[23]

That quote, from a 1949 inter-departmental committee memorandum, provides us with one explanation of why British leaders in office were suspicious of and, in the end, rejected, moves towards European integration in the 1950s. Where Britain was concerned, the Cold War was too serious a problem to justify earnest thoughts about a European Community which, in any case, was liable to fail. There were, of course, other reasons. Europe would mark a departure from the prudent, domesticist, national modernisation strategy. A Europe with supranational institutions and rules would interfere too closely and too publicly in domestic British government. Interdependence was one thing, and long accepted by British politicians: constant and public penetration of the Centre's autonomous shell was something else and should be rejected. In other words, Europe represented an attack on the whole statecraft of the British *ancien régime*'s strategy of prudent national modernisation, accompanied by the rhetoric of national greatness. In that sense, missing the Euro-bus (assuming it was ever scheduled to stop at Britain) was an exercise in rational decision-making by leading politicians in office. Europe threatened the whole basis Britain's post-1918 adjustment to democracy and external fragility.

BRITAIN AND EUROPE SINCE 1961

Some important problems of analysis have been considered and the *ancien regime* of British governing style, both domestic and external, described in broad outline. The task now is to examine Britain's relations with Europe in, and since, 1961, the year of the first application to join the European Economic Community. For present purposes we need to subdivide this period into four, relatively distinct phases, namely 1961–63, 1964–79, 1979–90 and 1990–95. Each subperiod will be devoted to answering different questions, but the answers will involve a consideration of the same issue, the relationship between the governing Britain problem, external affairs and Europe.

Great Reversals, 1961–63

Why, in 1961, did Conservative leaders in office reverse their previous strategy and apply for EEC membership?[24] The question, of course, has been posed many times before, but it cannot be ignored here simply because many of the motives and tactics surrounding the manoeuvre have persisted through to the 1990s.

The key figure in this episode was Harold Macmillan (Prime Minister, 1957–63) who, it should be noted, had been regarded by supporters of the National Governments of the 1930s with considerable suspicion and not a little pity and derision. At that time he was perceived to be fundamentally unsound on both economic and foreign policy and generally lacking in political seriousness. Like Churchill, however, who had been viewed in much the same way, Macmillan's political career was enormously helped by the anti-Chamberlain parliamentary coup of May 1940. In 1957 he took over the premiership in the difficult circumstances following the Suez debacle and Eden's enforced resignation through illness. He was certainly Washington's favoured candidate for the job, although the extent to which that support enabled him to defeat Butler ('a man of Munich') remains an open issue. Macmillan's initial objectives were three – to win the next election, repair Britain's relations with Washington and, in the longer term, conduct a revaluation of Britain's role in the world. By the end of 1959 he had achieved success on the first two counts. His problem (which, in effect, became the country's and his party's) was that although he thought often and seriously about the governing Britain problem, and was superb in presenting arguments and 'fixing' potential domestic opponents, he was rarely prepared to keep to a project when the going got tough. In short, he was a typical British party politician.

Three examples can be cited to support this point. First, Macmillan's response to Suez was a determination to rebuild the U.S. alliance. The Americans had made their point – Britain was not an equal, but a very junior, partner in the alliance – and were prepared to be accommodating. Nevertheless, this rush to Washington was the easy option and linked to the demands of domestic politics. It certainly took little account of the French, who regarded Suez as another British betrayal, like Dunkirk, and who turned away from America to pursue a European strategy. Secondly, in September 1957, the Cabinet accepted the proposals of its Treasury team that the balance of payments and inflation problems should be tackled, once and for all, by a monetary squeeze involving high interest rates and significant cuts in public expenditure. In January 1958, however, the Cabinet, guided by Macmillan, rejected some of the expenditure cuts proposed and, more importantly, the general notion that the time had come to confront inflation seriously. The outcome was the resignation of the entire Treasury team, Thorneycroft, Birch and Powell. Macmillan's response to this, that the whole affair was just a series of 'little local difficulties' was good politics, but left the Government without a coherent macroeconomic strategy.[25] Finally, at a crucial stage in the negotiations seeking EEC membership, Macmillan concluded the Polaris missile deal with President Kennedy, thus securing Britain's position as a nuclear power, assisting the Conservative's political position in Britain and his own position in the Cabinet. Once again this had an unfortunate impact on France, especially President de Gaulle.

It would be wrong, however, to confine the discussion of this period to Macmillan. After the resignations of 1958, the country was governed by a pliant Court of senior Conservative ministers. Consequently, there were few divisions among Conservative leaders regarding relations with Europe after the membership bid was announced in July 1961. This was important, given the fears of another split in the Party over the issue, like those over the Corn Laws and Free Trade and Protection. Before the bid was made public, every institution which needed to be 'squared' was 'squared' – the United States administration, the Commonwealth, the farmers, the City and the large scale manufacturing interest. Moreover, the case presented to support the new European strategy was plausible: EEC membership would benefit the British economy, boost Britain's status in the world, and yet amount in practice to little more than the Free Trade area, or Common Market, which Britain had always wanted. Less emphasis was put on the fact that the United States positively wanted Britain to be a EEC member. Similarly, the domestic party political reasons behind the entry bid were sidelined. Europe, for example, would provide Conservative leaders with a new and radical issue to present to the electorate after a decade of what was in danger of becoming a phase of stale or unpopular Conservative rule.[26] It would also protect Macmillan's position as Prime Minister. Europe, in short, was meant to provide a domestic, as well as external, zimmerframe for Conservative rule in Britain. To put the matter another way, the bid was launched because senior Conservative leaders were frightened: frightened of a new world order openly dominated by the superpowers, frightened of Europe's higher economic growth and its potential as a third force in the world, and frightened about the Conservative Party's electoral future.

Thus, the first great reversal, on European Community membership, was a good example of a Court playing domestic politics with foreign policy. Not surprisingly, the arguments employed were often economical with the truth. The other reversal came when the whole strategy was vetoed by de Gaulle in January 1963. The veto highlighted the mistakes made in implementing the strategy abroad: the continued obsession with the U.S., underestimating both French hostility and the strength of Franco–German ties, and overestimating the willingness of Britain's 'friends' in the Community to act against the French position.

The early 1960s were an important watershed in the development of British politics, and particularly the governing Britain problem. Europe was seen to be the easy solution to both domestic and external problems. The new strategy was rooted in the perceived demands of domestic politics. The outcome was greeted by Conservative leaders with their usual public aplomb. It was, in fact, a typically British/English cockup.

Engagement and Containment, 1964–79

In opposition, the bulk of the Parliamentary Labour Party had opposed the first EEC entry application by the Macmillan Government. By 1967, and in office, Wilson, with backing from his right-wing Cabinet colleagues, reversed this strategy and put in a second entry bid, which, once again, was vetoed by de Gaulle. This time, however, as a symbolic gesture of frustration, the bid was not withdrawn. Following de Gaulle's resignation in 1969, it was eventually picked up and successfully represented by the Heath-led Conservative administration. Following parliamentary approval, Britain entered the European Community in January 1973. Labour's two election victories in 1974 led to the renegotiation of the terms of entry obtained by Heath and his colleagues. In June 1975 a referendum was held on the issue of whether Britain should stay in the Community. Some 67 per cent of those who voted supported continued membership. Britain had finally engaged with Europe.

The entry process story is well-known.[27] What is more interesting is the intensity and scope of Britain's Euro connections in 1979, after some twenty years of sporadic elite debate on the subject, three entry applications, one referendum and six years of membership. It is clear that these connections did not amount to much. Europe had been engaged, but also contained in terms of its impact on the British polity. What were the reasons for this strange outcome? Why, in 1979, did the Britain and Europe relationship seem to be a classic case of premature ejaculation? One way of answering these questions is to remind ourselves of the four awkward dynamics behind the Macmillan Government's first entry bid. These were as follows:

(a) A perceived decline, or threat of decline, in what can be called the natural rate of governability. In other words, a worsening of the old governing Britain problem, particularly in the arena of macroeconomic policy.

(b) A perceived, or threatened, decline in Britain's world power status involving problems with the U.S. alliance, an increasing inability to stop the penetration of the Court's autonomy by inconvenient external forces, and its fear that public perceptions of these developments would have an adverse impact on voters.

(c) A takeoff, within Europe, of new ideas concerning increased integration, as the doctrine of 'ever closer union' begins to shift from the nominal to the real world in serious ways.

(d) External affairs cease to be a useful support for domestic strategies and becomes an opportunity for politicians seeking advantage in domestic party politics, and even within the Court.

What happens when these conditions are tested for their presence in the period 1964 to 1979? It is clear that both (a) and (b) were amply fulfilled. Apart from the first years of the Heath Government, the dominant economic strategy can be loosely labelled neo-corporatism, that is an attempt to achieve both economic modernisation and inflation control via a system of national level bargaining between the peak organisation of labour and business on the one hand and political leaders in office on the other. Although this strategy was popular in Europe and, indeed, was often supported by some politicians as a way of exhibiting their European orientation, it was, operationally, an essentially domesticist strategy, rooted in British conditions and designed to achieve national modernisation from within. Its problems, however, were many. It was always constrained by external account weaknesses and the fragility of sterling.[28] Moreover, in the 1970s, politicians in office were unable to take advantage of the freedoms offered by the new floating exchange rate regime. This was because of the stagflation resulting from commodity (especially oil) price rises and the growing unwillingness of grassroots trade unionists to accept the incomes policies or wage norms, which were the essential means of combating inflation under neo-corporatism. In media and academic comment, at home and abroad, neo-corporatism, perhaps unfairly, became associated with economic failure and 'ungovernability'.[29] If, to these economic failures, we add the general consensus that Britain's international power position had declined precipitously in the 1960s and 1970s, that foreign policy had become the management of that decline, then the situation seemed set for a more positive engagement with Europe.

In this period, however, few threats of integration emerged from Europe. There appear to have been two reasons for this. One resulted from the problems posed for the Community after 1973 by the enlargement process. The other was its inability to deal with the awkward global economic developments of the 1970s. Only at the end of that decade did Europe produce any further integration projects, namely the European Monetary System and the direct elections to the European Parliament. As a consequence, in 1979, Europe was still little more than an incomplete Common Market plus the Common Agriculture Policy. In short, it was EFTA with knobs on.

It follows that once the entry process, with its distinctive problems was completed, British politicians were able to avoid the full impact of Europe, especially since Labour's 'awkward partner' strategy pursued after 1975 was so popular with the Thatcherites. In so far as foreign policy was an object of party dispute in the late 1970s, it had settled into a very old groove, namely a consideration of what Britain's role should be in the Cold War. This was the framework which had provided custom and comfort for British politicians since 1945. Europe, therefore, had been engaged with and yet contained. The reasons, however, were to be found for the most part in Brussels, not in London.

Thatcherism and Europe, 1979–90

Thatcherism, to re-coin an aphorism, grew out of the bowels of the British trade union movement in the 1970s. Better, because fairer, it emerged from, and at the same time fostered, certain popular perceptions of British trade unionism in that decade. At the outset, then, Thatcherism was simply just another response to the governing Britain problem, namely the threat of inflation, external decline and the awkwardness of British democracy. It began as a modernisation strategy sweetened by the language of national greatness. It ended when the language of greatness had adversely affected the modernisation strategy. The discussion agenda for this particular part of the story proceeds as follows: first, an examination of the initial Thatcherite economic strategy, secondly, a consideration of foreign policy in the period and, thirdly, an assessment of Europe's impact on Thatcherism.

The initial economic strategy prioritised the defeat of inflation simply because, according to Thatcherite arguments at the time, inflation was the real cause of unemployment and its defeat the only basis from which to develop a more competitive economy. At the time, the orthodox means to confront inflation was still taken to be an incomes policy. This, however, was unavailable to the Thatcherites on doctrinal and, above all, political grounds. In doctrinal terms it interfered with market forces. In terms of practical politics, the experience of the 1970s seemed to suggest that the unions would never submit to a Conservative incomes policy. The winter of discontent in 1978–9 merely confirmed that political perception. So, the problem was to find a way of managing the economy and defeating inflation without having to rely on the support or acquiescence of the unions (or business for that matter). In other words, to find an economic strategy which would allow the new Conservative Court a degree of relative autonomy from awkward domestic forces. It was in this context that monetarism assumed significance.

Monetarism, as it was understood by the Thatcherites in 1979, offered a method of running the economy which was Court-based, that is, it would reduce the influence of both domestic and external forces by focusing on those matters the Court could control, monetary matters.[30] Indeed, handled correctly, it would reverse the usual order of influence: monetary policy would influence the inflation expectations of domestic actors and, if the pound was allowed to float, keep the influence of external forces to a minimum. There would be no repeat of the 1976 sterling crisis if the Court avoided an exchange rate target.

To be credible, a monetary strategy required a minimum of discretion and certainly no hint of 'U turns'. This could only be achieved, so the argument went, by a commitment to publicly stated rules. As Nigel Lawson put it, 'Rules rule, OK?'[31] Rules were best presented as targets in a rule book, albeit one that would necessarily appear in serial form. The rule book appeared at the 1980 budget as the Medium Term Financial Strategy.[32] This set rolling four year targets for the money supply and the Public Sector Borrowing Requirements. The principal instrument employed to reach the money-supply targets was the interest rate, an instrument which operated on the demand for money, rather than its supply. Note that in this scenario there could be no target for employment. Interestingly, there was no explicit target for inflation either.

This rules-based, domesticist-biased, path to national modernisation was subjected to a number of changes after 1980. Moreover, the targets were rarely reached and Mrs Thatcher, in particular, liked to insert sufficient discretion into the strategy for electoral purposes. Nevertheless, by mid-1985, it seemed to have worked, in the sense that other actors accepted the Court's commitment to the rules. The judge and jury of a rules-based strategy are other people's perceptions of it. In addition, the internal Conservative opposition to the strategy, the 'Wets', had been defeated. So, too, had the NUM, in a symbolic victory over the 'vanguard' of the trade union movement. Hence, by the summer of 1985 Thatcherism appeared to have resolved two of the three components of the governing Britain problem. In the process it could claim to have found a new method of economic management, one which could successfully reform Britain from within. The way seemed set to shift attention to the broader supply-side problems of the economy and other domestic aspects of the national rejuvenation project. In practice, this meant the reform of the welfare state and more privatisation.

On the surface, similar comments could be made about Thatcherite foreign policy. One way of approaching this matter is simply to list its triumphs – the Rhodesian/Zimbabwe settlement, the recapture of the Falklands, the Sino–British Agreement on Hong Kong, the purchase of Trident missiles and the successful reception given to Cruise missiles, the renewed vitality given to the special relationship by the Thatcher–Reagan friendship and the close contacts made with Gorbachev both before and after he assumed leadership of the Soviet Union. In fact, by mid-1985 Mrs Thatcher could claim to be on close terms with, and the principal intermediary between, the leaders of both the world's superpowers. This was something which Churchill had always aspired to and rarely achieved. Foreign policy, then, had provided essential support for the Conservative's domestic designs, which, initially, was the role it was supposed to fulfil. Indeed, it went further. Thatcherism, in terms of its resolute approach to problems, its monetarism and its privatisation schemes, had become major British 'exports'. The Conservative's campaign claims during the 1987 election, 'It's great to be great again', appeared only too plausible.

Of course, there were always doubts. There were doubts about some of the claimed successes, doubts, among the chattering classes, about South Africa, doubts, as the decade developed, about the increasing mismatch between defence roles and defence spending and, after 1989, very serious doubts about the Hong Kong settlement. More importantly, there were always some, including Geoffrey Howe in 1983, who were uncertain about the objectives of British foreign policy.[33] Others highlighted the difference between the traditional nature of British foreign policy, above all the Cold War rhetoric, and the emphasis on the special relationship, and the seemingly more radical domestic programme. After the 1987 election there could be no doubts. The decline and then collapse of the whole post-1945 Cold War structure of global politics produced complete confusion in Thatcherite foreign policy. Mrs Thatcher, perhaps unjustly, was perceived to be an old-fashioned, Cold War warrior. Moreover, she, and her political friends, seemed unable to deal with its consequences. What was the point of the special relationship when the Soviet Union had ceased to pose a serious threat to western Europe? Equally important, how could the Thatcherites respond to the French solution to the problems posed by a reunited Germany, namely to curb its power within the institutionalised constraints of a more integrated European Community? This, conveniently, leads us to Thatcherism's connections with Europe.

Early in their period of office the Thatcherites found Europe an easy, useful, even beneficial issue. Given Labour's increasing antagonism to the Community, the obvious ploy was to repeat, in parrot fashion, that the Conservative Party was the party of Europe, albeit, as the 1979 manifesto had put it, a party favouring 'a common-sense Europe'. Moreover, the issues Conservative leaders chose to stress, Britain's contribution to the Community budget and the necessary, and linked reform of the Common Agricultural Policy, were politically useful on three counts: they showed the Government fighting for 'British' interests, they obstructed talk of integration within the Community and, by avoiding the future of the European connection, they helped maintain Conservative unity. Following the final settlement of the budget issue in 1984, the Thatcherites were even persuaded to accept the Single European Act, designed to eliminate by 1992 the remaining (and significant) obstacles to the free movement of goods, services, capital and people throughout the Community. In 1985–6 this was sold to Mrs Thatcher, and then the party in Parliament, on the grounds that such an exercise in deregulation was a triumphant reflection of Thatcherism and raised no basic issues of sovereignty. Yet, by 1990, Europe represented a serious problem for the Thatcherites and played a major role in creating the conditions which produced Mrs Thatcher's enforced resignation in November of that year. Why?

The two major reasons were the saga of the ERM and the Commission's EMU project. In the late 1970s Mrs Thatcher, in opposition, had criticised the Labour Government's unwillingness to join the Community's Exchange Rate Mechanism, a fixed but adjustable currency bloc, designed to produce a zone of exchange rate stability and low inflation, dominated by the deutschmark and the monetary policy of the Bundesbank. In office, Mrs Thatcher rejected any notion of putting the pound in the ERM 'until the time was right'. Clearly, the whole scheme went against the domesticist principle of economic management outlined above – or so the Thatcherites argued at the time. However, in October 1985, Nigel Lawson, as Chancellor of the Exchequer, dropped monetarism and then, in a famous seminar, tried, and failed, to persuade Mrs Thatcher to put the pound in the ERM as an alternative macroeconomic strategy.[34] These developments had several awkward consequences. The first was that Lawson, probably from early 1986, covertly managed sterling so that it shadowed the deutschmark. In time, this caused a major public rift with Mrs Thatcher and probably made an important contribution to the return of inflation after 1987, a development which the Treasury found increasingly difficult to halt, despite higher interest rates. Subsequently, Lawson resigned and his successor as Chancellor, John Major, finally persuaded Mrs Thatcher to put sterling in the ERM in October 1990. The details of this sorry story are less important than its broad political implications.[35] First, the dispute between Chancellor and Prime Minister promoted divisions on the issue in the Court and among Conservative MPs. Lawson's arguments highlighted the ambiguities of the initial, domesticist, national modernisation, strategy. Unlike Howe, he did not see the ERM as a staging post to EMU. But he did feel that domesticism would gain from the anti-inflation record of the ERM and the Bundesbank. In an important sense, then, this dispute was about the appropriate means to domesticism, to domestic goals. Europe, by providing the ERM option, complicated the old arguments for and against domesticist and externalist monetary strategies.

European Monetary Union was an issue of a different order. It concerned the future of the Community as a more integrated economic and political union. It involved a single currency, a single Euro-Bank, and the consequent loss of control over monetary and currency policy by those states that signed up for membership. The important point here is that, as with the post-Cold War situation, the response of the Thatcherites was perceived to be entirely negative. EMU was rejected, but no viable alternative was developed if, as seemed likely in 1990, all other member states wished to go down this route. Specifically, there was no serious public discussion of a second-tier status, even less GITA (go it alone).[36] In short, the Thatcherites' weakness was not that they said 'No' to EMU, but that they said little else but 'No'. This not only showed a lack of imagination, it was also bad politics, especially at Westminster. It is hard not to conclude from this that the real difficulty lay with EMU's implications for Thatcherism's national rejuvenation strategy. National rejuvenation involved, in its external guise, a return to a Great Britain as a relatively autonomous global actor. EMU did not fit that game. It follows that, by 1990, both Euro-enthusiasts and Euro-sceptics shared one big thing: they both wanted Britain to remain a great power. They differed on the appropriate means to that objective. The language of greatness was still an essential feature of British politics.

Enigma Variations: The Major Governments and Europe

When Mrs Thatcher faced the press after her enforced resignation in November 1990, she justified her decision not to contest the second ballot of the Conservative leadership election by saying that the Conservative Party needed a new leader to heal its divisions and win the next election. These were certainly the two major tasks confronting John Major. Achieving them, however, was another matter. The new Conservative Court faced a number of very difficult problems. The first was that although Mrs Thatcher had constructed a viable coalition of voters and an effective governing strategy to deal with the problems of the 1970s, developments in the last years of her premiership had revealed the fragility of both that voter coalition and strategy in the new political circumstances of the late 1980s. Her one positive gift to Major was the sizeable majority of seats gained in 1987. Secondly, winning the next election involved confronting the economic recession which had started in Britain in the summer of 1990. Any measures designed to resolve that problem would have to take account of Britain's membership of the ERM. In practice, this meant that the remedies of the 1980s, allowing sterling to depreciate and managing interest rates, were no longer so easily available. An additional complicating factor was that Britain had entered the ERM shortly after the process of German reunification had begun. In consequence, Germany and Britain were facing two fundamentally different economic problems: for Germany the problem was the fear of inflation, for Britain it was recession and unemployment. Since it was the Bundesbank which set the rules for the ERM, it was unlikely that German interest rate policy would be adjusted to meet British needs. This was the crude logic of the ERM as an externalist economic strategy. Thirdly, the Maastricht Inter-Governmental Conference on European Union was due in December 1991. This would be a major test of the Government's diplomacy and Conservative Party unity. Finally, the Labour Party had continued its own re-modernisation process after 1987. On a number of domestic issues it was now more voter friendly. On the external front its old weakness, defence policy, was no longer so important after the Cold War, and, significantly, it had now adopted a more pro-European integration stance.

In these difficult circumstances, the Major led Court, after much that the press described as 'dithering', achieved its objectives. It is true the economy obstinately remained in recession. Nevertheless, the Poll Tax was ditched and Labour's own tax and inflation record could always be attacked. Moreover, the Gulf War, which temporarily resurrected the old special relationship, provided an additional boost. Most important of all, Major managed to conclude a deal at Maastricht which was good enough to settle the Conservative Party until after the General Election. The opt-outs from the social chapter and EMU, the stress on subsidarity not federalism, and the three-pillar structure for future Union activities all looked reasonable, so long as their essential short termism was pushed under the carpet, and the Treaty itself not read (thus allowing its strong integrationist language to continue unrecognised). Whatever, the Maastricht truce conveniently killed the issue for both the major parties at the 1992 election, which the Conservatives surprisingly won with a majority of twenty-one.

The Conservatives post-election honeymoon was quickly cut short by two Euro-developments – the Danes rejection of the Maastricht Treaty in a referendum on 2 June, and the withdrawal, or expulsion, of the pound from the ERM on 16 September, 'Black' or 'White' Wednesday, depending on your preferences. These events, together with the small parliamentary majority, were to cause the second Major Administration considerable problems. More generally, they were to set the framework for the governing Britain and Europe issues over the next three years.

The ERM debacle was not only embarrassing, it consigned to the dustbin the most important components of the Major Court's domestic and external governing strategies. Opinion poll support for the Conservatives registered an immediate decline. As an external shock it ranked with de Gaulle's veto in 1963 and the sterling crisis of 1976. Only the 1931 crisis had more immediate and intense political consequences. Yet, like 1931, 16 September 1992 was also a gift, albeit an uncomfortable one. It was a gift because it removed the external straitjacket on the British economy, namely a semi-fixed exchange rate allied to German monetary preferences. It was uncomfortable because its outcome, a return to a domesticist anti-inflation code, still severely constrained the Court's freedom of action in terms of fiscal and monetary policy. A degree of relative domestic autonomy was regained, but only at the price of imposing publicly constraining rules of economic management and an austerity culture, which affected all levels of the polity.

Confronted with the possibility of a collapse in international market confidence, Major and his Chancellor, Norman Lamont, moved rapidly to fill the yawning gap in their economic strategy. Within six weeks the new rules were in place.[37] They included inflation targets (below 2.5 per cent by the end of the Parliament), new public spending and public sector wage curbs, and a range of monetary indicators to be monitored. Above all, they inserted some transparency in British economic management by allowing a more positive role to the Bank of England, and its Governor, in the process of inflation control (specifically, interest rate policy). In one sense, the new strategy represented a return to the initial Thatcherite stance of the early 1980s. More plausibly, it is what the Thatcher Court should have put in place after Nigel Lawson's ERM-entry gambit was rejected in November 1985. The obvious benefits for British industry were lower interest rates and a considerable depreciation of sterling. There were also considerable costs, not least because political responsibility for these could no longer be offloaded onto foreigners. Constant attempts had to be made to curb public spending. Taxes were raised, the problems of the housing market ignored, and there was an ever-present fear (particularly in the Bank of England) that the depreciation of sterling would lead to inflation, an increase in interest rates, and a consequent surge in wage demands. Moreover, there were a number of ambiguities embedded in these rules. Initially, many Euro-sceptics feared they were merely designed to allow easy re-entry into the ERM. Later, some saw them as a means of qualifying to play the Maastricht EMU convergence game. Even if they did represent a long-term governing strategy, would the Court be able to sustain them when electoral politics and Conservative Party management became important? In short, would they, as the economists put it, become 'time inconsistent'?[38]

The (first) Danish referendum result led to the long saga of the Maastricht Bill's ratification in Parliament, a process which lasted from November 1992 to July 1993.[39] With hindsight, the whole imbroglio resembled a post-race scuffle between greyhounds for a hare which had already been withdrawn for a more important race at a later meeting. The real significance of the affair was the signals it gave about future troubles. Nevertheless, from the Court's point of view, what happened was bad enough. Getting the Bill on the statute book used up much time and energy, soured personal relations in the Parliamentary party, revealed to the world the intensity of its divisions over Europe and, embarrassingly, required considerable help from the opposition parties to get the legislation through. This was the sort of thing which was supposed to happen in the Italian parliament, not Westminster. Moreover, once the habit of dissent had developed on the issue it persisted after the summer of 1993, despite numerous appeals for a ceasefire. Indeed, at the end of 1994 eight Conservative Euro-sceptic MPs had the whip withdrawn after they had voted against a measure designed to increase Britain's contribution to the Euro-Union's budget. By that time, of course, the crux of the Euro-dispute was the wider, and more important, issue of Britain's response to new manoeuvres for Maastricht II and EMU. In the early summer of 1995, it was confidently reported that John Major would face a Euro-sceptic challenge to his leadership in the autumn. In a surprise move he forced the election to be held in July. The result was a creditable victory over the only Euro-sceptic challenger prepared to stand in the first ballot, John Redwood.

Europe, then, was undoubtedly a problem for the Major Court after the 1992 election. It revealed an intense fault line amongst Conservative MPs, and even in the Cabinet. Most MPs, however, were loyalists: they accepted the Court's case that there was no point in arguing over Europe until the precise blueprints for further integration were revealed in, or after, 1996. Moreover, these Westminster disputes did not extend to most constituency parties. The problem at that level was the fall in morale and party membership. In turn, that points to the more general problems confronting the Court in the mid-1990s. Media comment has concentrated on the symptoms of the problem: the ever smaller majority in the Commons, by-election defeats, local council 'wipe outs', sex and sleaze scandals, specific policy mistakes, the failure of the 'Back to Basics' strategy and the successful politicking of the Labour Party, notably under Tony Blair after July 1994.

The causes of these difficulties, however, lay elsewhere. Some were legacies of Thatcherism, the 'golden age that never was'. Many were to be found in other countries: weak and unpopular governments were not confined to Britain in the 1990s. The root problem, however, was the governing Britain problem in its *fin-de-siècle* guise. After 1992, the Major Court was confronted not only by the traditional dimensions of that problem – the management of inflation, Britain's external role and democracy – but possibly the last act in the old drama between national modernisation and national greatness. The economic measures of September and October 1992 probably represent the last chance for a successful domesticist modernisation strategy. They produced lower inflation and a fall in unemployment. What they did not produce is consumer/voter confidence. Equally important, they have yet to gain the confidence of the international money markets. Europe, on the other hand, seemingly offers so many advantages – shelter from global economic storms, the possibility of shifting responsibility for unpopular policies to Brussels, the comforting embrace of neo-corporatism and above all, a continuation of the national greatness game, a game which remains so popular with so many sections of the British political elite, above all in the Foreign Office. The problems of governing Britain in the 1990s are primarily those of a divided and frightened elite, divided between those who fear that an ancient, 'sovereign' polity is about to commit suicide and those who fear the consequences of remaining an ancient, 'sovereign' polity. In the 1990s, 'Europe' became the focus of that elite cultural divide, but the substance of the division was an old one, how to govern Britain, and who was to do the governing.

One final point remains. In the early autumn of 1995, when the political recession that had affected the Conservatives since 1992 was as strong as ever, the outlines of a possible future electoral lifeline for the Major Court began to emerge. On the domestic economic front, this seemed to amount to a determination to sustain the anti-inflation rules, modified by tax cuts and further public spending curbs (although not on health and education). Alongside this went a return to some old Conservative faithfuls, law and order, tighter prison and asylum regimes, plus steadfast opposition to political devolution for Scotland and Wales. In external affairs there appeared to be the beginnings of a serious rethink of Britain's overall strategy, no doubt stimulated by the vagaries of the Clinton Presidency on Northern Ireland and Bosnia and a desire to go beyond the simple banalities of Douglas Hurd's locust years at the Foreign Office.[40]

Where Europe was concerned several themes began to be stressed. One was to compare the Conservatives' cautious Euro-scepticism with Labour's Euro-centralism and the Liberal Democrats' Euro-federalism. Another was to attack Tony Blair's declaration that he would never allow Britain to be isolated in Europe, on the grounds that the effective defence of the country's interests might require isolation. Finally, there were signs of a significant time shift in the 'wait and see' or 'cunctation' tactics, regarding EMU.[41] The date for the final decision was moved from 1997 to 1999, or 2002, or the end of the next parliament.

No doubt there are many ways this emerging strategy can be explained. A popular one was to indicate it represented a 'lurch' to the right. However, it is becoming increasingly difficult to define right wing in the late 1990s. A more plausible explanation was to view the new strategy as a crude way of searching for policy space unoccupied by the Labour Party. In other words, it was simply following the rules of the British electoral game as understood by all intelligent leaders, especially those in trouble: find out where your opponents stand and then move to another spot on the line. After all, in Britain, national elections are very serious political affairs and to stay in business a Court has got to do whatever it takes. Ideas, and doctrinal consistency, are for amateurs. Serious politicians, as professionals players, must relegate them to their memoirs.

CONCLUSIONS

Macro polemics can score (sometimes own goals), but they rarely win. Their analysis can be too easily condemned as superficial, their conclusions dismissed as mere points of view. Where Britain and Europe is concerned the situation is even worse. Any exercise which moves away from the micro analysis of particular policies or institutions is liable to be regarded as contentious, especially if the perspective is Euro-sceptic. One curious feature of the British debate is the high propensity of Euro-enthusiasts to become very annoyed with, and rude to, their opponents. In these circumstances only four points are offered as conclusions, three of which are concerned with methodology. All, however, take sips from the Euro-sceptics' bowl of cream.

An initial assumption was that within the British structure of politics, ideas were likely to be employed as instruments of rule and party advantage rather than play any significant, independent role in the political process. Allowing for the ambiguity of the word 'ideas', that seems a plausible conclusion to draw from this survey.[42] It could be argued that the assumption is plausible only because the principal actor designation supports it. That is a valid point. Nevertheless, the ideas approach would not have received much support if a broader actor focus had been chosen. It is, perhaps, just as well that the wider debate had so little influence on politicians in office since, on the whole, it has been so poor. Like a cheap clockwork toy both sides have been going around the same old churned-up track for some thirty years. Increasingly, both resort to simple scare stories regarding future shock to support their rival cases. The whole affair represents an indictment of the British, especially English, intellectual 'class'. As the proponents of change, the Euro-enthusiasts must take most of the blame. At the beginning of the story they were economical with the truth, by the mid-1990s they were increasingly reluctant to clarify their vision of Britain in a future Euro-Union. If their root position is that they simply hold to a belief, or hunch, that European integration and Britain's association with it are good things, then they should say so. Given the difficulties surrounding the issue that is a perfectly reasonable stance.

The Euro-sceptics can also be criticised. As indicated below, Euro-Union is, in many ways, the easy future option for the British political elite. If Britain chooses not to join, or claim some special or variable status then, initially, there could be serious problems. Euro-sceptics are unwilling to debate these. That these territorial issues can be discussed seriously is indicated by the debate which the Old South conducted about its position in the United States Union between 1820 and 1860. It is embarrassing to recall that the Old South was a 'premodern', agricultural, and relatively poorly educated society, at the time.[43]

The major methodological ploy was to explicitly connect two agendas, the governing Britain problem and the Britain and Europe issue, and to grant analytical priority to the former. This provided some new interpretations of some very old topics. It cast doubt, for example, on the popular notion that in the past British politicians in office were seriously interested in sovereignty. Instead, it was suggested that British politicians merely sought a relative autonomy from external forces in a world they always accepted as awkwardly interdependent. Equally important, they exhibited a similar desire for relative autonomy in their operations on the domestic front. Hence, externally, it was not the substance of sovereignty which was pursued but its form, the form in which it could be presented to the British public. In turn, this highlighted the primacy of the tradition of domestic politics in British foreign policy, a tradition which, certainly since 1918, has involved a constant clash between the perceived need for national modernisation and an unwillingness to ditch the domestic benefits obtained from employing the rival public language of national greatness.

It was in this context that Europe became, and remains, such an awkward issue for British politicians. Europe exposes the ambiguous final logic of the primacy of domestic politics strategy. It conflates the old distinctions between domesticist and externally biased rules. It can claim to provide both modernisation and greatness, plus shelter from both domestic and external storms. Relative autonomy for politicians can be regained by increasingly locating key awkward decisions outside Britain, in Brussels, Frankfurt and, ultimately, Berlin. For a political elite which increasingly has lost its governing confidence, Europe represents the final, and easiest, solution to managing the awkward plantation. It offers the ultimate tranquilliser, the long-sought valium for Whitehall.

In these circumstances, assessing the behaviour of politicians in office on the European issue emerges as a major problem. The popular verdict is an unfavourable one: successive Courts have mishandled the matter. They began by missing the Euro-bus, they continued as awkward partners in the Euro-enterprise, and they have failed to produce an appropriate and explicit vision of Britain's relations with Europe. The assumption of a unitary, rational Court, dedicated, in the first instance, to the pursuit of its own, and its own party's interests, offers a somewhat different perspective. Given the awkward impact on the governing Britain problem, it could be argued that successive Courts have managed the issue exceptionally well. It has been confined to Westminster (apart from the 1975 referendum) and the major parties have avoided serious splits (apart from the SDP secession in the early 1980s). Moreover, if John Major manages to get his party to the next election in one piece it will be a significant political achievement. The whole story indicates what British politicians are exceptionally good at: not problem solving but problem management, at least on the domestic front. Of course, it is easy to demand something better than mere politicking. But you cannot demand from British politicians what the structure of British politics (including public opinion) only allows if they commit electoral suicide. The Labour leadership learnt that lesson in 1983. In any case, it is not at all certain that the break-up of the British party system would be a definite benefit. Liberal Democrats would say yes, so, too, would the SNP. But they would, wouldn't they? Did 1846 improve matters? Have the Italians and Canadians gained from such a development? Is Europe worth the domestic hassle? There are no easy answers to these questions.

One final point remains. What we can reasonably expect from our Courts is that they play away-games prudently. That is, they play intelligently in Europe. To do this you have to recognise your strengths and weaknesses. The language of national greatness precludes this. It generates constant ambitions to be a European great power, a constant desire to be 'at the centre' of things. But the political centre of Europe is already occupied by the Franco-German axis and its friends. Successive British Courts have tried to break that axis, or join it, or construct a rival axis. Thus far all such attempts have failed and they seem doomed to failure simply because, apart from the odd concession, it yields so many rewards to its members. In terms of high politics the Community/Union has moved only to tunes orchestrated in Paris and Bonn. In many ways European integration is only another episode in a very old story, the BGQ – bloody German question. This time, however, the French have climbed aboard the German raft. In doing so, they have exposed Britain's essential weakness in the wider European arena, something conveniently hidden since 1870. In crude realist terms, it may be that our only useful ally in that arena is Russia. At all events, the power map associated with European integration, and its connections with the BGQ, provide additional reasons for examining the alternatives more seriously than hitherto. At the very least we should be aware of which Euro-league we will be playing in for most of the time.

CHAPTER 11

Ideas are not Enough

Anthony Seldon[1]

I

Britain changed more in the fifty years from 1945 to 1995 than in any other fifty-year period.[2] The years 1895–1945 set the pace. Two world wars, the rise to respectability of organised labour, a Labour Party coming from nowhere to achieve an overwhelming election victory, votes for – and a transformation in the status of – women, independence for southern Ireland, the rise of the motor car, radio and film. But what is all of this alongside the transformation in so much more since the end of the Second World War? In 1945 Britain had a limited welfare state: by 1980 it was ubiquitous. In 1945 Britain was a great power, with the most far-flung empire of any country in history: it is now a second-rate power with but the tattered remnants of imperial glories. In 1945 her economy possessed formidable potential, and was still heavily dependent upon its traditional base in manufacturing industry: the 1980s laid waste to much of the manufacturing that had survived, and the balance of what is now a much smaller economy in world terms has tilted towards the service and financial sectors. Supranationalism since 1945 in the form of a drive towards European integration fuelled by Germany and France, and the rise of the global economy, has constrained Britain's national sovereignty and impeded freedom of choice in both the public and private sectors.

The power and scope of the central executive has swollen in peacetime beyond anything foreseen in 1939. The advent of computers has transformed the workplace and, together with television and an array of labour-saving, leisure-eating consumer durables, the home. The position of women in society, the nature of the family, the definitions and behaviour of youth, the racial complexion of the population, the influence of religious and traditional authority, the nature and stability of an individual's work, holidays and leisure, are just some of the other areas that have been transformed. In contrast to this broad-based trend, the political structure has changed little, to constitutional reformers appearing to be frozen in immobility.

Much of the history written on postwar Britain has concentrated on answering these questions: what has happened, when and where, who was responsible, and how were the changes introduced? Some postwar history has been mapped reasonably fully, especially individual episodes such as the Suez debacle in 1956 and the IMF Crisis in 1976: we have reliable studies of most governments, Prime Ministers and political parties. The post-Cold War opening of Soviet archives, and the slow but steady breath of *glasnost* wafting through the upper echelons of the Civil Service, and the 30,000 files released due to the Waldegrave initiative, have further facilitated the historian's work. Even with the thirty-year rule in place, the main events if not the fine print are fairly well established: there are few 'secrets' waiting to come out, at least not secrets that excite historians as opposed to the media. The purpose of this chapter in contrast, in line with many chapters in this book, is to explore the question of *why* changes have occurred. In so doing it will aim to penetrate below the surface of events and explanations and probe into the subconscious of postwar British history.

The chapter will begin by outlining briefly what the major shifts have been in economic and social policy, in industrial relations, in defence and foreign policy, in governments' policy towards science and in the administrative and spending habits of central government. The choice of turning points is necessarily opinionated, and will aim to move beyond the tired debates about decline and the existence of a postwar consensus.[3] The chapter will then examine the role of four factors in producing change: ideas, individuals, interests and circumstances, before reaching some conclusions about the particular role and importance of ideas in postwar British history.

II

Economic policy change began with the adoption of Keynesian policies in the partial commitment to full employment in the 1944 White Paper.[4] In 1947, the emphasis on central planning as an economic tool in running the economy was eased. The change of government to the Conservatives in October 1951 saw little fresh bar an increased stress on monetary policy.[5] In 1952 a plan, entitled 'Robot', to make the pound freely convertible at a floating rate of exchange was considered, and rejected. Two years later, following the failure of the 1953 US recession to make much impact on Britain, economic growth rather than full employment became the main goal of economic policy.[6] From 1961, with the growing perception that the British economy was not keeping pace with our competitors, the Conservative government became more interventionist. In 1975–76, control of inflation becomes the primary objective of economic policy. After 1979, privatisation and monetary targets began to receive higher priority.

In industrial relations, the voluntarist tradition, which had prevailed since Disraeli's Combination Act of 1875, began to be eroded in stages: the wage freeze of 1948 and the increase in regulation after 1961 including contracts of employment in 1963 chipped away at the principles of voluntarism, which was given legal protection by Disraeli's trade union legislation of 1875–6, began to be swept away.[7] Legalism was continued, in modified form, with Labour's Employment Protection Act of 1975, though some of the more interventionist measures such as the Industrial Relations Court had been abandoned by Labour in 1974. The Thatcher and Major industrial relations reforms were more gradualist than the 1971 Act, and relied on private companies, not the state, to activate legal proceedings. Eight Acts of Parliament from the 1980 Employment Act to the Trade Union Reform and Employment Rights Act of 1993 were passed by successive Conservative governments in an effort to re-regulate industrial relations. But there was no return to incomes policy.

Social policy saw its first clear policy shift with the publication of the Beveridge Report in December 1942. Although not containing radically new ideas, its key significance lay in the promotion of universalism (it applied to all) and comprehensiveness (it covered all aspects of an individual's loss of income). Assaults from the left, in 1951 when Nye Bevan tried to prevent the introduction of NHS charging, and from the right, in 1958 when Chancellor of the Exchequer Peter Thorneycroft tried to limit benefits, and from the left again after 1964, failed to change a basically bipartisan approach. The 1960s saw major liberalisations in divorce, homosexuality and divorce. In 1976 the Labour government was forced to abandon full employment, a major change which ushered in a period of reductions in social services.[8] Finally, with the Social Security Act of 1986, the Housing and the Education Reform Acts of 1988 and the NHS and Community Care Act of 1990 was introduced the purchaser-provider split. The state was still to finance the services, but independent agencies were increasingly to provide them.

Defence policy saw an early major change, which took time to work through. Britain had been the first country to demonstrate that a nuclear bomb was feasible, and had been deeply involved in the Manhattan Project. In 1947, Labour decided to build its own atomic bomb. Together with the important role it played in the Korean War (1950–53), this showed Britain's determination to continue to be a major international player after the Second World War. In 1957, the Sandys Defence White Paper indicated a change in balance away from conventional forces to nuclear weapons, and in 1962 the Conservative government purchased the Polaris missile system from the USA to deliver Britain's war-heads. Labour tinkered with changing Britain's defence policy but initially merely cut the number of Polaris submarines by one to four. The Healey Defence Review of 1967 then forced Britain to accept a reduced role in the post-colonial world. Policy remained largely bipartisan until divisions arose over Trident, Polaris' replacement, and the siting of US Cruise missiles in Britain in the early 1980s. The Nott Defence Review of 1981 tilted the service balance away from the Navy, and after the Cold War ended the King 1990 Defence Review further reduced force levels.

Foreign policy, which might be thought to dictate defence policy, has in practice often been conditioned by it, due in part to the difficulty in altering defence spending and jobs, at least in the short term. Commitments to foreign governments also militate against sudden changes, which further explains why alterations to British foreign policy have been infrequent since 1945. The importance to Britain of the Atlantic Alliance has remained throughout the postwar period, albeit with highs and lows. Britain has always been tentative in its relationship with Europe, rejecting joining supernatural bodies in 1950 (ECSC) and 1955–57 (EEC), attempting to join the latter in 1961 and 1967, and achieving it in 1973, but with an ambivalent and suspicious attitude for much of the time since. Britain's relationship with the Empire and Commonwealth has undergone the biggest change of all three of its main overseas relationships. Determined at first, despite the loss of India in 1947, to retain the Empire, governments then realised in a series of steps in the 1950s and 1960s that this would not be feasible, confirmed by the key decision in 1968 to withdraw from East of Suez. Nevertheless, Britain's decisive response in the Falklands War (1982) and its prominent role in the Gulf War (1991) and Bosnian conflict in the 1990s showed its determination to remain a major presence on the world stage, as guaranteed by its permanent seat on the UN Security Council and its place among the G7 group of leading industrial nations.

Science policy had been largely bipartisan after 1945, with only one difference in emphasis, Conservative governments being keener than Labour on supporting aerospace and military technology. The one major shift saw an abandonment of increasing expenditure on science policy (running at about ten per cent p.a.) from 1969, and an increasing prioritising of remaining investment in the most effective areas.[9] The size and shape of the government sector meanwhile saw a great expansion during the war. Total public expenditure (TPE) had been but 26 per cent of gross domestic product (GDP) in 1937: with the welfare state's creation between 1944–48 it rose to 37 per cent of GDP in 1948.[10] The ratio of TPE to GDP remained fairly constant until the Wilson government, when it rose to 43.9 per cent by 1968, in common with rises in other western countries. The Heath government of 1970–74 tried to reduce public expenditure, and to reorganise central government, both without lasting impact. Under Mrs Thatcher, the ratio fell from 45.9 per cent in 1979 to 41.4 per cent in 1989, but rose again to 46.8 per cent by 1993.[11]

III

Outlined above are some of the most significant policy changes initiated in Britain since 1945. But why did they occur? The field of motivation is relatively unexplored in Britain, in contrast to the more sophisticated analysis of government policy in many Western countries. Rose has been a major analyst of these questions in Britain.[12] Building on his work is the book which addresses itself most directly to our question, Brian Hogwood's *Trends in British Public Policy* (1992).[13] He analyses a mass of statistical data, in particular fluctuations in public expenditure, to analyse change but as he admits himself, much of what he says about the motives for changes is tentative.

The approach here is to examine the impact of four possible causes of change to assess how far ideas matter

- Ideas
- Individuals, internal, intermediate and external to government
- Circumstances, both internal and external to government
- Interests, both inside and outside government

Ideas are held to be powerful shapers of historical events, be it the Reformation or the Russian Revolution. A recent book edited by Michael Foley with the title *Ideas That Shape Politics* (1994) takes as a premise that ideas are absolutely crucial in shaping political choice and action.[14] Keynes' peroration in the *General Theory of Employment, Interest and Money* (1936) states that 'the world is ruled by little else [than ideas]'. Keynes hedged this statement with qualifications, not least concerning time, but he nevertheless helped confirm the view that ideas are fundamental to understanding the development of history.[15] George Bush and John Major were dogged in part by their failure to meet the enduring public expectation that leaders will produce a 'big idea'. Tony Blair says Labour is 'winning the battle of ideas'.[16]

Ideas as a subject are, it need hardly be said, fraught with complexity. To start: what is an idea? Ralf Dahrendorf has said: 'an idea is a notion of where we go from where we are ... a vision of the future state of affairs, which may or may not be desirable'.[17] This definition, of an idea being a scenario for the future, though imperfect, will suffice. Ideas exist on two levels. On an upper plane are over-arching ideas, that condition the entire way that a generation understands, models and interprets events. On a simplistic level the nineteenth century attachment to *laissez-faire* yielded to an era of mild interventionism for the first forty years of this century; a Keynesian period followed from the 1940s to 1970s, a more individualist era ensued and by the mid-to-late 1990s the mood seems ripe for another sea-change. Milton Friedman in similar vein argues that the last two hundred years have seen three great waves, an Age of Adam Smith, an Age of Keynes and now an Age of Hayek.[18] David Marquand has shown in Chapter One the limitations of such simple classifications. Nevertheless, the notion that each era has a dominant mentality – or 'conventional wisdom' (J. K. Galbraith) – is sound.

The London marketplace of ideas today is, in the eyes of Dahrendorf, 'the most fertile in Europe and perhaps the most fertile in the world'.[19] Some qualifications are necessary. Ideas are rarely new, as Plato acknowledged, and are equally rarely country-specific.[20] It is hard to pinpoint many purely-insularly initiated and developed ideas, especially since the whole post-war period has seen rapid transport of individuals and information. Christianity and syndicalism are but two of the innumerable foreign imports to Britain. The Mont Pelerin Society (MPS), founded in 1947 to combat what it saw as the widespread trend towards *dirigisme*, is a good example of the internationalisation of ideas since the Second World War. The MPS attracted liberal-minded scholars and writers from around the world, has held regular (usually annual) conferences, and has been a powerful influence disseminating anti-collectivist ideas and stimulating the establishment of free market institutions around the world such as the Institute of Economic Affairs.[21]

The MPS was a reaction against the dominant Keynesian consensus. Keynes, utilising both analytical and historical evidence, believed that the economy did not automatically tend towards equilibrium at a full (or at least an adequate) rate of employment and growth. Government action was thus needed to provide the stimulants and depressants to keep the economy growing on a relatively even course, much as the psychiatrist administers uppers and downers to keep a manic depressive in relatively stable health. But to the 'neo-classicists' or liberal economists like Friedman, the economy is not a manic depressive, but quite stable: they hold that the natural tendency of the economy, if freed from government intervention, is to allow markets to establish an equilibrium at least at an adequate or perhaps even a full level of employment and growth. Two positions, at polar ends.

This upper level of over-arching ideas often exists as sets of paired notions: individualism and collectivism; voluntarism and regulation; private welfare and the welfare state; devolution and centralisation; nationalism and internationalism. The finishing point at either end of the continuum may well never be fully reached: at any one given point in time, a country's policy in any one area will be somewhere along that line. The London-Gatwick shuttle service provides an analogy or, to be less metropolitan, the Stockton to Darlington railway. Going to Heathrow, or to Newcastle, is not an option. Will Hutton threatens to challenge this model with his argument, outlined in the next chapter, that his 'stakeholder' idea represents a third point, not mid-way between capitalism and socialism, but entirely separated from it, the third point of a triangle. Hutton's antecedents are many, such as the Marshall-Dahrendorf citizenship model. It remains to be seen whether Hutton's ideas will be enacted, and, if so, whether they will not prove to be merely, like Harold Macmillan's 'middle way', at a midway point along conventional lines, at the Croydon of British politics.[22]

Why might shifts between one paradigm and another occur?[23] Hirschman explains the movement back and forth between these two fixed points by saying that both the state and market solutions arouse expectations that they are bound not to be able to satisfy in the long term. Disappointment accumulates to the point where the alternative model (public or private) becomes the more attractive, and a shift in involvement from the one paradigm to the other occurs. As Hirschman himself notes in Chapter Two, there are limits on the explanatory value of his argument for recent British history. Nevertheless, even if one cannot state exactly why the shift from one dominant idea to another occurs, it is clear that the preponderance of one ideal or another at any given point in time conditions the entire way in which judgements are made by policy elites.

Hayek's *Road to Serfdom* (1944) and the early work of the Institute of Economic Affairs, founded in 1955, thus fell on stony ground.[24] Thorneycroft's resignation from the Treasury in 1958, Joseph's free market utterances during 1962–64,[25] similarly fell on deaf ears, in part as these views ran counter to the dominant idea, much as Oswald Mosley's push for a radical economic policy had done under the Labour Government in 1929–31, when orthodoxy and the 'Treasury view' was the order of the day.

At a lower level are ideas that are essentially facilitating rather than agenda-setting, and will only be taken up if they are in sympathy with the dominant idea. Environmentalism failed to make more impact on government thinking after its emergence at the end of the 1960s, when Greenpeace and Friends of the Earth were both founded, in part because the *dirigiste* state on which its presciptions were predicated was losing its hold.[26] Pressure for constitutional reform and a written constitution failed to make headway in the 1980s and 1990s partly because it was seen as *dirigiste*, thus anti the neo-liberal hegemonic principle.[27] Ideas which do not challenge the dominant idea, like nuclear deterrence, and may even facilitate it, will have far greater chance of acceptance.[28] Organisational reform failed to make much lasting impression in the 1960s and early 1970s, but made a major impact when in the 1980s and 1990s it chimed with the anti-statist instincts of the Thatcher and Major governments. Devolution is an idea that has failed to find favour less because it clashed with the dominant idea, but rather because it did not harmonise with the interests of the dominant party in power. Devolving power abroad, to British colonies, in contrast, was not viewed as a challenge to decision-takers in London, but was in any case rendered essential due to circumstances. All of this suggests, despite Keynes, that ideas are important, but have only a limited role in explaining change. For a more rounded understanding of postwar history, ideas must be seen in the context of the three other forces outlined above.

Individuals exert influence on three levels: persons operating within the government process, those in an intermediate position, and those external to government. The last have made arguably little impact on policy since 1945. Those working in universities, commentators and writers, whole disciplines indeed, have been largely ignored by government. Philosophy and philosophers have had startlingly little practical influence on government policy. The belief that philosophy has made a major impact on thinking is widespread. In October 1995, the *Times Literary Supplement* published a list of the hundred books which have most influenced 'Western public discourse' since 1945. Many philosophers have books listed, including Martin Heidegger, Jean-Paul Sartre, John Rawls and Ludwig Wittgenstein. But what government policy can one point to since 1945 that has been influenced by these? Why have the worlds of 'public discourse' and government decision-taking become so divorced? Or has philosophy failed to have the extensive influence even on 'public discourse' that the *TLS* pundits have claimed for it, as this author would (reluctantly) argue?

Bertrand Russell, A. J. Ayer, Bernard Williams and Mary Warnock have all had close connections with Labour politicians, as Karl Popper, Tony Quinton, Roger Scruton, Antony Flew and Anthony O'Hear to varying degrees have had with those on the right. Yet it is hard to find any discernible difference that philosophers have made to government policy or to politicians, aside from generalised influence of Karl Popper on Edward Boyle, and Hayek on Enoch Powell, Keith Joseph and Margaret Thatcher, or the influence of a select few like Mary Warnock and Bernard Williams who have sat on Royal Commissions (when they become insiders).[29] Key philosophical concepts such as rationality and objective appraisal of consequences have been notably absent from many policy decisions by government. The influence of Michael Oakeshott, the leading Conservative philosopher, has been minimal. It seems inevitable perhaps that the post-war British politician most influenced by logic and philosophy, Enoch Powell, should have become a maverick, not a political heavyweight. The influence of philosophy (via Greats and PPE at Oxford) on shaping the thought-processes of generations of civil servants, however, is incalculable.

Sociologists have had more impact on government policy.[30] The discipline's evolution postwar has gone through three principal phases. During the high point of Keynesian social democracy, from the 1940s to the 1960s, sociologists like T.H. Marshall showed how one could have an acceptable compromise between social justice and reasonable national prosperity, without the class polarisation foreseen by Marx. Marshall's work, according to Anthony Giddens, 'was probably almost as influential as Keynes' theories, because Keynesianism couldn't have worked without this filling in of the social or institutional side'.[31] Michael Young, Peter Townsend, Brian Abel-Smith and Chelly Halsey were four further sociologists with powerful connections with the Labour Party during this period, notably influencing Crosland in his social policies and discrediting IQ testing and the tripartite system of education. Sociology never recovered the influence it enjoyed in government circles in this period. In a second phase, coinciding with the internationalisation of sociology and its expansion at British universities in the later

1960s and 1970s, governments turned away from sociologists, a distancing that was reciprocated. Many sociologists turned on government, reserving especial derision for 'new right' ideology and its supposed ignoring of society. Right wing sociologists such as Julius Gould, Digby Anderson and David Green were in a narrow minority and were often in consequence disproportionately influential with Conservative governments. In the 1990s, sociologists such as Anthony Giddens, who are eclectic in their outlook, are again finding an (albeit limited) influence on 'New' Labour.

Economics, measured by numbers of British graduates, jobs for economists in the public and private sectors, and learned academic journals, has also mushroomed since the 1950s. Economists seek to explain how the economy and finance operate, and, with the development of econometrics since the 1960s, to provide government with tools and insights in order that they might manage the economy better. Yet economic historian cum public servant Eric Roll has concluded that 'if you compare the growth of the economics industry with the actual practical results of what used to be called "keeping the economy on an even keel", that relationship is very, very hard to demonstrate'.[32] No-one would deny the influence of Keynes (both an outsider and an insider) and Friedman (wholly an outsider) on British economic policy. Some Chancellors, like Hugh Dalton (1945–7), Hugh Gaitskell (1950–51) and Nigel Lawson (1983–89) have been gifted economists. Others like R. A. Butler (1951–55) and Geoffrey Howe (1979–83) have listened closely to trusted economists. Perhaps no academic economist had a greater influence on postwar economic policy than Robert Hall (chief economic adviser 1947–61).[33] Nicholas Kaldor and Thomas Balogh, also academic economists, had a powerful influence on Wilson when Prime Minister (1964–70), perhaps because Wilson's own economics background made him more open to such views.[34] Alan Walters (1983–89) had a profound influence on Mrs Thatcher, as did Sarah Hogg (1990–94), an economic journalist, on John Major. Neither achieved the central importance on economic policy of Terry Burns, outsider turned insider, in the 1980s and 1990s. Industrial relations economists, notably Derek Robinson and Hugh Clegg, had influence in the 1960s and 1970s. Bank of England economists such as Christopher Dow have engaged actively in academic writing. But, in general, Treasury ministers and officials since 1945 have had little time for or interest in the complexities of economic scholarship and debate. Kenneth Clarke, Chancellor of the Exchequer at the end of our period in the mid–1990s, denies being much influenced in his decisions by academic economics. It is a moot point whether economists have produced a much securer understanding of the economy and how to affect it than that possessed by economists in the 1940s.

Scientists have had more influence on government thinking, felt almost exclusively when scientists have been government insiders, or least least when their ideas have been mediated by government insiders, such as the Government Chief Scientist. None perhaps achieved greater influence than Solly Zuckerman (1964–71). The historical profession in contrast has made little impact on government. Despite preparing a number of its own internal histories of major events, such as the Suez crisis, government overall has shown little inclination to think historically or to analyse historical precedents in an attempt to reach better decisions.[35] Individual historians have been close to Prime Ministers, Bill Deakin and Churchill, or Martin Gilbert and Major, but their influence has been *ad hominem*, not as representatives of the historical profession. The maverick historian Correlli Barnett had disproportionate influence on Thatcherites in the 1980s.

The influence of political scientists and writers on contemporary politics has been similarly slight. Despite the existence of the Royal Institute of Public Administration until its demise in 1992, and committees like Redcliffe-Maud (local government) and Fulton (civil service), it is hard to see that many changes in Whitehall since 1945 being generated by the ideas of political scientists.[36] Where ideas have been taken up, such as Peter Hennessy's for publishing details of Cabinet committees and <u>Questions of Procedure for Ministers</u>, it has, unsurprisingly, been when these ideas have harmonised with the inclinations of insiders.[37] Bernard Donoughue, a political scientist at LSE before he became Head of the Number Ten Policy Unit, 1974–79, stands out as another rare representative of the discipline whose influence – albeit as an individual – has penetrated the heart of government.

Too much can be made of the failure of social sciences in the postwar world to have had more impact on government, or even to have met the claims that their more ardent supporters have advanced for them. Nevertheless, in a book assessing the importance of ideas in post-war Britain, it is salutary to note that the social sciences have failed to provide a convincing explanation of economic growth, the causes of crime, the motivation of electoral behaviour, or, it might be added, how change occurs in history and even to define 'ideas'. The failure of social science to live up to the expectations which it aroused for itself, especially in the 1960s, explains in part the only limited impact of these disciplines on government policy since the war.

Commentators in the serious press are a peculiar feature of British life: 'Op-Ed' page articles are far less prominent in the rest of Europe and in North America; according to Dahrendorf 'There are about two dozen commentators' who exercise real influence. He cites the *Guardian*'s Will Hutton and Hugo Young, though others on the centre right have often been as influential, such as Peter Jay in the 1970s and Samuel Brittan.[38] The two administrations since 1951 when intellectuals were most welcome at Number Ten were those of Wilson (1964–70 and 1974–76) and Thatcher (1979–90).[39] In contrast, the government of Major has seen an almost complete dearth of intellectuals at Number Ten.

The intermediate level refers to those bodies or functions

that facilitate individuals who are outside the government machine in injecting their thoughts into its heart. Royal Commissions, in abeyance during Mrs Thatcher's premiership, and departmental committees, provide forums for outside authorities to offer their ideas. Lord Percy's Royal Commission on Mental Illness and Sir John Wolfenden's departmental committee on homosexual law reform, both in the 1950s, provide two such examples, both helping to prepare the ground for significant changes in law.[40] The Central Policy Review Staff, or 'Think Tank', established to advise the Cabinet on all aspects of policy, enjoyed a fluctuating career from 1971–83, and one can exaggerate its importance. In a way novel for peace-time, it brought together outsiders, mainly from business and academe, and insiders, to produce a series of reports on subjects as diverse as the diplomatic service and the motor industry.[41] Some of its role after its demise was taken over by the Number Ten Policy Unit, founded by Wilson in 1974, and containing ten or less individuals drawn from inside and outside government. Several have been powerful influences, notably two heads, Donoughue and John Hoskyns (1979–82), and Nick True, the deputy head (1990–95), whose influence was felt in particular on the formulation of the Citizen's Charter in 1991 and the 'Back to Basics' policy in 1993.[42] Special advisers are political appointees drawn from outside Whitehall who become temporary civil servants. Isolated examples existed in the early postwar years, but it was only after 1964 that numbers grew, and after 1974 that the system of special advisers became institutionalised.[43] Often they have been marginalised by Whitehall, but some individuals have been powerful forces, such as Brian Abel-Smith on successive Labour Secretaries of State for Social Services in 1968–70 and 1974–78, Francis Cripps on Tony Benn from 1974–79 at the Department of Industry and then at Energy, and Andrew Tyrie on Nigel Lawson at the Treasury.[44]

Political parties and interest groups both provide the agency for individuals to influence policy. Both entities act like magnets, sucking in those with the ambition and ability to influence government policy. Into the Conservative Party's Research Department in the late 1940s came Iain Macleod, Enoch Powell and Reginald Maudling, all to have decisive influence on the party's postwar policy, in much the same way that Chris Patten did as Director of the Research Department from 1974–79 and Danny Finkelstein after 1995.[45] The Labour Party has provided the forum for two secretaries of Labour's Research Department, Michael Young (1945–51) and Peter Shore (1959–64) to exert their peculiar and powerful influence. Interest groups have been much studied as political entities, but little studied for their detailed impact on policy.[46] Nevertheless, it is clear that individuals as diverse as Jack Jones (General Secretary, Transport and General Workers' Union, 1969–78) and Rupert Murdoch (Chairman of News Corporation) have both exercised considerable influence on government policy, the former in the 1970s, the latter in the 1980s and 1990s.

Independent 'Think Tanks' have received increasing scholarly interest in the 1990s, notably in Richard Cockett's *Thinking the Unthinkable* (1994). His assertion is that thinkers in the New Right think tanks 'did as much intellectually to convert a generation of "opinion formers" and politicians to a new set of ideas as the Fabians had done with a former generation at the turn of the century'.[47] Cockett's thesis has been attacked for overstating the case, and for failing to demonstrate exactly how the influence of individuals in think tanks has been exerted.[48] This larger concern points to the problem this chapter has repeatedly found: how does one satisfactorily prove an influence on policy? This problem notwithstanding, one can assert that think tanks, which mushroomed in number during the 1970s, have had an influential role in collating the thoughts of like-minded intellectuals and funnelling them into governing circles. Dahrendorf indeed believes 'London is probably the outstanding place in

Europe for think tanks'.[49] Consultancies are an important new source of policy influence since the 1970s. The big six accountancy firms such as Arthur Andersen and Coopers and Lybrand proffer advice to government on a wide array of subjects including all major public sector restructurings.[50]

Judges can perhaps best be considered in this intermediate level. No understanding of postwar British history can be complete without considering Britain's senior judges. Judicial restraint over executive decisions dominated until the early 1960s when the promotion of two powerful judges, Lords Denning and Reid, heralded an era of judicial activism. The judges confronted the 1974–79 Labour government in some major cases such as Tameside schooling and Laker Skytrain. Judicial activism continued apace in the 1980s and 1990s, with judges increasingly applying a normative perspective, buoyed by the European Court of Human Rights (European Court of Justice).[51]

Individuals inside government consist in the main of permanent officials, and transient ministers. How much difference have they made? Each biography, and still more each memoir or autobiography, claims conclusive proof of the centrality of the subject. The sheer volume of political biography is testimony, however, not to the historical importance of the political class but to their economic muscle in publishing: political lives sell; the bigger the life, and the story, the greater the sales. Officials might well have been of more historical importance, but with very few exceptions they are not the subjects of biographies, nor outside the top echelons of the diplomatic service do they write their memoirs.[52] Yet certain officials have been utterly central to the development of policy in their areas, such as James Meade over economic policy when from 1940–47 he worked in the Economic Section of the Cabinet Office,[53] Norman Brook (Cabinet Secretary 1947–62) on successive Prime Ministers, Attlee, Churchill, Eden and Macmillan, Andrew Cohen and William Gorrell Barnes, Colonial Office civil servants, on decolonisation,

Richard ('Otto') Clarke of the Treasury on economic policy from the 1940s to the 1960s, Evelyn Sharp of the Ministry of Housing on housing policy from 1950–66, Leo Pliatzky of the Treasury on public spending control in the 1970s,[54] Michael Quinlan on defence policy, especially in the late 1980s and early 1990s, and Charles Powell, Private Secretary at Number Ten from 1984–91, on Mrs Thatcher's foreign policy. The contributions of these and many other officials goes far beyond passively advising ministers, yet the tendency in history books will always be to undervalue their importance. Regrettably, attempts in the early and late 1980s to set up a bank of in-depth interviews with all Britain's most senior officials failed to attract funding from the ESRC and Leverhulme Foundation. Such an archive would have gone a long way to setting the role of officials on a more secure footing, and provide reserach of *real* enduring value.

Few attempts to assess the role of individuals on recent British history have been made. Among the most important is Peter Clarke in his *A Question of Leadership* (1991), an analysis of the role and importance of leadership in British politics since Gladstone. Clarke finds that those individuals who have been successful in making a major impact in politics, like Attlee and Mrs Thatcher, managed to combine setting the agenda with mobilising political support. The former is partly a question of anticipating rather than merely chiming with the popular mood, the latter dependent *inter alia* upon 'rational persuasion, on executive efficiency, on charismatic oratory, on party organisation, on institutional power-broking or on high-political scheming'.[55]

Clarke is more concerned in the heart of the book, a series of biographical essays, to show *that* leaders change the agenda rather than *how* they do so. Howard Gardner addresses the latter question when he argues that a key ingredient of success in leadership is the ability of the leader to be able to 'tell a story' about the past and then to show how he or she is uniquely well qualified to bring about a resolution to the impasse. On this basis, Churchill had a strong story to tell in 1940 of little Britain's heroic stance against an evil dictator, as did Mrs Thatcher with the perils of consensualism and overmighty trade unions in the 1980s. But the *how far* and *how* questions about the individuals' impact on history need further probing than they have received so far in postwar British history books. Defeatism, as offered by political philospher Jerry Cohen when he wrote 'we don't and never will [have] a way of measuring the amount of impact that an individual can have on a political process', is premature.[56]

Those who believe the individual is important in shaping history emphasise contingency. Those who see history being formed more by circumstances and great historical forces concentrate on structural explanations: they suggest that changes would have occurred anyway regardless of the particular individuals in the limelight. The individual on this reading less makes history than is made by history. The great debates about Marxist and other determinist theories of history which render the individual largely irrelevant in causing change carry force. Impersonal forces, bad harvests, new methods of communication, the experience of war, certainly create the potential for change. There is also the more limited argument that the study of postwar history has suffered from an overfocus on individual leaders. Ben Pimlott has argued controversially that the most studied premier since 1945, Mrs Thatcher, and the only one to be daubed with an -ism after her name, is an overrated figure historically: her overall legacy, he writes, is 'mainly composed of developments that would have happened anyway, albeit with a different rhetoric, under Labour'.[57] Pimlott provides an essential reminder that an emphasis on any *one* of the four explanations of change (ideas, individuals, circumstances, interests) to the neglect of the others provides but a partial reading of events.

Circumstances can be defined as events which constrain policy options and in many cases dictate a certain course of action. They also come in two varieties, external and internal.

In both forms they provide opportunities, and in some cases the necessity, to recast policy. The former consist of shocks, originating from outside Britain, which have a profound influence within, war and economic traumas being the two principal varieties. The period since 1900 has been the first century of total war, with both world wars acting as powerful stimulants to change. The wars tested existing institutions, individuals and customs; they required total mobilisation of the country's resources devoted to one end, winning the war; they required replacement on a large scale of the country's human and physical resources. Finally, both aroused expectations on the part of those who participated and suffered for a better world to follow.[58] Measuring the impact of the wars is notoriously difficult, because one can never know for certain whether they speeded developments already in train, or caused them to come into being. In some cases, as with reforms to Whitehall, the *status quo ante bellum* rapidly reasserted itself once hostilities ceased. Nevertheless, albeit to a debatable extent, both wars had major impacts on the development of the welfare state, the evolution of political parties, the application of new scientific, technological and medical techniques, the position of women, and of the relative power of the upper, middle and working classes. The impact specifically of the Second World War in some areas is clear, for example boosting popular attachment to collectivism: in other areas, such as whether it enhanced the position of women, it is more uncertain.[59] On a smaller scale, the Korean (1950–53), Suez (1956) and Falklands (1982) Wars and the Bosnian conflict in the 1990s have provided the impetus for change, though the influence of these (bar Korea) is limited to the narrower area of defence policy and strategic thinking.

External economic shocks have had powerful influences since 1945. Memories of the profound interwar depression deeply affected those in power for many years after 1945. The failure of the American recession in 1953 to bite in Britain led to a new belief in Whitehall in the strength and potential of the British economy. In the 1960s the realisation that Germany, France, even Italy, were outperforming the British economy provided the boost for the search for new economic panaceas. Throughout the postwar period, and especially from the 1970s, decision-makers in Whitehall could not ignore what the financial markets and International Monetary Fund thought. Economic policy upheavals under the Heath government (1970–74) were caused at least as much by the break-up of the Bretton Woods system, the rapid rise in inflation and unemployment, and the OPEC crisis of 1973 as the death of the Chancellor of the Exchequer, Iain Macleod, in 1970.[60] Circumstances can again help explain the shift in economic policy in 1979–81. The very high unemployment levels, an international phenomenon of the period, helped the Thatcher government to the realisation that it could manage the economy with high unemployment levels, and still survive politically.[61]

Internal circumstances originate primarily within Britain, and include technological developments, such as nuclear energy, information technology, in nutrition and health or genetic engineering. They encompass changes in the religious make-up of the nation or certain regions, demographic change, the perception of governmental failure or 'overload', to windfall benefits like North Sea oil in the 1980s and 1990s. Hogwood rates the importance of such influences on policy change since 1945 highly: 'in terms of directly measurable impact, changes in demography and social characteristics have been responsible for far more change than overtly party political factors'.[62] But for the economic recession and the squeeze of spending after 1992, John Major's second government might have been far more adventurous in pursuing his ideal of an 'opportunity society'.[63] Chris Pierson in his chapter above has found that 'social, demographic and economic change'[64] have been far more significant than ideas to changes in social policy since 1945. Skidelsky concludes that Thatcherism's progress in the 1980s owed at least as much to the circumstances of the failure of government policy in the 1960s and 1970s as to an intellectual or ideological background.[65] Without the sense of breakdown and disillusionment with one model, the search for a new set of policies will not take place.

Norman Barry, the political philosopher, has written that 'there are only two serious competing explanations for change' in postwar Britain, ideas and vested interests.[66] The latter (which are in fact inseparable from ideas) forms the final influence. External interests include pressure groups, the media and political parties. Governments only allow themselves to be influenced by pressure groups when it is in their own interest to do so. Trade unions, arguably the most consistently powerful of all pressure groups in post-war Britain, derived their influence from government believing it had more to gain from consulting than from excluding them, as was the case before 1939.[67] After unions overreached their mark in the 1970s, and lost public backing, combining with economic changes undermining their powerbase, it was relatively painless for Mrs Thatcher to close the door to government on them.[68] The Liberal Party has made little impact on government policy since 1945, and the Labour Party's influence has been limited by the fact that in only nine of the fifty years between 1945–95 did the party have a solid working majority in the House of Commons. The Conservative Party's importance has been more extensive, though until 1975 it was the relatively calm centre rather than the radical ferment on the wings that dictated the agenda.[69] The media's influence lies more in its ability to influence public opinion rather than in it being a source of policy advice. The steely determination of Number Ten to ensure a favourable interpretation in the media of government policy is evidence of the importance that successive prime ministers have attached to its influence over public opinion. The jury remains out, however, whether the media really does have such a pervasive influence on public opinion: there is inconclusive evidence that it has shaped it for prolonged periods. The *Sun* and other mass circulation newspapers might influence some of the more impressionable sections of the public in the short term, as Martin Linton argues, was the case with the very close 1992 general election result.[70] The broadsheet press play a role – no more – in mediating ideas in a climate change.

Public opinion is not autonomous: it is informed by a mass of different influences. Ever since the franchise began to be extended in the early nineteenth century, it has wielded an important influence on policy choices by governments, the more so since techniques for monitoring and measuring it have become more sophisticated and immediate since the 1960s.[71] The public demand for social policies after both world wars, for economic growth in the 1950s and 1960s and for more economic freedom in the 1980s all fed through into policy programmes. Norman Blackwell's particular contribution as Head of the Number Ten Policy Unit since 1994 has been to reorientate Conservative policy back more towards the concerns of target voters.[72] The reorientation of the Labour Party since 1983 orchestrated by Neil Kinnock, Peter Mandelson and others has been fired more by the need to follow and satisfy public opinion rather than to lead it.[73]

The more important vested interests by far though are those internal to government. Public choice theory, which argues that civil servants are not just the willing and loyal implementors of ministerial wishes, but have their own agendas, has been very important here. The senior Civil Service as a whole can hold common views or a shared mentality, such as a belief that Britain's future lies in Europe and a resistance to change, whether from left or right. Mrs Thatcher spent enormous reserves of energy challenging Whitehall's notion that it was the better manager of public services than the private sector. More usually, a department holds a view, such as the Foreign Office which was Atlanticist-first in the 1950s, or the Treasury, with its attachment to Keynesianism up to the 1970s.[74] The Chiefs of Staff and the intelligence heads have been consistently powerful lobbies. It is ironic, and a telling comment on the gaps in British political science, that the most important and powerful single office in British government, Number Ten, has barely been studied.[75]

IV

The section above argues that all four factors – ideas, individuals, circumstances and interests – are potentially significant in explaining policy changes. Why then has this fact not been more generally recognised? Much of the responsibility lies with the literature. Despite over fifty thousand books and articles, many of them highly informative and valuable, the study of post-war British history remains in some ways incomplete. More robust and daring work is required if we are to have a surer appreciation of the complexities of British history in all its aspects since 1945.

Ideas and ideologies have been exhaustively discussed, but either they have been examined independently of policy, or the link with a particular policy or set of policies has been asserted rather than explained. General elections have again been much studied, yet with obvious exceptions like 1945 and 1979, they have often been insignificant milestones in pacing out post-war British history. Studies of individual governments would be more enlightening if they took account of all of the following five dimensions.[76] The inheritance on taking office: what was the legacy left behind by the outgoing government? What was the government's position immediately on taking office? Second, were factors – economic, social, international – beyond the government's immediate power to control generally benign, or malign? Third are parliamentary and electoral factors, such as how long the government had in office, what the size of its majority was, and what the quality of the opposition? Fourth: foreign governments' experience. How did governments overseas fare during the same experience? Finally, what was the legacy left by the government to its successors? How did it contrast with the inheritance?

Assessment of the proper role of individuals has been obscured by an excessive focus on the most visible political players, and by the tendency of biographers of postwar figures to see their subjects as free-standing individuals theoretically capable of achieving anything. They need instead to see the individual far more against the structural background in which they have operated at different times. Biographies should similarly be cognisant of five factors operating on their subject (and at different periods in their career). Was the economic environment positive in allowing the subject to achieve his or her aims, or did it constrict their options? Did the subject have the quality of support from staff and, where relevant, from parliamentary colleagues to allow him or her to maximise their opportunities? Did he or she nurture or deter that support? Was the media sympathetic or destructive? Was public opinion in sympathy with the individual's natural predispositions? Was the individual able to stake out a clear course that it was relatively easy to persuade colleagues and public opinion to follow? Were there widely agreed targets? Finally, did events present opportunities for the individual to display decisive leadership – for example a crisis or a war?

Because this approach has generally not been adopted, it is easy to see why Clement Attlee is deemed simplistically to be the better Prime Minister than James Callaghan, or indeed Mrs Thatcher than John Major.

Too much postwar history has been studied in isolated pockets, overlooking developments abroad and in other sectors of policy concurrently in Britain. The Institute of Contemporary British History has promoted a series of books which focus on particular policy sectors (economic policy, social policy, defence, etc.). Such studies of individual policy areas are important, but we also need policy histories to be written which are cognisant of and cross into other areas, above all economic policy, as economic constraints and policy affect all aspects of policy. The danger of atomisation in postwar British history, with specialists in one area, like international relations, knowing very little of others, is very real. It follows on the growing political science–history divide.

So what then is the correct weighting of ideas, individuals, circumstances and interests? To attempt any answer to this question we must return to the policy changes outlined at the start of the chapter. Figure 1 examines the influence of the four factors on some of the main changes in policy areas that occurred since 1945, and Figure 2 some initiatives that were aborted.

The diagrams below, inevitably representational rather than scientifically rigorous, show that the strongest correlation with policy success or policy rejection is not ideas, but 'circumstances'. This helps explain why the ideas that most affected policy since 1945, Fabian collectivism and the individualism of Hayek, had in both cases to wait thirty or forty years for the right set of favourable circumstances, interests and individuals for them to be put into policy.

The diagrams highlight three social policy 'successes' and two failures. In 1942, the Beveridge Report both chimed with but also helped channel the popular demand for a welfare state. As Jose Harris has argued, Beveridge was not an innovator, but the plan he put forward drew together disparate ideas and pulled them together into a common thread.[77] His particular contribution lay in his personal drive, the force of his personality and his gifts at promotion: 'Through his ability as a publicist he created the public mood which forced the establishment of the Civil Service and the Conservative Party to change their policies permanently'.[78] The balance of interests was thus against his proposals. The circumstances in contrast were very much positive, above all the public demand that there was to be no return to the 1930s with its unemploy-

Fig. 1 *The Four Factors and Successful Policy Change*

	Ideas	Individuals	Interests	Circum-stances
Social Policy				
1942	√	√	x	√
1976	√	–	–	√
1988	√	√	–	√
Economic Policy				
1944	√	√	√	√
1953–4	–	–	√	√
1961	–	–	–	√
1975–6	√	–	–	√
Industrial Relations				
1988	–	√	x	√
Foreign Policy				
Decolonisation	–	√	–	√
1972–3	–	√	–	√

Fig. 2 *The Four Factors and Unsuccessful/Aborted Policy Change*

	Ideas	Individuals	Interests	Circum-stances
Social Policy				
1952	√	√	–	x
1958	√	√	–	x
Economic Policy				
1952	–	–	–	x
Industrial Relations				
1969	–	√	x	x
1971	–	√	x	x
Foreign Policy				
1963	–	√	–	x
1967	–	√	–	x

Key: √ = a positive influence

x = a negative influence

– = a weak or a balanced influence

ment and poverty, the widely felt wish for a new start, a solid intellectual backing and above all victory in war.

In 1976, it was again circumstances which forced the realisation that existing Keynesian demand management ideas were not working. A new set of policy prescriptions based on new right ideas and cuts in welfare expenditure were available to be taken off the peg. The new ideas were all the more potent as they purported to show why the Keynesian ideas had broken down. Individuals and interests were of minor importance in this transition. The 1988 change, to the purchaser–provider split, was in contrast very much individual-driven. Mrs Thatcher had barely touched the welfare state in her first two terms in office: victory at the general election in 1987 gave her the opportunity to introduce some radicalism into social policy, and also to outwit the 'wets' in Cabinet who had argued against major change to welfare delivery. The ideas came from the new right think tanks such as the Institute of Economic Affairs and the Adam Smith Institute, and specifically from an American economist, A. Enthoven, who wrote a pamphlet when on a sabbatical in Britain.[79] In the case of 1988, circumstances were confined mainly to the fact of a third successive victory in 1987, and the opportunity, even the need, to set out in a new direction. The strength of interests helps explain why cuts fell harder on some sectors, such as unemployment benefit, rather than on student grants or on mortgage tax relief.

In contrast, circumstances were not propitious in the two false starts cited on the diagram under social policy. Bevan's resignation in 1951 over charges to the NHS was drawing on socialist ideas in the 1920s and 1930s. Both the ideas, and the individuals were present, but the circumstances of the Labour government needing to make savings were decisive. In 1958, Thorneycroft's resignation was aimed at taking spending in a proto-Thatcherite direction. The Conservative Research Department, and the newly-founded IEA, were furnishing the right wing ideas. Thorneycroft was joined by two able lieutenants at the Treasury, Enoch Powell and Nigel Birch, who resigned with him. But the circumstances of a government with an election on the horizon and no widespread concern about the need for cuts militated against Thorneycroft succeeding.

All of the shifts in economic policy identified earlier were present in the decision to adopt full employment.[80] The ideas were those of Keynes and other economists, James Meade was the key individual mediating the transition, vested interests were either neutral or positive, and the circumstances, including having on hand the instruments of economic planning from the war, were overwhelmingly positive. In the 1953–54 switch to economic growth, the failure of the US recession to make much impact on Britain, and the opportunism of the Conservatives realising that growth is a card that will out-trump Labour, were all-important: individuals and ideas were of tangential significance only. In 1961, again it was circumstance, in the shape of the ever-growing mountain of statistics, pamphlets and books announcing Britain's relatively poor economic performance, that dictated the change towards greater state intervention. The 1975–76 move towards inflation being the primary target of economic policy again sees circumstances to the fore: the break-up of the Bretton Woods system followed by the rapid increase in world inflation, the OPEC crisis, unemployment rising out of control and the influence of the International Monetary Fund all combined to make new right economic prescriptions suddenly look attractive. In 1952, the one economic policy failure highlighted, interests and individuals were finely balanced over the decision not to adopt the 'Robot' plan for making the pound freely convertible. Powerful economic ideas were marshalled on either side. What swayed the day was the circumstance of a small election victory in October 1951, and the Cabinet judging that the possibly deleterious effect on full employment provided a risk too far.

Foreign policy has been influenced less by ideas than other

policy areas since 1945: 'British foreign policy has had a void of ideas'[81] in the words of Christopher Hill. Despite the work of the Royal Institute of International Affairs at Chatham House, there has been less attempt by government to stand back and coolly assess Britain's overseas policy and future options than is the case of defence policy. Macmillan's working group in 1959–60[82] and the CPRS's Review of Overseas Representation of 1977 stand out as rare, and largely abortive, attempts to analyse critically and to think strategically about British foreign policy. Some individuals have been important, notably Ernest Bevin (Foreign Secretary 1945–51) and Heath (Prime Minister 1970–74), the first for defining Britain's post-war foreign policy, based on the three overlapping circles of Empire, Europe and the United States relationships, the latter for taking Britain into Europe. But there have been no foreign policy prophets on a par with Keynes or Beveridge. Even Mrs Thatcher, with all her power and longevity, failed to make foreign policy dance to her satisfaction. Political parties have been less influential than in other policy areas, and have often behaved counter-intuitively: Labour's leaders decided to build the atomic bomb and helped to create NATO; the Conservatives largely oversaw decolonisation; Heath was the coolest Prime Minister to the Americans since the war. Other interests have often balanced each other, notably lobbies for and against closer co-operation with Europe. It is thus circumstances which have been the most powerful force driving British foreign policy since 1945, above all the realisation that Britain no longer had the money, the troops or the resources to play the powerful role on the world stage to which governments of both parties since 1945 have been attached. The circumstances, above all of French opposition, explain Britain's failure to enter the EEC in 1963 and in 1967. Circumstances, notably increasing nationalism, relative economic decline and United States antipathy, combined to explain the unstructured and haphazard imperial decolonisation in the 1950s and 1960s.

Defence policy has been more ideas-driven since 1945 than foreign policy. The Global Strategy Paper of 1952, in which the Chief of Air Staff John Slessor played a seminal role, appreciated the mismatch between Britain's resources and its overseas commitments. It advocated a shift in emphasis from conventional warfare to nuclear deterrence, a policy which was confirmed by the Sandys White Paper of 1957. In the 1950s the British defence community was seething with ideas, on 'limited war', in which Basil Liddell Hart was crucial, and 'graduated deterrence', with Anthony Buzzard in a key role. A Chatham House study group in 1956, on which sat Denis Healey and Richard Goold-Adams, further refined these ideas. 'Escalation' as a concept was developed in Britain in the late 1950s and was first used by Wayland Young (later Lord Kennet). In the 1960s the Institute of Strategic Studies under its first director Alistair Buchan (1958–69), and academics such as Michael Howard and Lawrence Freedman, later became forces in the evolving debate on nuclear warfare. In the anti-nuclear movement British intellectuals Bertrand Russell and A. J. P. Taylor in the 1950s and E. P. Thompson in the 1980s had important roles. But British defence thinking has, in the post-war world, often been subordinate and reactive to American policies and wishes. Only with the end of the Cold War has there been the emergence of some distinctive British ideas, such as 'peace support operations'.[83]

It would be tempting to conclude this chapter with a determinist model of the conditions that must obtain if a proposed policy change is to be effective. The prospect is indeed too tempting to resist, however foolhardy the attempt, and tentative the proposals. It seems likely that change comes in history when the four factors present themselves in the following combination. Circumstances should be neutral or positive. Individuals should be present with either a coherent set of ideas, as Mrs Thatcher had from 1975, or capable of exploiting a change in circumstances, as Churchill did from 1940. If there are no individuals capable of exploiting a situation, change is less likely to occur, even if ideas are bubbling, circumstances are propitious and vested interests sympathetic. If internal interests are against a change, no change is likely to occur, even if the other three factors are positive. Ideas, to be successfully taken up, need advocates (individuals or interests), they need to square with the facts, to have a dominant idea or interest benign or positive, and to be launched into positive circumstances. The latter include a favourable financial environment, and time to see existing commitments and undertakings played out.

Such a conclusion however overreaches the more limited ambition of this chapter, which is to set ideas in some context. Even if maddeningly difficult to define, ideas clearly are crucial to an understanding of post-war British history, albeit in some areas such as economic policy than in others, notably foreign policy. Overall, though, and in contrast to the prevailing orthodoxy, this chapter finds that what is surprising about the impact of ideas on post-war British history is just how limited rather than great their impact has been. Even where their influence is demonstrable, they need to be seen in the context of the interplay of interests, individuals and circumstances. To understand what has shaped post-war Britain, ideas on their own are not enough.

CHAPTER 12

The Stakeholder Society

Will Hutton[1]

BRITAIN is not succeeding as it should. The difficulty is not its attachment to capitalism; market principles could hardly have been applied more fiercely over the last seventeen years. The problem is more complex, rooted in the highly unproductive way in which British social, economic and governmental structures lock together. The solution is neither to pursue the current path, nor to attempt any return to the failed corporatism of the 1970s. Rather it is to strike out in a new direction altogether, escaping the polarities of collectivism and individualism through which capitalism has so often been analysed and interpreted, towards a new conception of the stakeholder economy and society.

This chapter is a broad outline of the intellectual position I have been developing in newspaper commentaries over the last few years and articulate in my book, *The State We're In*. New Keynesian economic theories offer a new prism through which to interpret the market economy. This, together with the insight that capitalism comes in many forms, differentiated significantly by the ways investment capital is supplied and corporations are governed, provide the theoretical underpinnings both for a critique of the current system – and to guide a new way forward. In the balkanisation and demoralisation of British society, the consequences of the status quo are there for all to see – and without change the sustainability of British capitalism will ultimately come under threat.

But on balance, there are grounds for optimism. If the centre and the liberal-left can reawaken the tradition of British liberalism that was sundered by twentieth-century socialism, there is every chance that these 'stakeholder' prescriptions will be fulfilled in the years ahead.

THE STAKEHOLDING PERSPECTIVE

Capitalism comes in diverse forms. The simple proposition that the alternative to capitalism is socialism is an inadequate and misleading way of looking at the choices available. There are a multiplicity of capitalisms, configured by their institutional structures and the way the economic, social and political interconnect. Hence there are truly democratic choices available within a capitalist society. The way the left–right argument has been conducted during most of the twentieth century, between planning and the market, socialism and capitalism, is not particularly helpful now, if it ever was. Those are not the choices on offer, and one form of capitalism or another, is now the only game in town.

The way forward for the centre and the left is to reawaken a long and honourable progressive tradition, which splintered in the early years of the twentieth century. Just as in the past, the left has done itself a disservice by becoming stuck on the wrong road of public ownership, Conservatives do capitalism no favours with their obsession with a single, pure, free-market theory. It is obvious from the real world that different forms of capitalist system exist. There are varying combinations of the principles of commitment and flexibility, co-operative trust and competitive rigour, in economic life and, just as importantly, in the way states, private institutions and society at large are organised. The congruence of these elements defines the political economy of a capitalist society.

Three models of capitalist society

There are three basic models of capitalism extant in the world today, plus the British variant, which is a less productive form than those that prevail in the United States, east Asia and Europe. The neglected realm of political economy is the key to understanding the plurality of types of capitalism – an intellectual tradition to which *The State We're In* firmly belongs. When individual capitalist systems are seen as a whole, it is the way that the political, economic and social interlock that is striking. Moreover the varying shapes of those intersections determine their character as nations.

The United States is commonly seen as the most individualistic and libertarian of all economies. American financial, labour and product markets are very competitive and free, and public involvement in social welfare and direct ownership is comparatively small. But besides aggressive competition, the institutional structure of the American economy with, for instance the existence of over 10,000 regional banks and government support for high-technology research in the defence and space programmes, fosters some level of co-operative endeavour. Decentralised and participatory government is a yardstick for private action as well.

Social-market Europe, perhaps typified by Germany, represents another coherent way of structuring economic, political and social affairs. Unlike the United States, co-operation is entrenched through the mutual recognition of the rights of capital and labour, long-term relationships between borrowers and lenders and a political system based explicitly on formal power sharing. Regional government, and in parallel regional financial institutions, exist and are locked in to the national settlement. There is a generous social state. While this form has inflexibilities, it does conform to market imperatives.

East Asian capitalism takes the combination of co-operative behaviour in a competitive environment to its most extreme, in a way that confuses those accustomed to Anglo-American binary oppositions in logic and economics. Its financial system is regulated, traditional and long term. Labour is immobile, though trade unions are docile. Firms and the state promote inclusiveness and consensus among their members. Product markets are fiercely competitive but producers build up long-term relations of trust with their suppliers, financiers and workforces.

In each of these models, it is clear that actors such as firms, banks and workers behave in ways that are impossible to explain through classical assumptions about motivation. Behaviour *is* rational, but has to be placed within the context of the entire system of relations which makes up the political economy of the model.

British is not best

The British model is based on the same ideological theories as obtain in the US, but its institutional and political arrangements are vastly different, in ways that produce a less successful outcome for the overall system. In trying to copy America, we have ended up with the worst of both worlds. Britain has neither the dynamism of the USA, nor the institutions of social cohesion and long-term investment found in Europe.

The problems with the British approach date back to the way the country industrialised during the eighteenth century, in a largely spontaneous and market driven way, without state action (although there was more state support than most historians recognise). This contrasts sharply with industrial development in Germany and Japan. The institutions of British economy and society have never been configured to encourage industrial investment and progress. The relationship between British finance and industry has long been destructive, with finance usually triumphant. The City of London has always been dominant, both for domestic reasons and because of London's role as an international financial centre.

The property that defines the British financial system is its overarching preoccupation with liquidity (the capacity to turn loans and investments into cash rapidly). This flexibility is in the interests of finance and the markets that have been constructed to enable assets to be quickly cashed; but it is not in the interests of producers, who require more commitment. Short-term risks and high rates of return are the key features of British finance. This not only makes investment problematic, but puts companies under constant threat of takeover if they try to adopt other priorities than achieving high short-term returns.

Social values in Britain have long privileged finance over industry, and thus formed part of a failing overall system. The respect given to effortless superiority, the word of honour, the subtleties of rank and class, and aristocratic invisible income has a strong hold in British culture and accords with success at finance, commerce and administration rather than laboriously making products. Britain has been in thrall to 'gentlemanly capitalism' for most of this century, and only an interlude between 1931 to 1951, when depression and war forced the real economy's interests to be asserted, has offered partial relief.

British companies are subject to an arbitrary executive, to financial priorities above all others, and are subordinated to the pursuit of short-term profit. The function of the British company, in contrast to the Japanese firm, is to generate a high rate of return from trading activity, rather than to be a productive organisation embedded in a network of long-term trust relations – including financiers and work-force alike. The stock market's facilitation of hostile takeovers, and its inability to price future income rationally, police the firm's attachment to short-term returns. That the vast majority of important British firms are public companies largely owned by institutional shareholders whose aim is to extract dividends and capital gains is one of the most salient facts about the British economy. In Japan, shareholding is an expression of commitment and interlocking interests, and in other Asian economies the family firm is the primary unit.

The pre-modern, quasi-feudal British state is part of the systemic problem. Its economic institutions, the Treasury and the Bank of England, are part of the nexus of financial interests favouring gentlemanly rentierdom. Social, financial and governmental power are all centralised in London and the state has shown itself incapable of being other than *dirigiste* and centralised. It is the fount of the problems Britain has in defining responsible institutions. The state conforms to no agreed rules and has no clear set of principles governing its relationship with, and responsibilities to, its citizens. It need pay no heed to any concerns save the self-interest of the ruling party, malleable 'public opinion' and the book-keeping values of the Treasury. Attempts to create co-operative institutions, social rights and responsibilities, and regulation in the public interest have failed in Britain because of the fundamental lack of these values at the core of the state. This, again, is in sharp contrast to successful capitalist models, where the role of the state is delineated in a written constitution.

In Britain, unlike America, Europe or east Asia, the political, social and economic systems form a whole which is not conducive to industrial success and social cohesion. This is not to argue that everything in Britain is failing and everything is working perfectly abroad; but it *is* to assert that enough is going wrong in Britain to arouse powerful concern – and overseas models offer insights and structures, which although they cannot be imported wholesale, need to be carefully examined for their lessons.

Conservative Britain has followed the wrong track . . .

Many of the faults with the British system have been accentuated by the policies of successive Conservative governments since 1979. Conservative supremacy was used for the single-minded pursuit of free-market economic doctrines: the retreat of the state and the ungloving of the invisible hand of market forces were supposed to create a new era of prosperity free from the 'distortions' caused by government intervention.

The results have proved different, and have not been due to a lack of thoroughness in the implementation of free-market reforms. The state has been purged of people and institutions which supported other priorities and the possibilities inherent in a system of government unregulated by written norms have been exploited to the full.

The financial system was almost completely deregulated in a series of changes, such as the lifting of exchange controls and the scrapping of banks' reserve requirements. Instead of a new age of investment, this led to a surge in consumer and housing lending, while industry's capital stock per unit of output declined. The dominance of finance over the real economy was strengthened, as high real interest rates – the only lid on credit once controls had gone – inhibited investment and rewarded the rentier.

Labour market reforms were intended to bring it closer to the classical ideal of a market, by allowing workers to 'price themselves into jobs' and causing the market to clear. Therefore, trade unions' powers were systematically restricted, and benefits cut to try to eliminate 'scrounging'. After nearly two decades of this process, the promised results have still not appeared – the numbers unemployed or economically inactive remain high and wages are still unresponsive to changes in unemployment. The theory was fundamentally wrong in imagining that the labour market was a market like all others, that wages are compensation for work which is inherently unpleasant, and that the human values of fairness and motivation are irrelevant. Exhaustive academic research has found, for example, that employers pay wages above the lowest possible level and are slow to sack workers in recessions because they place a high value on loyalty, fairness and the construction of effective teams. Free-market theory has proved inadequate at explaining such apparently irrational behaviour.

... and created a new world of them and us

Poverty and insecurity have resulted from Conservative labour market and social security policies. The segmentation of the labour market has created a new and pernicious form of social stratification: the 30–30–40 society. Approximately 30 per cent of the population are disadvantaged; the unemployed, those excluded from the labour market and those with only the most marginal participation. As in the US, the poverty and social stress experienced by this group of people causes acute misery and has consequences for the rest of society. Crime, family breakdown, a growing army of only partially socialised young men and vast social security spending on propping up inequality are the result.

The next 30 per cent are the marginalised and the insecure, whose jobs, for one reason or another, do not provide any tenure. This includes households dependent on part-time earnings (up to two years), those under short-term contracts with few employment rights, and those who have become involuntarily self-employed. This category is particularly exposed to the spread of marketisation and the displacement of risk onto individuals, who have found it extremely difficult to cope with the necessity for private pensions, health insurance and transport.

The remaining 40 per cent are the privileged, with tenured employment, although this group are by no means uniformly wealthy. They are often the insiders of more sophisticated labour market theories, who have enough power to do well.

This sort of society is economically unproductive as well as morally repugnant. Keynesian economists have always pointed out that unequal societies are more prone to underconsumption and hence harsher fluctuations of the economic cycle, because higher savings rates among the rich lower general effective demand. The tax system has become systematically less progressive, with particular bonanzas for wealthy individuals and the corporate sector, most notably oil companies. For the poorest in society, spending is skewed towards VAT-exempt and zero-rated goods and the informal economy. The result has been a severe deterioration in the growth of tax revenues and the ability of the government to afford its programmes without increasing taxes on those in the middle of the range.

. . . because it has followed bizarre economic doctrines.

The theoretical concepts that have been adduced in support of this policy direction are almost embarrassingly flimsy. The first building block has been the so-called 'rational economic man', a creature unknown to anyone who has spent half an hour studying human psychology. This imaginary creature values work negatively and leisure positively; he exists to maximise his own utility and has a clear concept of how this can be achieved given the alternatives available.

Supply and demand certainly interact in markets, but the elegant classical pattern of scissors crossing at an equilibrium point is not supported by the observations of real-world research. Indeed the marginal costs of production can fall when greater quantities are supplied, across a wide range of industries – so that both demand and supply curves actually end up sloping in the same direction.

In some ways the worst error is to believe in a general competitive equilibrium; that a free-market system will itself arrive at an unimprovable optimum point under its own steam. The assumptions required to reach this result in pure theory are extremely distant from the conditions pertaining in real markets, and involve bizarre abstractions like omniscience, a universal auctioneer, and the suspension of the passage of time. This is so extreme that competitive equilibrium theory tells us nothing about the dynamics of market economies.

Britain should adopt the concept of stakeholding.

Economics instead should be based on the realities of capitalist societies. This involves explaining phenomena such as the business cycle, corporate behaviour, and the way in which economic systems interlock with the social and political. The work of John Maynard Keynes is at the root of this alternative economic tradition.

The prescriptions of such an approach are very different from those of free-market theory. They involve an observation of what differentiates successful from unsuccessful forms of capitalism, a question that revolves around investment. This in turn is crucially linked to the organisation of the financial system, which in Britain should be reformed in order to lower the cost of capital and lengthen the payback period required of investment projects. It would involve wholesale restructuring under the aegis of a reformed Bank of England, to establish patterns of more committed ownership and more long-term lending.

A multiplicity of small reforms, ranging from the role of non-executive directors to the tax treatment of short-term capital gains, would help to push the system towards generating more committed, patient owners and bankers. A network of thriving regional and specialist banks could be encouraged, but that, in turn, is predicated on the way shareholding is regarded and whether it can be transformed into a stable relationship of commitment; and an end to the way in which a single loan can make a firm the prisoner of the bank, without the bank in turn having any responsibility or stake in the firm's success. The tax system should promote long-term shareholding and penalise speculation, and there should be other legal and financial obstacles to takeovers. Company accounts should become more transparent, and corporate governance reformed to reflect the various interests that converge on the firm – suppliers, workers and trade unions, banks, as well as shareholders and directors. This is the central idea of the stakeholder economy.

The choice now is not to return to the debased corporatism of the 1970s, but to develop a capitalism that is socially cohesive and economically productive. Part of the process of ideological self-definition is finding a word to describe the variety of capitalism one is championing, and stakeholding is an attractive choice. The idea has long been deployed in management literature and various firms have described themselves as stakeholder companies. The best types of overseas forms of capitalism have been achieved by striking the right balance between commitment and flexibility. Stakeholding is a neat way of encapsulating just that.

The welfare state should be restructured.

The success of a stakeholder economy is dependent on the creation of a stakeholder society. The welfare state is a potentially powerful means of expressing national social solidarity, but is progressively at risk as it becomes organised around means testing and creeping marketisation. Yet a welfare system worthy of the name depends upon a national consensus, and this is unlikely to develop around either a flimsy safety net or an overly restrictive and uniform system. Stopping the fragmentation of society, by imbuing the successful with a sense of common social citizenship, requires recognising their desires for self-advancement.

This means that equality of provision needs to be surrendered before the larger necessity of universal inclusion; that some measure of inequality has to be traded off against universality of membership. The state should offer supplementary social insurance systems in unemployment benefit and health which would take provision beyond the universal minimum, in a similar way to the pension system offered under the old SERPS. Catering for excellence in the public sphere also means recognising that while access to schools should be egalitarian, setting and streaming need to be introduced as key exams are approached to emphasise that academic excellence rather than social engineering is the objective of the state education system. Much better to have the middle class attending grammar schools and streamed comprehensives than opting out into elite-forming private schools.

Stakeholding means a written constitution too ...

Social and economic developments are obviously embedded in the character of the political system. Britain's lack of a written constitution, and the behaviour of its state, is a prime generator of the values and practices that are prevalent throughout society. For many years the pressure for constitutional reform has been directed at individual issues, whether it is a proportional voting system or a Bill of Rights, and the arguments used have been specific. Now they are coming together. As British ministers try to claim that European justice should have 'variable geometry' and the Scott Report and the BSE fiasco highlight the failures of secretive and unaccountable government, constitutional reform has been brought into the mainstream of peoples' concerns and made into the subject of political debate.

Co-operative, successful forms of capitalism do not arise spontaneously, but are the product of conscious design. To engage in such a reform programme government must have the democratic legitimacy – based on the principles of proportionality, inclusiveness and openness rather than winner-take-all triumphalism. In consequence, unions, companies and other private interests might just accept regulation and intervention as being more than just the imposition of a partisan state. Britain needs to acquire a republican attitude – not in terms of abolishing the monarchy, but rather in reclaiming the idea that government is a matter for the public, not a secretive elite.

The poverty of British constitutional arrangements is apparent when one considers their inability to enable effective mediating institutions between the central state and the citizen. An independent Bank of England under current arrangements would be a shadow of central banks elsewhere, most likely falling under the even more total control of London finance and the Conservative Party power network. A democratised Bank should reflect the political, regional and economic pluralism of a democratised polity. Diffused executive power in Britain, through institutions such as Training and Enterprise Councils, hospital trusts and quangos need not be a pernicious development, as it is when party bias, bookkeeping values and secrecy pervade their operations. A decentralisation of political power would foster a decentralisation of financial power.

The British state has no rules or guiding principles, and it is not surprising that this lacuna is found elsewhere in society – we are subjects and workers, not citizens and members of productive teams. Running a company is a reflection of running the nation – it is dominated by the executive, audit is weak, an extremely feeble form of shareholder democracy is the nominal final arbiter, and a narrow view is taken of wider responsibilities to stakeholders.

This is the prescriptive part of the argument that economic, political and social systems should work hand in hand. It is about reinventing the liberal, Whig tradition in British politics. Liberals at the turn of the century fragmented and variously allied with labour or 'gentlemanly capital', but at the end of the twentieth century there is the opportunity to regroup. John Monks, of the TUC, for example, and Iain Vallance of BT come from a bigger shared tradition than the camps of twentieth-century socialism or free-market purism. The dormant Whig tradition is one that can be productive and progressive.

... and engagement with foreign affairs

There are certainly consequences for foreign policy and international economic relations if Britain is to be changed in this fashion. The stable post-war order was underpinned by international co-operation around American leadership, within the stable exchange rate system of Bretton Woods. International financial flows are now so large as to be beyond the control of any government; in order to allow countries to make their own choices there has to be an international structure of control. Private capital does need freedom of movement, but within a framework of standardised environmental and employment rights, which would prevent a destructive auction of immiseration in the interests of unaccountable finance. The restoration of the European ideal – and the creation of a popular democratic consciousness within Europe – is necessary if sovereignty over economic life is to be reasserted. It also implies a commitment to international order, through resistance to aggression rather than the weak policies seen during the wars in the former Yugoslavia. Economic and political order are indivisible – sustaining a moral diplomatic order is a vital precondition of economic prosperity.

ORIGINALITY AND INFLUENCES

The State We're In is a work of synthesis, of my own ideas and those of others. Its objective is to draw the connection between the failure of corporate and political systems of governance and the effect that has had on the labour market and therefore British society generally. But I couldn't make any of those steps of the argument without having the facts, theory and research of hundreds of people at my disposal as support for what I am saying. When a tide of ideas is turning, the intellectual enquiry of people in many different areas links up in sometimes surprising ways. For example, sociologists of the family have become interested in what is happening in the labour market because of the effects of deregulation – the commitment to being a good parent in market societies is becoming more and more difficult. Equally, geographers have taken an increasing interest in my concerns about the centralisation of the British financial system, and its effect on regional economies. I have been very privileged in my years at the *Guardian* to have seen the products of a lot of different intellectual supply lines cross my desk, and to try to knit the strands together.

Keynes offers the outstanding alternative to free-market theory, and much of the underpinning of my economic analysis is due to him, augmented by the insights of modern game theory. His *General Theory* is the book that has had the largest single influence on my thought. In contrast to the unreal abstractions of free-market theory, Keynes attempted to account for the actual realities of capitalism. The focus of his attention was on the place where time, money and uncertainty – all crucial facts about life that classical theorists assumed away – intersect and have the greatest impact. This is the financial system, which is supposed to reconcile the conflicting interests of savers and investors, and therefore has a powerful influence on the most volatile element of the economy, namely investment. This is the origin of my concern with the financial system as a determinant of economic success. The Keynesian tradition is much richer and has more explicatory power than the bastardised versions which have reached textbooks, and the straw man created by its intellectual opponents. As interpreted by Axel Leijonhufvud and James Meade it is simply the economics of reality. In recent years, some American economists have pioneered a remarkable resurgence of these ideas, based on new insights, which have started to transform academic thinking. Part of my work in my columns has been to disseminate this thinking to a wider audience.

Professor John Kay wrote *The Foundations of Corporate Success*, which focused on company architecture as a determinant of company growth, a good year before I wrote *The State We're In*. David Goodhart wrote a good paper for the IPPR (The Institute of Public Policy Research) on German stakeholder capitalism, while David Marquand's important book, *The Unprincipled Society*, was a forerunner of some of the principal arguments. All three were important intellectual influences.

My ideal, in terms of the traditional spectrum between collectivism and individualism, is different, forming the third point of a conceptual triangle:

This is different from, say, a classic compromise position such as that found in Harold Macmillan's famous book *The Middle Way*, which struck a balance between the traditions of collectivism and individualism. He would compromise with socialists over nationalisation, arguing that a public good should be in public ownership. In contrast, I would dispute that public ownership is necessary on those grounds. If you can structure a firm well, you do not need public ownership. A stakeholder firm incorporates the social partnership and dialogue that you are trying to achieve. There may be technical reasons for a public monopoly to be publicly owned, but these are entirely technical.

I hope stakeholding can reawaken the liberal tradition and escape collectivism. For example, it should be possible to criticise British company law for being inadequate because it does not define the job of non-executive directors without being accused of promoting socialism. This is a liberal reformist statement, not, as it is interpreted by many businessmen, a death threat to modern British capitalism.

THE PROSPECTS FOR SUCCESS

In the past, only traumatic events like defeat in war, economic collapse or revolution have given a country a sufficient shock to adopt the wide ranging and radical change which Britain must choose now. Britain failed, for historical reasons, to renew itself, while America, France, the rest of Europe, and east Asia have performed this feat in the last 250 years. Over two centuries late, it is time for the spirit of 1789 to arrive in Britain and democratise government and society; the euthanasia of the rentier can be achieved without the guillotine.

Confronting an established order, even when it has demonstrably failed, is always a daunting process. Centuries of power and privilege have embedded the elite networks which underpin Conservatism and the rentier state. Consecutive years of power have entrenched Conservative ideological hegemony and spread its supporters throughout the media and business worlds, as well as the ramshackle maze that comprises the British state. Politicised influence is now entwined with the old networks. An entire failed system needs to be reshaped, requiring effort across the range of policy areas. It is entirely predictable that the resistance to a reform programme would be determined and hysterical, and election campaigns fought during such a confrontation will be brutal.

But Britain has the opportunity to achieve change and the prospects should be a cause for optimism. The country led the world in industrialisation and parliamentary democracy, and can lead in peaceful democratic renewal. The conditions now are positive. The failure of the Conservative project to produce the results it promised, on its own terms, let alone when subjected to a wider critique, strip away the economic reasons which may have generated support. The Conservative revolution is consuming its own; the monarchy and other traditional institutions are in decline, and the little platoons, such as voluntary organisations and even English counties, are being disbanded as the market and the centralising state apply their inexorable formulae. The Conservative Party has been in internal crisis, with Britain's role in Europe serving as a focus for deeper incoherence.

Under the leadership of Tony Blair, the Labour Party has attempted to build a wider consensus around the progressive pole in British politics, although perhaps at the cost of a radical reforming vision. The next election may mark the start of the programme, although the mandate for a full radical reform might not take shape until after a first term of more cautious progress. Blair is trying to convey the idea that the Labour party is travelling in an individualist direction while espousing collective values, but only occasionally does he travel into a new ideological space, by talking about political reform and the enabling state as the handmaiden of economic an social change. He is by no means a consistent follower of the entire agenda, and has made it known that his espousal of stakeholding is not the same as buying the programme of *The State We're In*. On the other hand, he uses the same language and concepts, and setting the agenda is the first battle in politics.

Some of the finest academic economists in Britain – John Kay, Steve Nickell and Richard Layard – are trying to elaborate a theoretical programme of research which have shared preoccupations with these lines of thought, linking the structure of finance and corporate government to investment and growth. Extraordinarily, given its importance to the way the world works, this is a research area that economics has neglected over the last twenty years. In the United States, some Democrats have been considering radical change to corporate governance and the tax system to promote responsibility from private firms.

The concepts and preoccupations outlined in *The State*

We're In, and the growing body of writing and research on its themes, are reaching a wider and wider audience. My hope is that it can contribute to the change it advocates, and I am very optimistic about success. Stakeholding is finding an increasingly positive reception among industrial and even financial audiences. Whether it is private seminars in the City of London or strategy meetings of the police force, the ideas are debated – and more sympathetically than ever seemed likely on publication. It may be written from the centre-left tradition, but immense numbers of the British immediately understand its themes – and relate to it. Even the right have to concede that it is passing the market test.

On balance, it is probable that we will get the political change that is necessary. Economic restructuring can happen. Britain could become the dynamic and socially cohesive place which its population yearns to live in – but it will take nerve and grit. The rewards could be immense.

CONTRIBUTORS

DAVID MARQUAND is Principal of Mansfield College, Oxford.

ALBERT HIRSCHMAN is Professor of Social Science Emeritus at the Institute for Advanced Study, Princeton.

ROBERT SKIDELSKY is Professor of Political Economy at the University of Warwick and Chairman of the Social Market Foundation.

PETER CLARKE is Professor of Modern British History at the University of Cambridge and Fellow of St John's College, Cambridge.

ROBERT TAYLOR is Employment Editor of the *Financial Times*.

JOSE HARRIS is Professor of Modern History at the University of Oxford and Fellow of St Catherine's College, Oxford.

CHRIS PIERSON is Professor of Politics at the University of Nottingham.

RAYMOND PLANT is Master of St Catherine's College, Oxford.

GEOFF MULGAN is Director of Demos.

JIM BULPITT is Professor of Politics at the University of Warwick.

ANTHONY SELDON is Founding Director of the Institute of Contemporary British History.

WILL HUTTON is Editor of the *Observer*.

NOTES

1. MORALISTS AND HEDONISTS

1 I am grateful to the Leverhulme Trust for supporting the research on which this essay is based.

2 J. M. Keynes, *The General Theory of Employment, Interest and Money* (Macmillan & Co., 1936, reprinted 1954), pp. 383–4.

3 Antonio Gramsci, *Selections from the Prison Notebooks* (Lawrence & Wishart, 1971), pp. 57–8.

4 I first discovered the term in David Heald, *Public Expenditure* (Robertson, 1983).

5 Cherwell to Churchill, 18 March 1952, PREM 11/37. Public Record Office.

6 For the ministers, see Edmund Dell, *A Hard Pounding, Politics and Economic Crisis 1974–76* (Oxford University Press, 1991); for the officials, see Leo Pliatzky, *Getting and Spending: Public Expenditure, Employment and Inflation* (Basil Blackwell, 1984).

7 A seminal exposition of these varieties is Michel Albert, *Capitalism against Capitalism* (Whurr Publishers, 1993).

8 *Report on Wealth Creation and Social Cohesion in a free society* [The Dahrendorf Report], The Commission on Wealth Creation and Social Cohesion (July, 1995); *Growth, Competitiveness, Employment, Commission of the European Communities*, COM (93) 700 (December, 1993).

9 Francis Fukuyama, *Trust: The Social Virtues and the Creation of Prosperity* (Hamish Hamilton, 1995); Ernest Gellner, *Conditions of Liberty: Civil Society and Its Rivals* (Hamish Hamilton, 1994); Ralf Dahrendorf, *The Modern Social Conflict: an essay on the politics of liberty* (Weidenfeld and Nicolson, 1988); Amitai Etzioni, *The Spirit of Community: Rights, Responsibilities and the Communitarian Agenda* (Fontana Press, 1995).

10 David Willetts, *Civic Conservatism* (Social Market Foundation, 1994); Will Hutton, *The State We're In* (Jonathan Cape, 1995); The Dahrendorf Report, *op. cit.*

11 John Gray, *The Undoing of Conservatism* (Social Market Foundation, 1994), p. 22.

12 Robert Skidelsky, 'Thatcher's Unfinished Business', *Prospect* (January, 1996), pp. 38–45.

13 J. M. Keynes, 'The End of Laissez-Faire', in John Maynard Keynes, *Essays in Persuasion* (W. W. Norton & Company, 1963 edition), p. 312.

14 Susan Howson and Donald Moggridge (eds.), *The Collected Papers of James Meade*, vol. IV, *The Cabinet Office Diary 1944–46* (Unwin Hyman, 1990), p. 115.

15 Quoted in D. A. Riesman, 'Introduction', in David Riesman (ed.) *Theories of the Mixed Economy*, vol. I, R. H. Tawney, *Equality* (William Pickering, 1994), p. xix.

16 T. H. Marshall, *Citizenship and Social Class and other essays* (Cambridge University Press, 1950).

17 Albert O. Hirschman, *The Rhetoric of Reaction: Perversity, Futility, Jeopardy* (Harvard University Press, 1991), pp. 154–9.

18 Riesman, *Theories of the Mixed Economy*, vol. IV; Harold Macmillan, *The Middle Way* (Macmillan & Co., 1938), p. 109.

19 Reisman, *Theories of the Mixed Economy*, vol. V, E. F. M. Durbin, *The Politics of Democratic Socialism* (William Pickering, 1994), p. 361.

20 For a stimulating discussion of this aspect of Hayek's doctrine, see Andrew Gamble, 'Hayek and the Left', *The Political Quarterly* (January–March, 1996).

21 For selected examples of the 'overload' thesis, see Anthony King, 'Overload: Problems of Governing in the 1970s', *Political Studies*, vol. 27 (1979), pp. 351–70; Richard Rose and Guy Peters, *Can Government Go Bankrupt?* (Macmillan, 1979); Samuel Brittan, *The Economic Consequences of Democracy* (Temple Smith, 1977); and Gordon Tullock, *The Vote Motive*, Hobart Paperback 9 (Institute of Economic Affairs, 1979).

22 For whom, see Albert O. Hirschman, *The Passions and the Interests: Political Arguments for Capitalism before Its Triumph* (Princeton University Press, 1977). For the social and cultural context in which they flourished, see Harold Perkin, *The Origins of Modern English Society 1780–1880* (Routledge and Kegan Paul, 1981), pp. 38–44.

23 J. G. A. Pocock, *The Machiavellian Moment: Florentine Political Thought and the Atlantic Republican Tradition* (Princeton University Press, 1975), pp. 486–7.

24 David Howell, *Blind Victory, a study in income, wealth and power* (Hamish Hamilton, 1986), p. 4.

25 Alan S. Milward, *The European Rescue of the Nation-State* (Routledge, 1992).

26 A. V. Dicey, *Lectures on the Relation Between Law and Opinion*

in England during the Nineteenth Century (Macmillan, reprinted 1963); W. H. Greenleaf, *The British Political Tradition*, vol. II (Methuen, 1983); Robert Skidelsky, *The World After Communism: A Polemic For Our Times* (Macmillan, 1995); Albert O. Hirschman, *Shifting Involvements: Private Interest and Public Action* (Martin Robertson, 1982).

27 Quoted in Nicholas Timmins, *The Five Giants: a biography of the welfare state* (Fontana Press, 1996), p. 58.

28 Lord Beveridge, *Full Employment in a Free Society*, Second Edition (George Allen and Unwin, 1960), p. 258.

29 For the first, see James Hinton, *Shop Floor Citizens: Engineering Democracy in 1940s Britain* (Edward Elgar, 1994); for the second, see *Economic Survey for 1947* (HMSO, Cmd. 7046).

30 Keith Middlemas, *Power, Competition and the State*, vol. I, *Britain in Search of Balance, 1940–61* (Macmillan, 1986), p. 116.

31 For the clerisy, see Stefan Collini, *Public Moralists, Political Thought and Intellectual Life in Britain 1850–1930* (Clarendon Press, 1991). For the attack on the professional ethic, see Harold Perkin, *The Rise of Professional Society: England Since 1880* (Routledge, 1989), pp. 472–519.

32 For this technocratic managerialism, see Samuel H. Beer, *Britain Against Itself, The Political Contradictions of Collectivism* (Faber and Faber, 1982), pp. 120–26.

33 David Riesman, *Theories of the Mixed Economy*, vol. VII, Anthony Crosland, *The Future of Socialism* (William Pickering, 1994), pp. 521–4.

34 Shirley Letwin, *The Anatomy of Thatcherism* (Fontana Press, 1992), p. 33.

35 The phrase was Mrs Thatcher's. Quoted in Peter Jenkins, *Mrs Thatcher's Revolution: The Ending of the Socialist Era* (Jonathan Cape, 1987), p. 66.

36 Kenneth Minogue, 'The Emergence of the New Right' in Robert Skidelsky (ed.), *Thatcherism* (Chatto and Windus, 1988), pp. 125–42.

37 Margaret Thatcher, *The Path to Power* (HarperCollins, 1995), p. 565.

3. THE FALL OF KEYNESIANISM

1 In his speech to the Labour Party conference, Callaghan said that the option of 'spending our way out of recession no longer existed' and had worked in the past only by 'injecting bigger and bigger doses of inflation into the economy'. Quoted in Wyn Grant and Shiv Nath, *Economic Policymaking* (Blackwell, 1984), p. 144. In his Mais Lecture of 1984, Nigel Lawson said that 'the conquest of inflation . . . should . . .

be the objective of macroeconomic policy': see 'The British Experiment', Fifth Mais Lecture, City University Business School (1984). In the White Paper, *Employment: The Challenge for the Nation, 1985* (HMSO, Cmnd. 9474), the government's responsibility is specified as controlling inflation to provide a stable framework for economic activity; deregulation and other improvements to the labour market; and employment aid for particular groups. For a discussion, see Jim Tomlinson, *Employment Policy: The Crucial Years 1939–1955* (Clarendon Press, 1987), pp. 162–5.

2 Don Patinkin wrote that 'Friedman's analytical framework is Keynesian' in 'Friedman on the Quantity Theory and Keynesian Economics' in Robert J. Gordon (ed.), *Milton Friedman's Monetary Framework* (University of Chicago Press, 1974), p. 173.

3 On 'New Keynesian' economics, see N. G. Mankiw and D. Romer (eds), *New Keynesian Economics* (MIT, 1991).

4 Albert O. Hirschman, *The Rhetoric of Reaction*.

5 Donald N. McCloskey, 'The Literary Character of Economics', *Daedalus*, 113 (1984).

6 J. M. Keynes, *The General Theory of Employment, Interest and Money*, pp. 383–4. Reference is to the edition published in *The Collected Writings of John Maynard Keynes* [henceforth *JMK*], 30 vols (Macmillan for the Royal Economic Society, 1971–89), vol. VII.

7 M. Friedman, 'A Monetarist Reflects', *Economist* (4 June 1983).

8 H. G. Johnson, 'Keynes and British Economics', in Milo Keynes (ed.), *Essays on John Maynard Keynes* (Cambridge University Press, 1975), p. 109ff.

9 F. A. Hayek, 'The Austrian Critique', *Economist* (11 June 1983).

10 J. Viner, 'Mr. Keynes on the Causes of Unemployment', *Quarterly Journal of Economics*, 51 (November, 1936).

11 T. W. Hutchison, *Keynes versus the 'Keynesians'*, Hobart Paperback (Institute of Economic Affairs, 1977).

12 J. R. Hicks, 'Mr. Keynes and the "Classics": A Suggested Interpretation', *Econometrica* (5 April 1937).

13 See T. W. Hutchison, *Economics and Economic Policy in Britain 1946–1966* (George Allen & Unwin, 1968), pp. 121–2.

14 See J. M. Buchanan, John Burton and R. E. Wagner, *The Economic Consequences of Mr Keynes*, Hobart Paper 78 (Institute of Economic Affairs, 1978).

15 James Macmillan, *Daily Express* (24 May 1966), quoted in A. P. Thirlwall, *Nicholas Kaldor* (Wheatsheaf, 1987).

16 J. M. Keynes to R. F. Harrod (4 July 1938); see *JMK*, vol. XIV, p. 296.

17 Alan Walters, 'Milton Friedman', in John Eatwell, Murray Milgate, Peter Newman (eds.), *New Palgrave Dictionary of Economics* (Macmillan, 1987), 2, p. 425.

18 Angus Maddison, *Dynamic Forces in Capitalist Development* (Oxford University Press, 1991), p. 168.

19 Herbert Stein, *The Fiscal Revolution in America* (University of Chicago Press, 1969), p. 171.

20 Stein, *The Fiscal Revolution*, p. 172.

21 See Peter A. Hall (ed.), *The Political Power of Economic Ideas: Keynesianism Across Nations* (Princeton University Press, 1989), pp. 93, 190, 219.

22 Elizabeth Durbin, *New Jerusalems: The Labour Party and the Economics of Democratic Socialism* (Routledge & Keegan Paul, 1985), p. 159.

23 Jim Tomlinson, *Employment Policy*, p. 102.

24 See the table on p. 34 in Buchanan, Burton and Wagner, *op. cit.*

25 Samuel Brittan in *What is Left of Keynes?* (Social Market Foundation, 1994), p. 17.

26 Robert Rhodes James, *Anthony Eden* (Weidenfeld & Nicolson, 1986), pp. 415–6.

27 Quoted in Alistair Horne, *Macmillan 1957–1986* (Papermac, 1989), p. 76.

28 For a good account of how the neo-classical synthesis came about, see Axel Leijonhufvud, *Keynes and the Classics*, Occasional Paper 30 (Institute of Economic Affairs, 1969).

29 A point forcefully made by Alan Coddington in his *Keynesian Economics: The Search for First Principles* (Allen & Unwin, 1983), pp. 42–3.

30 Friedman's December 1967 Presidential address to the American Economic Association was published as 'The Role of Monetary Policy', *American Economic Review* (March, 1988).

31 See the entry on Abba Lerner by Tibor Scitovsky in the *New Palgrave Dictionary of Economics* (Macmillan, 1987), 3, p. 168.

32 David Marquand, *The Unprincipled Society* (Jonathan Cape, 1988), ch. 2.

33 'Economic Measures', Labour Party Talking Points Nos. 15/16, 1966, p. 15, quoted by Wilfred Beckerman, *The Labour Government's Economic Record 1964–1970* (Duckworth, 1972), p. 44.

34 For the debate on the 'causes of Britain's slow growth rate' see Michael Stewart, *The Jekyll and Hyde Years: Politics and Economic Policy since 1964* (Dent, 1977), pp. 43–5; for a recent, technical discussion see N. F. R. Crafts, 'Economic Growth', in N. F. R. Crafts and

Nicholas Woodward (eds.), *The British Economy since 1945* (Clarendon Press, 1991).

35 Sir Donald MacDougall, *Don and Mandarin: Memoirs of an Economist* (John Murray, 1987), p. 189.

36 For the consequences of the Bank's new policy see Tim Congdon, *Reflections on Monetarism* (Edward Elgar, 1992), pp. 14–17.

37 Robert Bacon and Walter Eltis, *Britain's Economic Problem: Too Few Producers* (Macmillan, 1978), p. 118.

38 Milton Friedman, 'Keynes's Political Legacy' in *Keynes's 'General Theory': Fifty Years On*, Hobart Paperback 24 (Institute of Economic Affairs, 1986), pp. 52–3.

39 Quoted in A. Malabre Jr, *Lost Prophets* (Harvard Business School Press, 1994), p. 77.

40 For an extensive discussion, see Robert Skidelsky, 'The Decline of Keynesian Politics', in Colin Crouch (ed.), *State and Economy in Contemporary Capitalism* (Croom Helm, 1979).

4. THE KEYNESIAN CONSENSUS

1 I have dealt with this debate in *The Keynesian Revolution in the Making, 1924–36* (Clarendon Press, 1988) and 'The Treasury's analytical model of the British economy between the Wars', in Barry Supple and Mary Furner (eds.), *The State and Economic Knowledge* (Cambridge University Press, 1990), pp. 171–207. I am grateful to Stefan Collini, John Thompson and Maria Tippett, as well as to members of the Sheffield conference, for their criticism of an earlier draft.

2 Citations from the entry by Hal R. Varian, *The New Palgrave*, sub 'microeconomics'.

3 *JMK*, vol. VII, p. 85.

4 *JMK*, vol. VII, p.xxxii.

5 *JMK*, vol. XXI, pp. 387, 390 ('How to avoid a slump', Jan. 1937).

6 For an expansion of the points in this and the previous paragraph, see my essay, 'The historical Keynes and the history of Keynesianism', in T. C. W. Blanning and D. N. Cannadine (eds.), *History and Biography: essays presented to Derek Beales* (Cambridge University Press, 1995). In both that and the present essay, I lean on the fine studies of policy-making by Alec Cairncross, *Years of Recovery: British economic policy, 1945–51* (Methuen, 1985); Alan Booth, *British Economic Policy, 1931–49: Was There a Keynesian Revolution?* (Harvester Wheatsheaf, 1989); Susan Howson, *British Monetary Policy, 1945–51* (Clarendon Press, 1993).

7 'Social Insurance and Allied Services': Report by Sir William Beveridge, Cmd 6404 (November, 1942), par. 8.

8 Cf. Albert O. Hirschman, *The Rhetoric of Reaction*, p. 151.

9 Cmd 6404, par. 441.

10 Cmd 6404, par. 440.

11 'Employment Policy', Cmd 6527 (May, 1944), foreword.

12 See Nigel Lawson's introduction to Walter Eltis and Peter Sinclair (eds.), *Keynes and Economic Policy* (Macmillan, in association with the National Economic Development Office, 1988), pp. xv-xvi; also quotations from pars. 49 and 77.

13 Cmd 6527, par. 66.

14 *JMK*, vol XXVII, pp. 377-9 (Keynes to Sir Alan Barlow, 15 June 1944).

15 Cmd 6527, foreword.

16 *Ibid*, par. 40.

17 *Ibid*, par. 68.

18 *Ibid*, par. 17. Correlli Barnett has tendentiously glossed this episode as a triumph for the 'glib confidence' of 'New Jerusalemism'; see *The Audit of War* (Macmillan 1986), pp. 257-63.

19 John Parker, *Labour Marches On* (Penguin, 1947), p. 55.

20 James Edward Meade, *Planning and the Price Mechanism: the liberal-socialist solution* (George Allen & Unwin, 1948), p. v.

21 Cairncross, *Years of Recovery*, pp. 308-9.

22 Cmd 6527, par. 41.

23 *Ibid*, par. 80.

24 *Ibid*, par. 87.

25 Hirschman, *Rhetoric of Reaction*, pp. 110ff.

26 Hayek, *Road to Serfdom* (G. Routledge & Sons, 1944), p. 50.

27 *Ibid*, pp. 151-2.

28 *Ibid*, p. 148.

29 See Quintin Hogg, *The Case for Conservatism* (Penguin, 1947), pp. 220-1.

30 Hayek, *Road to Serfdom*, p. 31.

31 *JMK*, vol XXVII, pp. 386-7 (Keynes to Hayek, 28 June 1944).

32 Hayek, *Road to Serfdom*, p. 154.

33 *Ibid*, p. 154.

34 *Ibid*, pp. 151-2.

35 Cmd 6527, par. 80.

36 Hogg, *Case for Conservatism*, pp. 220-1.

37 Parker, *Labour Marches On*, p. 56.

38 Hogg, *Case for Conservatism*, pp. 219, 223-4.

39 John Strachey, 'Tasks and achievements of British Labour', in R. H. S. Crossman (ed.), *New Fabian Essays* (Dent, 1970), pp. 189-90.

40 *JMK*, vol. VII, p. 378.

41 Austen Albu, 'The organisation of industry', in Crossman (ed.), *New Fabian Essays*, p. 127.

42 *JMK*, vol. VII, p. 378.

43 Sir Stafford Cripps, quoted in Edward Bridges, *The Treasury* (Oxford University Press, 1966), p. 93.

44 *JMK*, vol VII, p. 376.

45 See pp. 409–14 and the authoritative treatment in Howson, *British Monetary Policy*, pp. 291–2, 305–7.

46 C. A. R. Crosland, 'The transition from capitalism', in Crossman (ed.), *New Fabian Essays*, pp. 39–40.

47 Parker, *Labour Marches On*, p. 56; cf Howson, *British Monetary Policy* (Clarendon Press, 1993), pp. 25, 50, 120, 146–7.

48 Meade, *Planning and the Price Mechanism* (1948), p. 12.; cf Howson, *British Monetary Policy*, p. 163.

49 I have substantiated this point in 'The historical Keynes and the history of Keynesianism', in T. C. W. Blanning and D. N. Cannadine (eds.), *History and Biography: essays presented to Derek Beales*.

50 Strachey, 'Tasks and achievements of British Labour', Crossman (ed.), *New Fabian Essays*, p. 185.

51 Crosland, 'The transition from capitalism', in Crossman (ed.), *New Fabian Essays*, pp. 38, 41.

52 Strachey, 'Tasks and achievements of British Labour', in Crossman (ed.), *New Fabian Essays*, p. 196.

53 *Ibid.*, p. 197.

54 Harold Macmillan, 'The Middle Way – 20 Years After', in *The Middle Way* (Macmillan, 1966), p. xxv.

55 Samuel Brittan, *The Treasury under the Tories* (Penguin, 1964), p. 162.

56 A. W. Phillips, 'The relation between unemployment and the rate of change of money wages in the United Kingdom, 1861–1957', *Economica*, vol. xxv (1958).

57 Milton Friedman, 'The role of monetary policy', in *The Optimum Quantity of Money* (Macmillan, 1969), p. 104.

58 Hirschman, *Rhetoric of Reaction*, pp. 45, 74.

59 Friedman, *Optimum Quantity of Money*, p. 109.

60 Sir Keith Joseph, speech at Preston, *The Times* (6 September 1974).

61 Nigel Lawson, *The View from No.11. Memoirs of a Tory Radical* (Bantam, 1992), pp. 414–15.

62 Friedman, *Optimum Quantity of Money*, p. 107.

63 Cmd 6527, par. 80.

5. INDUSTRIAL RELATIONS

1 A. Flanders in *Management and Unions* (Faber and Faber, 1975), p. 40.

2 O. Kahn-Freund, 'Legal Framework', in A. Flanders and H. A.

Clegg (eds.), *The System of Industrial Relations in Great Britain* (Oxford University Press, 1956), p. 44.

3 TUC evidence to the Donovan Royal Commission 1966, p. 69.

4 R. Hyman in P. Edwards (ed.), *Industrial Relations: Theory and Practice in Britain* (Blackwell, 1995), p. 31.

5 A. Fox, *History and Heritage: The Social Origins of the British Industrial Relations System* (Allen and Unwin, 1985), p. 388.

6 H. M. D. Parker, *Manpower: A Study of War-Time Policy and Administration* (HMSO, 1957), p. 476.

7 B. Turner, *Citizenship and Capitalism*, ATU (1986), p. 69.

8 D. King, *Actively Seeking Work?* (University of Chicago Press, 1995), p. 115.

9 P. Davies and M. Freedland, *Labour Legislation and Public Policy* (Clarendon Press, 1993), p. 647. This admirable book provides a lengthy analysis of the tensions between *laissez-faire* collectivism, regulated voluntarism and the radical individualistic approach developed by Margaret Thatcher and John Major. Also see Robert Taylor, *The Trade Union Question in British Politics since 1945* (Blackwell, 1993) and David Marquand, *The Unprincipled Society* (Jonathan Cape, 1988).

10 J. Hinton, *Shop Floor Citizens: Engineering in 1940s Britain* (Edward Elgar, 1994), pp. 203–4.

11 F. Zweig, *The British Worker* (Pelican, 1952), p. 180.

12 *Economic Consequences of Full Employment* (HMSO, Cmnd 1417, 1957), p. 17.

13 Labour party conference report (1963), p. 78

14 G. Goodman, *The Awkward Warrior* (Davis Poynter, 1979), p. 369.

15 *Ibid.*, p. 382.

16 J. Goldthorpe *et al*, *The Affluent Worker*, Vol III (Cambridge University Press, 1969), p. 215.

17 Donovan Royal Commission, (HMSO, Cmnd 3623, 1968), p. 36.

18 Ministry of Labour evidence to the Donovan Commission, 1965, p. 2.

19 *In Place of Strife* (HMSO, June 1969), p. 23.

20 See W. McCarthy (ed.), *Legal Intervention in Industrial Relations* (Blackwell, 1992), p. 213.

21 *Ibid.*, p. 56.

22 E. Hobsbawm, *The Forward March of Labour Halted?* (Verso, 1981), p. 14.

23 See W. Brown (ed.), *Changing Contours of British Industrial Relations* (Blackwell, 1981), p. 66.

24 Hansard Parliamentary Debates, vol. 974 (17 December 1979) cc 59–61

25 F. A. Hayek, *The Constitution of Liberty* (Routledge and Kegan Paul, 1960), p. 276.

26 F. A. Hayek, *1980's Unemployment and The Unions*, (Institute of Economic Affairs, 1980), p. 52.

27 *People, Jobs and Opportunity* (HMSO, Cmnd 1810, February 1992), p. 11.

6. CONTRACT AND CITIZENSHIP SINCE 1945

1 This paper is part of a wider study on the intellectual history of modern social policy, supported by the British Academy and the Nuffield Foundation. A slightly different version has appeared in French in *La revue française de Science Politique*, 45, 4 (Août 1995).

2 H.C. Deb. (1945–6), vol. 418, cols. 1895–6; (1947–8), vol. 443, cols. 31–2, 419; vol. 444, col. 1693.

3 M. Reddin, 'Universality versus Selectivity', in William A. Robson and Bernard Crick (eds.), *The Future of the Social Services* (London, 1970), pp. 23–35.

4 Peter Baldwin, *The Politics of Social Solidarity* (Cambridge, 1990), p. 51.

5 B. Webb, *Our Partnership* (London, 1948), pp. 373–4; *Royal Commission on Unemployment Insurance, minutes of evidence* (HMSO, 1932), evidence of Mrs. Sidney Webb; Fabian Society MSS, 'Royal Commission on Unemployment Insurance', memorandum by Mrs. Sidney Webb, 30 Nov. 1931.

6 Sidney Webb, 'Social Movements', in *Cambridge Modern History, vol. 12: The Latest Age* (Cambridge, 1910), pp. 730–65; H. H. Asquith Papers, vol. 78, f.169, summary of reports of Royal Commission on the Poor Laws, 1909; S. and B. Webb, *English Poor Law History: Part II: The Last Hundred Years*, (Longmans, 1929) vol. II, pp. 995–6.

7 Parliamentary debates, H.C. Deb. (1933–4), vol. 283, cols. 1073f. Ironically, Labour opposition to national insurance and demand for a non-contractual, non-means-tested, unemployment benefit was led by Arthur Greenwood, who ten years later as Minister of Reconstruction sponsored and promoted the Beveridge report.

8 Keir Hardie, *John Bull and His Unemployed Problem: A Plain Statement on the Law of England as it Affects the Unemployed* (ILP, 1905). A rather similar position had been taken up by Sidney Webb in his earliest writings on the Poor Law, before his conversion to its abolition; see Sidney Webb, 'The Reform of the Poor Law', *Contemporary Review*, 58 (1890), pp. 95–120.

9 Tony Cutler, Karel Williams and John Williams, *Keynes, Beveridge and Beyond* (Routledge, 1986), pp. 9–19.

10 *Social Insurance and Allied Services*, Cmnd. 6404, (1942), pp. 249–276.

11 James W. Nisbet, *Britain and Social Security. An Appraisal of the Beveridge Plan* (Society of Individualists, 1943); Sir Arnold Gridley, *Deceiving the People* (Society of Individualists, 1943); C. Clive Saxton, *Beveridge Report Criticised* (G.G. Harrap & Co, 1943).

12 Nuffield College Reconstruction Survey, local reports (1942–3), *passim.*

13 M. A. Crowther, 'The Later Years of the Workhouse 1890–1929', in Pat Thane (ed.) *The Origins of British Social Policy* (Croom Helm, 1978), pp. 36–55; P. A. Ryan, 'Popularism 1894–1930' in Thane (ed.) *Origins*, pp. 56–83.

14 H.C. Deb. (1940), vol. 357, col. 2305.

15 On the extent of this intellectual migration, see Stephen Brooke, *Labour's War: The Labour Party During the Second World War* (Oxford University Press, 1992), pp. 162–7.

16 Dorothy Sheridan (ed.) *Wartime Women: An Anthology of Women's Wartime Writing for Mass-Observation 1937–45* (Heinemann, 1990), pp. 215–226.

17 Susan Pederson, *Family, Dependence, and the Origins of the Welfare State: Britain and France 1914–1945* (Cambridge University Press, 1993), pp. 5–6; R. M. Titmuss, 'War and Social Policy' in *Essays on the Welfare State*, (Allen and Unwin, 1963), pp. 75–87.

18 This issue is extensively discussed in Kristy Parker, 'Women M.P.s, Feminism and Domestic Policy in the Second World War', (Oxford D.Phil. thesis, 1995), chaps 4–5.

19 PRO, CAB 87/76, 'Basic Problems of Social Security with Heads of a Scheme', 11 Dec. 1941.

20 *Social Insurance and Allied Services. Memoranda from the Organisations*, (HMSO, 1942) Paper 7; London Women's Parliament, reports, (London Women's Parliament, 1941–3); Lady Juliet Rhys Williams, *Something to Look Forward To* (Macdonald, 1943).

21 H.C. Deb. (1933–4), vol. 283, col. 1313.

22 Nuffield College Reconstruction Survey, local reports (1942–3). In nineteen out of the twenty seven regions covered by the survey, the limited coverage of health insurance was mentioned as the major area of popular dissatisfaction with the social services.

23 PRO, CAB 87/79, 'Trades Union Congress. Replies to Questions Submitted by Sir William Beveridge', 3 Apr. 1942.

24 Harold Laski, *A Grammar of Politics* (Allen and Unwin, 1925), pp. 520–3.

25 *Social Insurance and Allied Services*, p. 11; Nuffield College Reconstruction Survey, *passim*.

26 H.C. Deb. (1945–6), vol. 418, cols. 1733–1993.

27 For Beveridge's dismissal of such proposals as not practical politics and inseparable from means-tests, see PRO, CAB 87/76, minutes of Social Insurance committee, 15 Oct. 1941.

28 The vulnerability of tax-financed benefits is underlined by the fact that Beveridge's initial proposals for family allowances were far more savagely pruned down in response to Treasury pressure than any of his other, contribution-based, proposals.

29 Hubert Henderson papers, memorandum on 'The Beveridge Proposals', J. M. Keynes, 20 July 1942.

30 PRO, T.230/100, J. E. M. Meade to D. N. Chester, 15 June 1941.

31 Beveridge Papers, VIII 29, 'Internal Measures for the Prevention of General Unemployment' (n.d.), and PRO, CAB 87/78, Social Insurance committee, minutes, 24 June 1942.

32 J. M. Keynes, *How to Pay for the War* (Macmillan, 1940).

33 Beveridge Papers, IXa, 37(1), J. M. Keynes to Beveridge, 17 March 1942.

34 Geoffrey Finlayson's *Citizen, State, and Social Welfare in Britain 1830–1990* (Oxford University Press, 1994) touches upon debates of the 1940s, but leaves much to be further explored.

35 H.C. Deb. (1945–6), vol. 418, col. 1896.

36 This is an aspect of wartime and post-war social reconstruction that deserves closer discussion than I have been able to give it here. It is arguable that the surprising lack of concern with vertical redistribution that characterises social policy debates of the period was linked to the fact that many people thought that such redistribution was happening anyway. Certainly much of Beveridge's perception of post-war problems was coloured by his belief that there would never be a return to the kind of pre- and post-tax income differentials that had prevailed before the war.

37 Quentin Skinner, paper on 'Classical' and 'Gothic' perceptions of civic virtue, Keble College, May 1993. See also Quentin Skinner, 'The republican ideal of political liberty', in Gisela Bock, Quentin Skinner and Maurizio Viroli, *Machiavelli and Republicanism* (Cambridge University Press, 1990), pp. 293–309; and David Marquand, 'Civic republicans and liberal individualists: the case of Britain', *Arch, europ. sociol.*, XXXII (1991) pp. 329–44.

38 Rodney Lowe, *Adjusting to Democracy: the Role of the Ministry of Labour in British Politics 1916–39* (Oxford University Press, 1986).

39 I have discussed this more extensively in 'Political Thought and the Welfare State 1870–1940: an Intellectual Framework for British

Social Policy', *Past and Present*, 135 (May, 1992), pp. 116–141.

40 W. H. Beveridge, *Unemployment. A Problem of Industry* (Longmans, 1930), pp. 294, 305, 317–23, 373–400.

41 Beveridge's numerous references to the 'British race' should not be read as having ethnically exclusive overtones: it meant, rather, those fortunate enough to share in a common inheritance of constitutional freedoms.

42 See, for example, PRO, T230/100, R. C. Tress to D. N. Chester on 'The Methods of Finance of Social Insurance', (n.d.); H.C. Deb. (1945–6), vol. 418, cols. 1733–6. On 'Gothic democracy' as a key element in wartime political thought see Angus Calder, *The Myth of the Blitz* (Pimlico, 1991), esp. chaps 5 and 9.

43 Barbara Wootton, 'Before and After Beveridge', *Political Quarterly*, xiv, 4 (Oct–Dec., 1943), pp. 361–2.

44 Jose Harris, 'Did British Workers want the Welfare State?', in J. M. Winter (ed.) *The Working Class in Modern British History* (Cambridge University Press, 1983), pp. 200–14; Jose Harris, 'War and Social History: Britain and the Home Front during the Second World War', *Contemporary European History*, i, 1 (1992) pp. 31–2.

45 Beveridge Papers, IXa 15, Employment investigation, report of a meeting with the TUC, 9 Feb 1944.

46 Royal Commission on Unemployment Insurance, Paper No. 100, para. 45–7, pp. 1327–8 (HMSO, 1932).

47 The belief that compulsory training schemes had become politically unacceptable lay behind the Cabinet decision in December 1945 not to adopt Beveridge's proposal that the unemployed should be entitled to benefit for an indefinite period, subject to submission to compulsory re-training (PRO, CAB 134/697, 'Period of Unemployment Benefit in Relation to Training Schemes', 17 Nov 1945).

48 Richard Titmuss papers, 'Beveridge 1942 and 1954', paper in R. M. T.'s ms., 1954.

7. SOCIAL POLICY

1 See, for example, R. Mishra, *The Welfare State in Crisis* (Wheatsheaf Books, 1984).

2 P. Gregg, *The Welfare State* (Harrap, 1967).

3 W. Beveridge, *Social Insurance and Allied Services* (HMSO, 1942), p. 17.

4 C. Barnett, *The Audit of War* (Macmillan, 1986).

5 J. Dryzek and R. Goodin, 'Risk-Sharing and Social Justice', *British Journal of Political Science*, 16 (1) (1986), pp. 1–34; P. Thane, *Foundations of the Welfare State* (Longman, 1982).

6 R. Lowe, *The Welfare State in Britain Since 1945* (Macmillan, 1993), p. 130.

7 W. Beveridge, *Social Insurance and Allied Services*, p. 7.

8 P. Addison, *The Road to 1945* (Cape, 1975), p. 213.

9 W. Beveridge, *Social Insurance and Allied Services*, p. 122.

10 J. Hills, *The Future of Welfare* (Joseph Rowntree Foundation, 1993), p. 41.

11 J. Hills, *The Future of Welfare*, pp. 51–2; *Social Justice* (Institute for Public Policy Research, 1994).

12 Lowe, *The Welfare State in Britain*, pp. 134–5

13 D. Kavanagh, *Thatcherism and British Politics* (Clarendon Press, 1987); P. Taylor-Gooby, *Public Opinion, Ideology and State Welfare* (Routledge & Keegan Paul, 1985).

14 T. H. Marshall, *Social Policy in the Twentieth Century* (Hutchinson, 1975), p. 97.

15 C. Schottland, *The Welfare State* (Harper and Row, 1969).

16 R. Mishra, *The Welfare State in Crisis*, p. 1

17 T. H. Marshall, *Sociology at the Crossroads* (Heinemann, 1963), pp. 70–4.

18 D. Donnison, 'Social Policy since Titmuss', *Journal of Social Policy*, 8 (2) (1979), pp. 146–7.

19 P. Addison, *The Road to 1945*, pp. 245–6.

20 P. Addison, *Churchill on the Home Front: 1900–1955* (Pimlico, 1992), pp. 405–6.

21 P. Taylor-Gooby, *Public Opinion, Ideology and State Welfare*, pp. 55–9.

22 B. Pimlott,'The Myth of Consensus' in L. M. Smith, (ed.), *Echoes of Greatness* (Macmillan, 1988); Lord Fraser, cited in T. Raison, *Tories and the Welfare State*, (Macmillan, 1990), p. 15.

23 R. Lowe, *The Welfare State in Britain*, p. 85.

24 J. Hills, *The Future of Welfare*.

25 R. Lowe, *The Welfare State in Britain*, p. 165.

26 See C. Pierson, *Beyond the Welfare State?* (Polity Press, 1991), pp. 141–78.

27 A. Gamble, *The Free Economy and the Strong State* (Macmillan Education, 1988), p. 43.

28 D. Selbourne, *Against Socialist Illusion* (Macmillan, 1985), p. 117.

29 N. Johnson, 'The Break-up of Consensus' in M. Loney, (ed.), *The State or the Market* (Sage in association with the Open University, 1987), p. 155.

30 P. Golding and S. Middleton, *Images of Welfare* (Martin Robinson, 1982).

31 P. Taylor-Gooby, *Public Opinion, Ideology and State Welfare*; P. Taylor-Gooby, 'The Role of the State' in R. Jowell, S. Witherspoon and L. Brooks, (eds.), *British Social Attitudes*, 6th edition (Gower, 1989); P. Taylor-Gooby, 'Attachment to the Welfare State' in R. Jowell, L. Brooks, B. Taylor, G. Prior (eds.), *British Social Attitudes, the 8th report* (Gower, 1991).

32 J. Hills, *The Future of Welfare*, p. 8.

33 *Social Trends* (HMSO, 1995).

34 N. Barr and F. Coulter, 'Social Security: Solution or Problem?' in J. Hills, (ed), *The State of Welfare* (Clarendon Press, 1990), p. 333.

35 J. Hills, *The Future of Welfare*; R. Goodin and J. Le Grand, *Not Only the Poor* (Allen & Unwin, 1987).

36 Department of Social Security, *Annual Report*, (HMSO, 1993), p. 7.

37 Department of Social Security, *Annual Report*, (HMSO, 1993), p. 2.

38 M. Mann, 'The Social Cohesion of Liberal Democracy', *American Sociological Review*, 35, (3) (1970), pp. 423–39.

9. CULTURE

1 For an excellent history of the arts council, see Robert Hutchinson, *The Politics of the Arts Council* (Sinclair Brown, 1982).

2 See Geoff Mulgan and Ken Worpole, *Saturday Night or Sunday Morning: from arts to industry – new forms of cultural policy* (Comedia, 1986).

3 For the best history of arts policies, see Janet Minnihan, *The nationalization of culture: the development of state subsidies to the arts in Great Britain* (Hamish Hamilton, 1977).

4 A good example of the problems of achieving clarity about goals and criteria can be seen in the otherwise broadly progressive document, *Towards a National Arts and Media Strategy*, produced under the aegis of the Arts Council in 1992.

5 The most trusted groups of professionals tend to be those with most day-to-day contact with the public: doctors, police, teachers. See the data of Henley Centre, *Planning for Social Change 1995/6*, or MORI.

6 A comprehensive account of public policy and the cultural industries, which unfortunately has not been repeated, was published by the GLC. *The state of the art or the art of the state* (Greater London Council, 1985).

7 James Curran and Jean Seaton, *Power without Responsibility* (Methuen, 1985).

8 Daniel Bell precisely sees the identification of modernist culture as

the key legitimator of the social order as one of the most dangerous threats to the cultures on which capitalism depends; *The Cultural Contradictions of Capitalism* (Basic Books, 1976), p. xxiv.

9 Robert Hughes, *The Culture of Complaint* (Oxford, 1993)

10. THE EUROPEAN QUESTION

1 R. Holland, *The Pursuit of Greatness: Britain and the World Rule, 1900–1970* (Fontana Press, 1991), p. 342. Holland's argument is that a disdain for, and fear of, the language of national modernisation, was a distinguishing feature of the 'fatalism' present in large sections of the British political elite from the early twentieth century. It preferred the language of national greatness.

2 There is no one label which can be employed to describe all the manifestations of the Europe issue. I have used several as deemed appropriate and to avoid boring repetition. This is unsatisfactory, but convenient.

3 Perhaps it should be added that the writer is a member of the Conservative Party. I accept that membership of a more integrated European Union may be of benefit to many countries. Euro-enthusiasts, however, have failed to persuade me that Britain, or rather England, is definitely one of them.

4 See, for example, S. George, *An Awkward Partner: Britain in the European Community* (Clarendon Press, 1990) and Simon Bulmer's chapter in S. George (ed.) *Britain and the European Community: the Politics of Semi-Detachment* (Clarendon Press, 1992).

5 See S. Davis, *The Federal Principle* (University of California Press, 1978), p. 205 and J. Bulpitt, *Territory and Power in the U.K.* (Manchester University Press, 1983) ch. 1.

6 See, however, J. Peterson, 'Subsidiarity: A Definition to Suit Any Vision?' *Parliamentary Affairs*, 1994, and, L. Blickner and L. Sangolt, 'The Concept of Subsidiarity and the Debate on European Co-operation', *Governance*, 1994.

7 For doubts about the novelty of interdependence see D. Henderson, 'International economic integration: progress, prospects and implications', *International Affairs* (1992) and D. Gordon 'The Global Economy', *New Left Review* (1988). Interdependence is a far more subtle concept than its crude use in this debate suggests. See, for example, R. Keohane and J. Nye, *Power and Interdependence: World Politics in Transition* (Little, Brown, 1977) for a more complex approach.

8 A. Moravesik, 'Preference and Power in the European Community', *Journal of Common Market Studies* (1993).

9 In sequence see A. Milward, *The European Rescue of the Nation State* (Routledge, 1992), Helmut Kohl's speech in October 1995, *Guar-*

dian (26 October 1995) and B. Connolly, *The Rotten Heart of Europe* (Faber and Faber,1995).

10 P. Ludlow, 'Maastricht: the View from Brussels', *Journal of Common Market Studies* (1993). For similar certainties, see Tony Blair, 'Britain in Europe', *Royal Institute of International Affairs* (5 April 1995), especially pp. 8 and 9.

11 See D. Daiches, *Andrew Fletcher of Saltoun: Selected Political Writings and Speeches* (Scottish Academic Press, 1979). B. Levack, *The Formation of the British State* (Clarendon Press, 1987) and L. Paterson, *The Autonomy of Modern Scotland* (Edinburgh University Press, 1994).

12 For good short surveys of the rationality problem, see K. Monroe (ed.) *The Economic Approach to Politics* (HarperCollins, 1991), Intro.; G. Almond, *A Discipline Divided* (Sage, 1990), chapter 4. On the collective action problem and rationality, see K. Dowding, 'Collective Action and Group Theory' in P. Dunleavy and J. Stanyer (eds.), *Contemporary Political Studies* (Political Studies Association of the United Kingdom, 1994), vol. II. For bounded rationality and satisficing, see H. Simon, 'Rationality as a Process and as a Product of Thought', *American Economic Review* (1978).

13 See Jim Bulpitt, 'Historical Politics: Macro, In-Time, Governing Regime Analysis' in J. Lovenduski and J. Stanyer (eds.) *Contemporary Political Studies*, vol. II.

14 For a general discussion of rules in politics, see W. R. Keech, Rules, Discretion and Accountability in Macroeconomic Policymaking', *Governance* (1992).

15 At the December 1910 election, the electorate was 7.7m. At the December 1918 election it was 21.3m. By the 1929 election it had reached 28.8m. See D. Butler and G. Butler, *British Political Facts, 1900–1994* (Macmillan, 1994), pp. 214–15.

16 Cited in P. Williamson, 'The Doctrinal Politics of Stanley Baldwin' in M. Bentley (ed.) *Public and Private Doctrine: Essays in British History Presented to Maurice Cowling* (Cambridge University Press, 1993).

17 On the Coalition see, K. Morgan, *Consensus and Disunity* (Clarendon Press, 1979) and M. Cowling, *The Impact of Labour, 1920–1924* (Cambridge University Press, 1971).

18 The literature on the inter-war treasury view is now considerable. The following items are useful surveys (although none of them support directly the line taken here): R. Middleton, *Towards the Managed Economy* (Methuen, 1985); A. Booth, 'Britain in the 1930s: A Managed Economy?' *Economic History Review* (1987); and P. O'Brien, 'Britain's Economy Between the Wars: A Survey of a Counter-Revolution in Economic History', *Past and Present* (1987). For the link between domestic

economic management and appeasement see, G. Peden, *British Rearmament and the Treasury, 1932–1939* (Scottish Academic Press, 1979) and R. Parker, *Chamberlain and Appeasement* (Macmillan, 1993) ch. 13.

19 For surveys of post-war economic policy, see A. Cairncross, *The British Economy Since 1945* (Blackwell, 1992) chaps 2 and 3; J. Tomlinson, *Public Policy and the Economy Since 1900* (Oxford University Press, 1990) chaps 7 and 8; S. Brittan, *The Treasury Under the Tories, 1951–1964* (Penguin, 1964), chaps 5 and 6. Once again, none of these books gives explicit support to the arguments presented here.

20 The outstanding sceptic's case on this matter is still R. Matthews, 'Why has Britain had Full Employment Since the War?' *Economic Journal* (1968).

21 Neville Chamberlain never believed the Americans would give any support to Britain in a European war. Churchill, of course, rejected this view. In many ways, the principal division between appeasers and anti-appeasers in the 1930s was over their attitudes to the United States, not Germany.

22 On post-war 'imperial' policy see, J. Gallagher, *The Decline, Revival and Fall of the British Empire* (Cambridge University Press, 1982) and J. Darwin, *The End of the British Empire* (Blackwell, 1991). In fact, Britain took its African empire more seriously after 1945 than after 1918.

23 The quotation comes from D. Reynolds, '1940: fulcrum of the twentieth century?', *International Affairs* (1990).

24 On the first EEC application, see D. Dutton 'Anticipating Maastricht: The Conservative Party and Britain's First Application to Join the E.C.' *Contemporary Record* (1993); J. Young, *Britain and European Unity* (Macmillan, 1993) ch. 3; A Horne, *Macmillan, 1957–1986*, (Papermac, 1989) and R. Holland, *The Pursuit of Greatness*, ch. 8.

25 On this episode, see Brittan, *The Treasury under the Tories*, pp. 185–196 and A. Horne, *Macmillan, 1957–1986*, pp. 70–79.

26 Six days before the membership bid was made public, the Chancellor, Selwyn Lloyd, had announced a severe credit and wage squeeze.

27 On the 1960s and 1970s, see Young, *Britain and European Unity*, chaps 4 and 5. On Heath's bid see U. Kitzinger, *Diplomacy and Persuasion* (Thames & Hudson, 1973). On the 1975 referendum, see A. King, *Britain Says Yes* (American Enterprise Institute, 1977).

28 See S. Brittan, *Steering the Economy* (Penguin, 1971), ch. 8. Wilson is often cited as the classic 'discretion' politician. In fact, between 1964 and 1967, he adhered to one big political rule, namely that the Labour Government should not be associated with a devaluation.

29 For critical reviews of the ungovernability thesis see A. Birch, 'Overload, Ungovernability and Delegitimation: the Theories and the British Case', *British Journal of Political Science* (1984), and R. Rose, 'Ungovernability: Is There Fire Behind the Smoke?' *Political Studies* (1979).

30 See my 'The Discipline of the New Democracy: Mrs Thatcher's Domestic Statecraft', *Political Studies* (1986). It should be noted that there were several other domesticist strategies in the early 1980s – Labour's Alternative Economic Strategy, the Mitterand experiment in France and Reagonomics.

31 See G. Howe, *Conflict of Loyalty* (Macmillan, 1994), p. 155.

32 On the Medium Term Financial Strategy, see N. Lawson, *The View from No. 11* (Bantam, 1992) chaps 5–8; G. Howe, *Conflict of Loyalty*, chaps 12–14, and C. Thain 'The Education of the Treasury: the Medium Term Financial Strategy, 1980–1984', *Public Administration* (1985).

33 P. Riddell, *The Thatcher Government* (Blackwell, 1985) p. 227.

34 Lawson's version of this episode is found in chapter 39 of his memoirs, *The View From No. 11*. Mrs Thatcher's version is in *The Downing Street Years* (HarperCollins, 1993), pp. 693–8.

35 They are discussed in M. Thatcher, *The Downing Street Years*, ch. 24; D. Smith, *From Boom to Bust* (Penguin, 1993) chaps 4–8; and H. Thompson, 'Joining the ERM: Analysing a Core Execution Policy Disaster' in R. Rhodes and P. Dunleavy (eds.), *Prime Minister, Cabinet and Core Execution* (Macmillan Press, 1995).

36 For GITA see Young, *Britain and European Unity*, p. 99.

37 For the emergence of the new rules see, 'The 1992 Autumn Statement and the Conduct of Economic Policy', *Treasury and Civil Service Committee, First Report, 1992–93*.

38 F. Kydland and E. Prescott, 'Rules Rather than Discretion: The Inconsistency of Optimal Plans' *Journal of Political Economy* (1977).

39 For the details of the Parliamentary story, see, D. Baker *et al*, 'The Parliamentary Siege of Maastricht 1993: Conservative Divisions and British Ratification', *Parliamentary Affairs* (1994).

40 An example may be the speech Malcolm Rifkind, Hurd's successor as Foreign Secretary, gave at Chatham House in September 1995. See *The Times*, editorial, 'Palmerston's Duty' (22 September 1995).

41 Cunctation was Sir Robert Vansittart's term for 'wait and see'. Vansittart was Permanent Under Secretary at the Foreign Office, 1930–37.

42 The outstanding exception to this rule, at least in terms of relations with the European Community, was Edward Heath. Mrs Thatcher was far more flexible. On the other hand, it could be argued

that Heath was not an ideas man, but a man who had one idea – to get Britain into the Community.

43 For the general debate in the Old South see Jesse T. Carpenter, *The South as a Conscious Minority, 1789–1861* (New York University Press, 1930). For the interesting debate in Georgia, not exactly the intellectual centre of the section, see W. H. Freehling and C. D. Simpson (eds.), *Secession Debated: Georgia's Showdown in 1860* (Oxford University Press, 1993).

11. IDEAS ARE NOT ENOUGH

1 The title implies my dissent from Keynes's peroration that 'the world is ruled by little else' than ideas. The author is grateful for his two year visiting lectureship at the School of History and International Relations at the University of Kent at Canterbury in 1991–3, when many of these ideas were gestated. He would also like to thank John Barnes, Lewis Baston, Brian Brivati, Peter Hennessy and David Marquand for comments on an earlier draft of this chapter.

2 P. Catterall, *British History 1945–87: An Annotated Bibliography* (Blackwell, 1989) lists some 50,000 books and articles.

3 H. Jones and M. Kandiah (eds.), *The Myth of Consensus? New Views on British History 1945–64* (Heinemann, 1996). A. Seldon, 'Consensus: A Debate Too Long?', *Parliamentary Affairs*, vol. 47, no. 4, pp. 501–14. See also H. Jones, 'The Postwar Consensus in Britain: Thesis, Antithesis, Synthesis?', in B. Brivati, J. Buxton and A. Seldon (eds.), *History Handbook* (Manchester University Press, 1996), pp. 41–9.

4 J. Tomlinson, *Democratic Socialism and Economic Policy: the Attlee Years* (Cambridge University Press, 1996), ch. 5. See also A. Booth, *British Economic Policy 1931–49: Was There a Keynesian Revolution?* (Harvester Wheatsheaf, 1989); A. Cairncross, *Years of Recovery: British Economic Policy, 1945–51* (Methuen, 1985).

5 N. Rollings, 'Poor Mr Butskell: A Short Life Wrecked by Schizophrenia?', *Twentieth-Century British History*, vol. V, no. 2 (YEAR), pp. 183–205.

6 PRO, CAB 134/852 'World Trade and Economic Conditions', 21 July 1954. Quoted in Tomlinson, *Contemporary British History*, Vol. X, no. 2 (forthcoming).

7 R. Taylor, *The Trade Union Question in British Politics: Government and Unions Since 1945* (Blackwell, 1995).

8 H. Glennerster, *British Social Policy Since 1945* (Blackwell, 1995), p. 167.

9 See T. Wilkie, *British Science and Politics Since 1945* (Blackwell,

1991). See also author's interview with David Edgerton, *Contemporary British History*, vol. X, no. 2 (forthcoming).

10 R. Middleton, 'The Growth of Government, 1945-95: Another British Peculiarity', ICBH Conference paper (July, 1995).

11 Interview with Richard Rose, *Contemporary British History*, vol. X, no. 2 (forthcoming); P. Hennessy, *Whitehall* (Fontana Press, 1989), pp. 88-125; K. Theakston, *The Civil Service Since 1945* (Blackwell, 1995), p. 83.

12 Rose summarises his own *oeuvre* in R. Rose, *The Art of Writing About Politics* (Centre for the Study of Public Policy, 1995). See also his interview with Michael Kandiah in *Contemporary British History*, vol. X, no. 2 (forthcoming).

13 B. W. Hogwood, *Trends in British Public Policy* (Open University Press, 1992). See also C. Hood, 'The Marketplace for Ideas', BBC Radio 4 *Analysis* programme, reprinted in *Contemporary British History*, vol. X, no. 2 (forthcoming), explaining economic reversals; P. Hall, *The Political Power of Economic Ideas* (Princeton University Press, 1986); J. Kingdom, *Agendas, Alternatives and Public Policies* (HarperCollege, 1995).

14 M. Foley (ed.), *Ideas That Shape Politics* (Manchester University Press, 1994).

15 See Arthur Seldon, 'Economic Scholarship and Political Interest', in Andrew Gamble *et al.*, *Ideas, Interests and Consequences* (Institute of Economic Affairs, 1989), pp 79-80.

16 D. Kavanagh and A. Seldon (eds.), *The Major Effect* (Macmillan, 1994), especially pp. 3-17.

17 Author's interview with Lord Dahrendorf, *Contemporary British History*, vol. X, no. 1, pp. 137-43.

18 Cited in A. Gamble, 'Ideas and Interests in British Economic Policy', *Contemporary British History*, vol. X, no. 2 (forthcoming).

19 Lord Dahrendorf in 'The Marketplace for Ideas'.

20 'It is quite difficult to say that there is such a thing as a really new idea in many areas of public policy.' C. Hood in 'The Marketplace for Ideas'.

21 See R. M. Hartwell, *A History of the Mont Pelerin Society* (Liberty Fund, 1995).

22 Croydon is midway between London Victoria and Gatwick airport. H. Macmillan, *The Middle Way* (Macmillan & Co., 1938).

23 W. H. Greenleaf, *The British Political Tradition*: vol. I, *The Rise of Collectivism*; vol. II, *The Ideological Heritage* (Methuen, 1983).

24 This subject is examined in R. Cockett, *Thinking the Unthinkable: Think Tanks and the Economic Counter-Revolution* (Fontana Press, 1995), pp. 57-199.

25 J. Ramsden, *The Winds of Change: Macmillan to Heath 1957–75* (Longman, 1996), pp. 181–2.

26 A. Dobson in Foley, *Ideas*, pp. 103–10.

27 See R. Holme and M. Elliot, *Time for a New Constitution* (Macmillan, 1988). The argument expressed at this point – that some ideas failed because they were unsympathetic to the small state mentality then in vogue – has been challenged variously by A. Gamble, *The Free Economy and the Strong State* (Macmillan Education, 1988) and S. Jenkins, *Accountable to None: The Tory Nationalisation of Britain* (Hamish Hamilton, 1995).

28 Author's interview with Lawrence Freedman, *Contemporary British History*, vol. X, no. 2 (forthcoming).

29 'The hundred most influential books since the war', *Times Literary Supplement* (6 October 1995). Author's interview with Antony Flew, *Contemporary British History*, vol. X, no. 2 (forthcoming).

30 Martin Bulmer, 'The Contribution of Sociology to the Understanding of Postwar British History', ICBH Summer School Conference paper (10 July 1995).

31 Author's interview with Anthony Giddens, *Contemporary British History*, vol. X, no. 1, pp. 144–51.

32 Author's interview with Eric Roll, *Contemporary British History*, vol. X, no. 1, pp. 186–98.

33 Author's interview with Jim Tomlinson, *Contemporary British History*, vol. X, no. 2 (forthcoming).

34 A. Graham, 'Thomas Balogh (1905–85)', *Contemporary Record*, vol. VI, no. 1, pp. 194–207.

35 'Learning from History', ICBH Conference, Nuffield College, Oxford (1988).

36 See Ivor Shelley, 'What Happened to the R.I.P.A.', *Public Administration*, vol. 71 (1993), pp 471–89.

37 Private information from a Whitehall insider.

38 Author's interview with Lord Dahrendorf, *Contemporary British History*, vol. X, no. 1, pp. 137–143.

39 Brian Harrison, 'Intellectuals and Mrs Thatcher', *Twentieth Century British History*, vol. 5.

40 Cmnd 169 and 247 respectively.

41 See T. Blackstone and W. Plowden, *Inside the Think Tank: Advising the Cabinet 1971–83* (Heinemann, 1988).

42 See B. Donoughue, *Prime Minister: The Conduct of Policy under Harold Wilson and James Callaghan* (Cape, 1987), and A. Seldon (ed.), 'The Number Ten Policy Unit', *Contemporary British History*, vol. X, no. 2 (forthcoming).

43 K. Theakston, *The Civil Service Since 1945*, pp 14–15.

44 Peter Townsend, 'Professor Brian Abel-Smith', *Independent* (9 April 1996). Further details in S. James (ed.), 'Political Advisers: A Witness Seminar', ICBH seminar (April, 1995).

45 J. Ramsden, *The Making of Conservative Party Policy: The Conservative Research Department Since 1929* (Longman, 1980), pp. 104–5.

46 One of the better recent books is D. Marsh (ed.), *Pressure Politics* (Junction Books, 1983).

47 R. Cockett, *Thinking the Unthinkable*, p. 5.

48 A. Denham and M. Garnett, 'The Nature and Impact of "Think Tanks" in Contemporary Britain', *Contemporary British History*, vol. X, no. 1, pp 43–61. Denham and Garnett have in their turn been attacked for understating the influence of think tanks by M. Oliver, 'The Nature and Impact of "Think Tanks" in Contemporary Britain: A Comment', *Contemporary British History*, vol. X, no. 2 (forthcoming).

49 Author's interview with Lord Dahrendorf, *Contemporary British History*, vol. X, no 1, pp. 137–143.

50 Geoff Mulgan in 'The Marketplace for Ideas'.

51 J. Griffith, *Judicial Politics Since 1920: A Chronicle* (Blackwell, 1993). S. Lee, 'Law and the Constitution', in D. Kavanagh and A. Seldon (eds.), *The Major Effect* (Macmillan, 1994), pp. 122–44.

52 A rare exception is A. Danchev, *Oliver Franks: Founding Father* (Clarendon Press, 1993).

53 See J. Meade in J. Howson and D. Moggridge (eds.), *The Cabinet Office Diary, 1944–46* (Unwin Hyman, 1990).

54 Leo Pliatzky, *Getting and Spending: Public Spending, Employment and Inflation* (Blackwell, 1984) and *Paying and Choosing* (Blackwell, 1985).

55 P. Clarke, *A Question of Leadership* (Hamish Hamilton, 1991), pp. 1–7, and 'Political Leadership', *Modern History Review*, vol. III, no. 1, pp. 13–14.

56 J. Cohen *et al.*, 'Individuals in History', *Modern History Review*, vol. II, no. 3, pp. 12–14.

57 B. Pimlott, 'The Unimportance of "Thatcherism"', *Contemporary Record*, vol. III, no. 1, p. 14.

58 See A. Marwick, *Britain in the Century of Total War: War, Peace and Social Change 1900–67* (Bodley Head, 1968) and *War and Social Change in the Twentieth Century* (Macmillan, 1974).

59 See for example P. Summerfield, 'Approaches to Women and Social Change in the Second World War', in B. Brivati and H. Jones (eds.), *What Difference Did the War Make?* (Leicester University Press, 1993), pp. 63–79.

60 See A. Cairncross, 'The Heath Government and the British Economy', in S. Ball and A. Seldon (eds.), *The Heath Government of 1970–74: A Reappraisal* (Longman, 1996), forthcoming.

61 See author's interview with Jim Tomlinson, *Contemporary British History*, vol. 10, no. 2 (forthcoming).

62 B. Hogwood, *Trends in British Public Policy*, p. 208.

63 Private Information.

64 See C. Pierson above, chapter 7.

65 R. Skidelsky, 'The Origins of Thatcherism', *Contemporary Record*, vol. III, no. 1, pp. 12–13.

66 N. Barry, 'Ideas and Interests: The Problem Reconsidered', in *Ideas, Interests and Consequences*, pp 53–4.

67 R. Taylor, *The Trade Union Question in British Politics*.

68 B. Roberts, 'Trade Unions', in D. Kavanagh and A. Seldon (eds.), *The Thatcher Effect: A Decade of Change* (Oxford University Press, 1989), pp 64–79.

69 Author's interview with John Ramsden, *Contemporary British History*, vol. 10, no. 2 (forthcoming).

70 M. Linton, 'Was it the Sun wot won it?', 7th Guardian Lecture, Nuffield College, Oxford. But see also M. Harrop and M. Scammel, 'A Tabloid War', in D. Butler and D. Kavanagh, *The British General Election of 1992* (Macmillan, 1992).

71 See R. M. Worcester, *British Public Opinion: A Guide to the History and Methodology of Political Opinion Polling* (Blackwell, 1991).

72 Private information.

73 See E. Shaw, *The Labour Party Since 1945* (Blackwell, 1995).

74 A. Seldon, 'The Heath Government in History', in *The Heath Government of 1970–74*, p. 14.

75 Under the Whitehall Programme, Number Ten and the influence of the Prime Minister will be analysed by at least three projects, by George Jones, Richard Rose and in a joint project by Dennis Kavanagh and Anthony Seldon.

76 A. Seldon, 'Assessing Governmental Performance: Britain's Administration since 1945', ICBH Tavistock Paper series (1991).

77 J. Harris, 'Political Ideas and the Debate on State Welfare', in H. L. Smith (ed.), *War and Social Change* (Manchester University Press, 1986), pp. 248–49.

78 Author's interview with Rodney Lowe, *Contemporary British History*, vol. X, no. 2 (forthcoming).

79 A. Enthoven, *Reflections on the Management of the NHS* (Nuffield Provincial Hospitals Trust, 1985).

80 I am indebted in this section to Jim Tomlinson in the interview

in *Contemporary British History*, vol. X, no. 2 (forthcoming).

81 Author's interview with Christopher Hill, *Contemporary British History*, vol. X, no, 2 (forthcoming).

82 Cmd 4107.

83 Author's interview with Lawrence Freedman, *Contemporary British History*, vol. X, no. 2 (forthcoming).

12. THE STAKEHOLDER SOCIETY

1 This chapter was based on interviews with Will Hutton and reading of his work by Anthony Seldon and Lewis Baston.

INDEX

Abel-Smith, Brian 150, 268, 272
ability 178–9, 187–8, 190–1
activism 5–6
  civic 16, 23, 27, 195; in economic
    policy 59–60; judicial 274;
    moral 21–2, 26, 27–8
Adam Smith Institute 285
Addison, P. 143
advisors 272
Advisory, Conciliation and
  Arbitration Service (ACAS) 106,
  113, 119
Albu, Austen 80
Anderson, Digby 269
Andreski 127
appeasement 230
approved societies 124, 130–1
Arnold, Matthew 199
Arts Council of Great Britain 198–9,
  201
arts policy see culture
Attlee, Clement 22, 132, 275, 282
Attlee Government, see Labour
  Governments: 1945–51
Audit of War (Barnett) 142
Ayer, A.J. 172, 267

Bacon, Robert 62
Bagehot, Walter 35
Baldwin, Peter 123
Baldwin, Stanley 228
Balogh, Thomas 269
Bank of England 61–2, 248–9, 270,
  295, 299, 302
Barber, Anthony 60–1
Barnes, William Gorrell 274
Barnett, Corelli 142, 270
Barry, Norman 279

BBC 205–7
benefits 154–5, 160–1, 296
  see also social insurance; social
    security
Benn, Tony 272
Bentham, Jeremy 20
Bernstein, Eduard 166–7, 169
Bevan, Aneurin 7, 126, 129, 260, 285
Beveridge, William 23, 141–2, 283
  on citizenship 133–4; and post-
    war consensus 36;
    Unemployment: a Problem of
    Industry 134; view of women 128
Beveridge Report 28, 139, 141–5,
    147, 163, 283
  and citizenship 134; social
    insurance scheme 22, 94, 122,
    125, 129–31, 133, 137, 141,
    260; unemployment in 70–2
Bevin, Ernest 93, 96, 287
Birch, Nigel 7, 53, 235, 286
Black, Peter 206
Blackwell, Norman 280
Blair, Tony 9, 28, 250, 252, 263, 307
Blum, Leon 80
Bosnian conflict 262, 277, 303
Bow Group 99
Boyle, Edward 268
Bretton Woods system 52, 231, 278,
    286, 303
British Council 208
British Empire 261–2, 267
British Museum 199
Brittan, Samuel 84, 271
broadcasting 205–7
Brook, Norman 274
Brown, William 108
Buchan, Alistair 288

Budgets
  (1947) 50, 82; (1972) 60–1; (1980)
  241; shadow (1992) 175–6
Bulpitt, Jim 214–56
bureaucracy, welfare 180–1, 185,
  189, 199
Burke, Edmund 34
Burns, Terry 270
Bush, George 263
business cycle, political 45, 51
Butler, R.A. 36, 234, 269
Butskellism 36, 84, 148, 231
Buzzard, Anthony 288

Cabinet, Inner 224
Cabinet Office 131
Cairncross, Sir Alec 74
Callaghan, James 41, 153, 282
Callaghan Government, *see* Labour
  Governments: 1974–9
Can You Forgive Her? (Trollope)
  34–5
Canova, Antonio 212
capitalism
  British model 293–5; Crosland on
  83; defence of 125; diversity of 9,
  291; full employment and 48;
  Marx's account of 167–8; and
  social democracy 167–9;
  stakeholding variety 299–300
Castle, Barbara 104–5
Central Arbitration Committee 106
Central Policy Review Staff 272
centralism 17
Certification Office 106
Chamberlain, Joseph 67
Chamberlain, Neville 230, 232
Cherwell, Lord 7
Churchill, Winston 7, 98, 234, 242,
  270, 276, 288
Churchill Governments, *see* Coalition
  Government; Conservative
  Governments: 1951–55
cinema 204, 209, 257
circumstances 46–7, 276–9, 281,
  283–9; Fig. 1, 2
citizenship
  civil 12; and class 132; classical
  view of 133–4; and duties

133–4; and gender 127–8; and
  markets 12–13; Marshall on
  12; rediscovery of 9; and
  resources 190–1; rights 122,
  124, 126, 130, 133–4, 146, 183,
  190; shop floor 95; social 12,
  14, 22, 94, 98, 114, 154; and
  social welfare 122, 124, 126–7,
  132–4
'Citizenship and Social Class'
  (Marshall) 12, 146
civic activism 16, 23, 27, 195
civic conservatism 10
civic culture 204–5
civic virtue 22, 128, 135
civil rights 12, 192–3
Civil Service 7, 8, 274–5, 277–8, 280
Clarke, Kenneth 270
Clarke, Peter 173, 275
Clarke, Richard 275
class 90, 128, 132, 169
Clegg, Hugh 270
Clinton, Bill 252
Coalition Government
  and Beveridge Report 141, 143;
  social contract with trades
  unions 94; social policies 147
Coalition of National Unity 228
Cockett, Richard 273
Cohen, Andrew 274
Cohen, Jerry 276
Cold War 9, 232–3, 240, 243, 247,
  288
collective bargaining 90
  and incomes policy 118, 136; and
  planning 96; Thatcherite version
  of 110, 112, 120; voluntarist
  nature of 88–9, 92–4, 97, 116
collectivism
  economic 23; hedonistic 23–6, 28;
  and individualism 2, 19–21,
  265, 290, 305; and
  Keynesianism/monetarism 64–5;
  liberal 6, 27, 28; moral 21–2,
  24, 26–7; post-war 135, 277,
  283; public attitude to 162; state
  96; trades union support for
  91–2; welfare 23
Collins, Cannon 206

Combination Act (1875) 259
Commission for Racial Equality 106,
    113
Commissioner for the Rights of Trade
    Union Members 113
Common Agriculture Policy 239, 243
Common Market, *see* European
    Union
Commonwealth 232, 236, 261
communism 101
  collapse of 9, 38
Communist Party 95
community 9–10
competitive equilibrium 298
Conservative Governments
    (1951–55) 148, 259
    (1957–63) defence policy 261; and
      EEC 234–8; foreign policy
      working group 287; and
      macroeconimcs 235, 238; and
      social expenditure 148; Treasury
      resignations 235
    (1970–74) 238; economic policy
      278; EEC membership
      application 237; industrial
      relations 104–6, 119; public
      spending 262; unemployment 60
    (1979–90) 267, 271–2; abandons
      full employment 140; arts under
      202–3, 207, 211; and demise of
      Keynesianism 62; economic
      policy 240–2; and Europe
      240–6; foreign policy 242–3,
      287; housing policy 156–7;
      industrial relations 110–12, 120,
      260; public spending 262;
      privatisation 154; and social
      democracy 166; social policy
      140, 154, 156, 159, 163; and
      trades unions 110–13, 240–2,
      279; and unemployment 278;
      and welfare state 285; and
      Whitehall 280
    (1990–) 8, 267, 271, 278
    and Europe 246–52; industrial
      relations 260
Conservative Party
  anti-welfarist agenda 140; and
    culture 210, 206–7, 212;

economic policy 7, 51, 58, 60–1;
  and Europe 216, 235–7; and
  failure 295–8, 306–7; foreign
  policy 287; ideological
  transformation of 152; and
  industrial relations 260; influence
  of 279; internal disputes 8, 307;
  and Keynesian consensus 7,
  149; and labour market 161,
  296–7; New Conservatism 231;
  and NHS 147; and poverty 184;
  Research Department 273, 285,
  287; science policy 262; and
  welfare state 148, 152–3, 155–6,
  158; Wets 242, 285; *see also*
  New Right
Constant, Benjamin 32–3
Constitution of Liberty (Hayek) 111
constitutional reform 266, 301–2
consultancies 274
consumerism 31–2, 73, 81, 258
Contract of Employment Act (1962)
    100
corporatism 17, 94–5, 97, 101, 119,
    290, 300
  neo-corporatism 238–9, 251
Council for the Encouragement of
    Music and the Arts (CEMA)
    197–8, 208
Cousins, Frank 101–2
Covent Garden Opera House 201
crime 10, 297
Cripps, Francis 272
Cripps, Sir Stafford 7, 22, 81
*Critique of the Gotha Programme,
    The* (Marx) 167
Crosland, Anthony
  on capitalism 83; collectivism of
    21, 23–4; on full employment 82;
    The Future of Socialism 81, 165,
    168, 170, 172; revisionism of
    166–7; *Social Democracy in
    Europe* 175; social democracy of
    165–94, 268; *Socialism Now*
    170, 172
culture 1, 9, 195–213
  amateurism 208; arts policy
    201–5; as conflict 210–11;
    cultural resistance to

consumerism 31–2; exclusivity of
196; funding of 203, 207, 209;
high versus popular 197–9, 201,
205; municipal role in 204, 212;
public and private 208–9;
remoteness from politics 211

Dahrendorf, Ralf 263, 264, 271,
273
Dalton, Hugh 49, 81, 82, 269
'De la liberté des Anciens comparée à
celle des Modernes' (Constant)
32–3
Deakin, Bill 270
decentralisation 302
decolonisation 287; Fig 1
defence policy 247, 260–1
influences on 288; nuclear deterent
235, 242, 261; Reviews 261
Defence White Paper (1957) 261,
288
deference 202, 206, 209
Delors, Jacques 114
demand management 17, 49–51, 58,
81–4, 95, 97, 118, 285
democracy
in capitalist society 291; in culture
196; Europe and 216–17;
industrial 109, 119–20; and
interventionism 15–16; and
modern capitalism 168–9; and
private/public ethos 32–3, 35
Denning, Lord 274
dependency 140, 193
and citizenship 133–4; culture of
25, 182; working class hostility
towards 154
devolution 267
De Wolff, P. 68
Dicey, A.V. 19
disappointment 31–2, 266
distribution
and culture 199–200; and social
justice 176–80, 190–1
domesticism 231, 244–5
economic 248, 251; Europe and
233, 236–7, 245, 255; and
external affairs 215–16, 227,
230, 232, 235–6, 238, 242,

254; and policy rules 226; of
Thatcherism 241; of Treasury
View 229–30
Donnison, David 146
Donoughue, Bernard 271–2
Donovan Royal Commission 103–4,
119
Dow, Christopher 270
Durbin, Evan 13–14, 49
duties 9, 21, 23–4, 133–4

Eady Levy 204
East Asia 292–3, 295, 306
Economic Journal 68
economic policy 231, 259
influences on 264–5, 269–70,
277–8, 283, 286, 289; Fig. 1, 2;
influence of economists 269–70;
Keynesian 41–66; Majorite 248;
rules of 226; stakeholder 10,
190–308; stop-go 51, 58, 84;
Thatcherite 240–2; *see also*
macroeconomics
Eden, Anthony 53, 99, 234
education
comprehensive 171; and equality
174, 191; funding 153, 155;
inclusivity of 195; internal
market 160, 163, 185; private
159; in stakeholder society
300–1
Education Act (1944) 147
Education Reform Act (1988) 260
egalitarianism, *see* equality
Eltis, Walter 62
Emergency Powers Act (1920) 90
employment, *see* full employment
Employment Act
(1946, USA) 48; (1980) 260;
(1982) 111
Employment Appeals Tribunal 106
Employment Protection Act (1975)
106, 260
Employment Rights Act (1993) 260
Employment White Papers
(1944) 48, 72–3, 75, 78–9, 82, 87,
147, 259; (1985) 41–2
'End of Laissez-Faire, The' (Keynes)
11

English Constitution, The (Bagehot)
35
*English Culture and the Decline of
the Industrial Spirit* (Wiener)
33–4
Enthoven, A. 285
environmentalism 266
Equal Opportunities Commission
106, 113
Equal Pay Act (1970) 105
equality
of condition 191; neo-liberal view
of 176–85; of opportunity
170–1, 191; of outcome 172;
public expenditure and 174–5,
181–2; social 175–6, 181; in
social democracy 23, 165–8,
170–4, 178, 190–1; and
taxation 173
Equality (Joseph) 177, 179
ethics 172
Euro-scepticism 215, 250, 252–4
Europe 303, 306
Britains relations with 9, 214–56,
261, 287; capitalism in 292–3;
culture in 210, 212; industrial
relations in 102, 107, 109, 115,
116, 119; nation states 18–19;
social insurance in 123
European Commission 217, 219
European Court of Justice 115, 217,
219, 274
European Exchange Rate Mechanism
(ERM) 8, 244–9
European Monetary System 239
European Monetary Union (EMU)
222, 244–7, 249–50, 252
European Parliament 217, 239
European Union 53, 215, 215, 217,
233
advantages/disadvantages 220–3;
British entry 234–9, 261, 287;
English interests 221; integration
215–16, 219–23, 227, 232,
238–9, 244, 254, 256, 257;
labour regulations 114–15, 121;
Major Governments and
246–52; as power system
219–20; principal actor 223–4;

Thatcherism and 240–6;
workings of 219–20
Evolutionary Socialism (Bernstein)
166
exchange rate 7, 51, 52,
existence goods 200
external affairs, *see* foreign policy

Factory Acts 116
Fair Wages resolution (1891) 90
Falklands War 262, 277
Family Allowance Act 147
family allowances 130, 143
Family Endowment Society 128
Federal Writers/Arts Project 210
federalism 217–20
Festival of Britain 212
financial system 293–4, 296, 299,
304, 307
Finkelstein, Danny 273
firm 294–5, 299, 302, 305
First World War 90, 228
fiscal policy 49–50, 84
Flanders, Allan 88
Flew, Anthony 267
Foley, Michael 263
Foreign Office 251–2, 280
foreign policy 239, 261–2
domesticism in 215–16, 227, 230,
232, 235–6, 238, 242, 254;
influences on 286–7, 289; Fig. 1,
2; Majorite 252; rules 226–7; and
stakeholding 303; Thatcherite
242–3
*Foundations of Corporate Success,
The* (Kay) 305
Fox, Alan 90
France 306
Britain's relations with 235–6,
243; culture in 210; and EU
219–20, 256, 257, 287; French
Revolution 32, 33;
industrial relations in 101; private/
public ethos in 33
Fraser of Kilmorack, Lord 148
Free Trade 67
Freedman, Lawrence 288
Friedman, Milton 2, 264, 269
comparison with Keynes 63–4; on

inherent fallibility 86–7; on
Keynes 44; on monetarism 85; as
neo-classicist 170, 265; quantity
theory of money 55, 63; and
unemployment 45, 56–7, 61, 63
full employment 60, 136, 286
abandoned 62, 120, 140, 153, 260;
in Beveridge Plan 71–2, 143;
Crosland on 82; high and low
56–7; and inflation 83–5;
Keynesianism and 48, 50–2,
54–6, 61, 63, 259; and labour
market 93, 94–5, 97, 100, 117;
planning for 74–7, 79–81
Fulton committee 270
Future of Socialism, The (Crosland)
81, 165, 168, 170, 172

G7 group 262
Gaitskell, Hugh 23, 36, , 49, 81, 169
Gamble, Andrew 153
Gardner, Howard 275
Gaulle, Charles de 235, 236–7
Geertz, Clifford 36
Gellner, Ernest 197
gender 127–9
*General Theory of Employment,
Interest and Money* (Keynes)
44–5, 46, 54, 56, 63, 68–9, 78,
80–1, 263, 304
gentry values 33–5, 294
Germany
capitalism in 292–3; and EU
219–20, 256, 257; industrial
relations in 101; reunification
243, 246; state power in 18;
student protests 31
Giant's Strength, A 99
Giddens, Anthony 268–9
Gilbert, Martin 270
Gladstone, William 67
Global Strategy paper 288
Gold Standard 67–8, 81, 230
Goldthorpe, John 103
Goodhart, David 305
Goodman, Lord 207
Goold-Adams, Richard 288
Gould, Julius 269
government

Court's role in 224–6; governing
Britain problem 215–16, 227–8,
234, 237–8, 240, 242, 251,
254–5; principal actor in 223–4;
statecraft 224–30; studies of
281–2
Government and Opposition 37
Gramsci, Antonio 5, 6
Gray, John 10
Great Depression 44, 63
Greater London Council 212
greatness, national 230, 242, 246,
251, 255–6, 257
Green, David 269
Greenleaf, W.H. 19
growth 41, 57–8, 175, 259, 286, 307
Guardian 271
Guild Socialists 92
Gulf War 247, 262

Haldane 178
Hall, Robert 269
Halsey, Chelly 268
Harris, Jose 22, 122–38, 283
Hart, Basil Liddell 288
Hayek, Friedrich A. 15, 26, 44, 45,
87, 150, 170, 264, 268
anti-Keynesian arguments of 76–8;
Constitution of Liberty 111;
critique of social justice 167,
176–8, 187, 189; individualism
of 283; *Road to Serfdom* 49,
75–6, 266; on trades unions
111
Healey, Denis 261, 288
health care 153, 155
inclusivity of 195; insurance 124,
129; private 159, 185, 196; and
social right 183; *see also*
National Health Service
health and safety at work 90, 116
Health and Safety Commission 106,
119
Heath, Edward 287
Heath Government, *see* Conservative
Governments: 1970–74
hedonism 21, 23–6, 28
Henderson, Hubert 49
Hennessy, Peter 271

Heritage, Department of 212
Hicks, John 45, 63
Hill, Christopher 287
Hinton, James 95
Hirschman, Albert 13, 19, 29–40,
    70, 75, 85, 265–6
  on public services 196; *The
    Rhetoric of Reaction* 2, 29, 36,
    42; *Shifting Involvements* 2,
    29–36
historians 270
historicism 13, 17
history 258, 276, 281–3
Hobhouse 178
Hobsbawm, Eric 108
Hogg, Quintin 79
Hogg, Sarah 269
Hogwood, Brian 263, 278
Hong Kong 242, 243
Hoskyns, John 272
housing 148, 156–7, 249
Housing Act (1988) 260
housing benefit 156
Howard, Michael 288
Howe, Geoffrey 243, 245, 269
Howell, David 17
Huntington, Samuel 36
Hurd, Douglas 252
Hutchinson, Terence 44
Hutton, Will 265, 271, 290–308

idealism 224
Idealists 178
ideas 5–6, 253, 263–7, 279, 281,
    283–9; Fig. 1, 2
Ideas That Shape Politics (Foley)
    263
ideology 27, 281
  impact of Keynesianism 69–70;
    reactionary/progressive 36–40;
    of Thatcherism 36
In Place of Strife 105
income
  growth 41; inequality 156, 171–2;
    maintenance of 154, 159–60
Income Support 143–4, 161
incomes policy 55, 57, 59, 62, 101,
    103, 107, 118, 120, 180, 239,
    240, 260

individualism 264, 283
  acquisitive 98, 112, 119;
    authoritarian 8–9; and
    collectivism 2, 19–21, 265, 290,
    305; hedonistic 26; and
    Keynesianism/monetarism 64; in
    industrial relations 112–14,
    120–1; moral 24–5, 26; public
    attitude to 162; under Thatcher
    112
individuals 267–8, 282, 285–9; Fig.
    1, 2
Industrial Charter (1947) 98
industrial democracy 109, 119–20
industrial relations 3, 88–121,
    259–60; Fig. 1, 2
  formal/informal 103–4; historical
    perspective 90–3, 116–21; *In
    Place of Strife* White Paper 105;
    legislation 99, 104–7, 109–11,
    118, 120, 260; social contract
    106; state role in 89–94, 96–7,
    100–1, 103; voluntarist
    tradition 88–93, 95–117;
    White Paper (1956) 99
Industrial Relations Act (1971)
    105–6, 260
Industrial Realtions Court 260
Industrial Training Act (1964) 100
industry 293, 295–6
inflation 59, 60–1, 82–3, 235, 239,
    259, 286
  and demand 81; ERM and 245;
    German 247; and Keynesianism
    41, 44, 46, 49, 50, 53–5, 64, 69;
    and macroeconomic policy 60,
    84, 86; Majorism and 248; and
    quantity theory of money 55;
    statecraft and 228; Thatcherism
    and 240–1; and unemployment
    55–7, 60, 61, 63, 77, 83–5, 240;
    wage 53, 98–9, 100, 103,
    131–2
information revolution 17–18, 66,
    258
injustice 176–7, 186–7
insecurity 113–14, 121, 297
Institute of Contemporary British
    History 282

Institute of Economic Affairs (IEA)
150, 170, 264, 266, 285
Institute of Strategic Studies 288
institutions 10, 293, 295
interdependence, European 217–18,
233
interest groups 272–3
interest rates 84, 241, 245
interests
national 216–17, 220–2; vested
interests 5, 43, 279–81, 283–7,
289; Fig. 1, 2
international factors 51–2, 277–8
International Monetary Fund 278,
286
interventionism 264, 286, 301
Conservative 259–60; in culture
198; Keynesianism and 46, 265;
in markets 11–12, 14–16
Invalidity Benefit 161
investment 80–1, 293–4, 296, 299,
304, 307
Ireland 257
Isaacs, George 95
ITV 206

Japan 293, 294–5
Jay, Peter 271
Job Seeker's Allowance 161
Johnson, Harry 44
Jones, Jack 102, 109, 273
Joseph, Sir Keith 85, 152, 177, 179,
266, 268
judges 274

Kahn-Freund, Otto 89
Kaldor, Nicholas 46, 58, 269
Kay, John 305, 307
Keynes, John Maynard 11, 36, 269,
286, 299
chairman of CEMA 198; on
Employment White Paper 72;
General Theory 44–5, 46, 54,
56, 63, 68–9, 78, 80–1, 263,
304; on ideas and vested interests
5, 43–4; and Keynesians 44–5;
and moral activism 22; on social
insurance 131
Keynesianism 259, 264

'bastard' 54; consensus on 48–9,
145, 264; Crosland and 165, 175,
185; demise of 8, 18, 24, 41–66,
153, 285; exogenous events and
46–7; fiscal 49–50; flaws in
42–3, 44–5; and Friedmanism
63–4; and growth 58;
ideological impact of 69–70; and
investment 80–1; as
macroeconomic theory 68–70,
169; 'new' 66, 290; opponents of
76–7; and planning 74–7; policy
and 45–6, 59, 62, 64–5;
revisionists 83–4; social
democracy 6–17, 21–2, 28, 65,
184; and socialism 48–9, 65, 74;
special theory of 63–4; and
unemployment 41–2, 44–5, 46,
53, 70, 74
King, Tom 261
Kinnock, Neil 280
Kohl, Helmut 220
Kondratieff cycle 47
Korean War 261, 277

labour exchanges 90, 136
Labour Governments
(1945–51) 231, 257; and
Beveridge Report 141; defence
policy 260–1; economic policy
7; and Keynesian social
democracy 9, 49; nationalisation
80–1, 148; NHS charges 148;
planning 80–1; social insurance
125–6; and trades unions
94–7, 117; welfare state 139
(1964–70) 271; and EEC 237;
economic policy 57–8;
industrial relations 59, 104–7;
introduces redundancy
payments 100; planning 58–9;
public spending 262
(1974–9) 8, 271; abandons full
employment 62, 260; adopts
monetarism 62; and EEC 239,
244; incomes policy of 62;
public spending 153–4
labour market 9, 304
and benefit levels 161;

labour market – *cont.*
  Conservatives and 154, 296–7;
    flexibility 161; and full
    employment 97, 100, 117;
    insecurity 113–14, 121, 297;
    regulation of 90, 93, 96,
    99–101, 106, 108
Labour Party 28
  and class 132; conference (1976)
    41, 62, 153; and culture 201–2,
    206, 208, 212; defence policy
    260–1, 287; and dependency
    culture 182; and Europe 243,
    247, 252; and incomes policy
    101; limited influence of 279;
    New Labour 3, 9, 307;
    philosophy of 149; and planning
    76; remodernisation of 247,
    280; Research Department 273;
    science policy 262; social
    contract 106–7; and social
    insurance 124, 126–7, 129–30,
    136
Lamont, Norman 248
Language, Truth and Logic (Ayer)
    172
Laski, Harold 129
law, rule of 180, 192–3
Lawson, Nigel 241, 269, 272
  on Employment White Paper 72;
    and ERM 244–5, 249;
    individualism of 21; Mais lecture
    41, 86
Layard, Richard 307
leadership 6, 275
Lee, Jenny 196
legislation
  industrial relations 99, 104–7,
    109–11, 118, 120, 260; trade
    union rights under 89; workplace
    90–1, 100, 114
Le Grand, Julian 196
Leijonhufvud, Axel 304
Lerner, Abba 56
liberal collectivism 6, 27, 28
Liberal Democratic Party 252, 256
Liberal Party 279
liberal socialism 12, 76
liberalism 170, 178, 291, 302, 305

Liberals and Social Democrats
    (Clarke) 173
liberty
  and ability 178–9, 187–8, 190;
    positive and negative 178, 187–8;
    and private/public ethos 32–3;
    and social justice 178–9, 187
Libraries Act (1845) 199
limited liability statecraft 229–30,
    232
Linton, Martin 280
Little, I.D.M. 170
Lloyd, Selwyn 59
Lloyd George, David 228
London Women's Parliament 128
Lowe, Rodney 144, 148

Maastricht Treaty 115, 247, 249–50
McCloskey, Donald 42
MacDonald, Ramsay 80
MacDougall, Sir Donald 60
Macleod, Ian 273, 278
Macmillan, Harold 13, 23, 98, 265
  forms NEDC 100; and
    Keynesianism 84; *The Middle
    Way* 305; and trades unions 99
Macmillan Government, *see*
  Conservative Governments:
  1957–63
macroeconomics 3, 67–8
  and demand 81; demise of 41–2;
    Hayek on 44; and inflation 60,
    84, 86; Keynesian 54, 63,
    67–87; Macmillan Government
    and 235, 238; and modern
    capitalism 169; and monetary
    policy 50; novelty of 75; and
    planning 73, 75–6; and
    Treasury View 229; and
    unemployment 72, 84
Maddison, Angus 48
Major, John 210, 245, 255, 263, 270,
    282
Major Government, *see* Conservative
  Governments: 1990–
management 168
Mandelson, Peter 280
Manhattan Project 260
Mann, Michael 162

Manpower Services Commission 106, 113, 119
manufacturing industry 58, 66, 67, 98, 103, 236, 257
market economics 27, 264–5, 290–1
and citizenship 12–13; and culture 208, 211; failure of 11, 15, 296–8; interventionism 11–12, 14–16, 65; and moralistic individualism 25–6; New Right and 8, 14–15, 25; public attitude to 162; role of trust in 9–10; social effects of 10; and social justice 176–7, 179, 186–7; within welfare state 159–64, 185
Marquand, David 5–28, 57, 264, 305
Marshall, Tom H. 94, 127, 146, 183, 268
'Citizenship and Social Class' 12, 146
Marx, Karl 167, 268
Marxism 45, 170, 167–70, 276
Maudling, Reginald 273
Meade, James 12, 73, 74, 82, 131, 274, 286, 304
means-testing 126, 131, 143, 300
media 271, 279–80, 282
Medium Term Financial Strategy 241
middle class 196, 202
Middle Way, The (Macmillan) 305
Milward, Alan 18
Ministry of Labour 104
Ministry of Labour and National Service 93, 95
Mishra, Ramesh 146
mixed economy 7, 12
modernisation, national 114–15, 229, 231–3, 238, 240–1, 245, 251, 254
monetarism 61–2
abandoned 244; adopted 62, 66, 241, 259; Friedman on 85; and Keynesianism 42, 45, 47, 85–6, 184
monetary policy 50–1, 81, 84, 259
Monks, John 107, 302
Mont Pelerin Society 264

Moore, John 184
moral/mechanical reform 173–5
moralism 21
and capitalism 9; Friedman's 63; and market forces 25–6; moral activism 21–2, 26, 27–8; moral collectivism 21–2, 24, 26–7; moral individualism 24–5, 26; and social democracy 179–80, 186
Mosley, Oswald 266
Mulgan, Geoff 23, 195–213
Murdoch, Rupert 273
Music Travellers 197
Myrdal, Gunnar 38

nation state, *see* state
National Arts and Media Strategy 210
National Council of Women 128
National Economic Development Council 100, 113, 118
National Government 123, 230–1, 234
National Health Service 147–8, 150
in Beveridge 143; charges introduced 148, 260, 285; expenditure 151; internal market 160, 163, 185, 260; popularity of 157–8
National Health Service and Community Care Act (1990) 260
National Incomes Commission 100
national insurance, *see* social insurance
National Insurance Act (1911) 124
National Insurance Bill (1945) 130, 147
National Lottery 201
National Plan (1965) 59
National Union of Mineworkers (NUM) 242
nationalisation 80–1, 148, 168, 231, 305
TUC calls for 92, 94, 117
nationalism 197, 265, 287
NATO 232, 287
neo-classicists 54, 265
neo-corporatism 238–9, 251

neo-functionalism 219
neo-liberalism 3, 163, 166, 170, 174,
    266
  critique of social democracy
    176–94
New Fabian Essays 80, 81, 82
New Labour 269
  anti-welfarist agenda 140; and
    Europe 9; and New Right policies
    9; stakeholding 307
New Liberals 178
New Right 8–9, 18, 28, 269, 285–6
  inverted historicism of 17; and
    Keynesian social democracy
    14–15; moral vision of 24–6;
    think tanks 273; and welfare
    state 152, 159, 163; world view
    of 18–19
Nickell, Steve 307
1968 student protests 29–31
Nixon, Richard 60
Northern Ireland 221, 252
Nott, John 261
nuclear weapons 235, 242, 260–1,
    266, 287–8
Nuffield College Reconstruction
    Survey 130
Number Ten Policy Unit 271–2, 280

Oakeshott, Michael 78, 268
officialdom, resentment of 135–6
officials 274
O'Hear, Anthony 267
OPEC crisis 43, 61, 152, 278, 286
opera 201, 209
Open University 196
organisational reform 266–7
Orwell, George 211

Parker, H.M.D. 92
Parker, John 74, 79, 82
patronage 196, 199, 201
Patten, Chris 273
Pedersen, Susan 127
PEP 128
Percy, Lord 272
Phillips curve 55, 85
philosophers 267–8
Pierson, Chris 139–64, 278

Pimlott, Ben 148, 276
planned economy 13, 17, 98, 259
  and demand 84; democratic
    planning 79; during economic
    decline 101; and full employment
    74–7, 79–1; for growth 100;
    Labour and 58–9; supply-side
    49; trades unions and 92, 96
Plant, Raymond 24, 165–94
Pliatzky, Leo 275
pluralism 224–5
Pocock, J.G.A. 16
policy 1, 224
  changes in 259–62, 283; Fig.1, 2;
    and circumstances 276–9, 283;
    histories of 283; and ideas
    263–7, 281, 283; influence of
    individuals on 267–76; influence
    of interests 279–81; influences
    on 283–8; Keynesian 43, 45–7,
    59–60, 64–5
political economy 292
political parties 1, 255, 287
  and ideas 253; individual's role in
    272–3; statecraft of 225–6; and
    vested interests 279
political reform 194
political scientists 270–1
politics
  private/public ethos 30–5;
    reactionary/progressive ideologies
    36–40; as spectacle 36
Poll Tax 247
Poor Law 122, 124, 126–7
Poor Law Amendment Act (1834)
    161
Popper, Karl 267–8
popular music 208
populism 224
post-war consensus 36
poverty 134, 137
  and class 132; under Conservatives
    156, 297; Conservative view of
    184; deserving and undeserving
    poor 155; and freedom 179;
    working poor 9
Powell, Charles 275
Powell, Enoch 7, 53, 150, 235, 268,
    273, 286

press commentators 271
pressure groups 279
Priestley, J.B. 212
Prior, Jim 110
private/public
  issues 30–5
  provision 140
privatisation 154, 159, 242, 259
professions 23, 202–3
progressives 36–40, 44, 70, 199–200
public assistance 126–7, 130, 134
public choice theory 280
public domain 9, 12, 14, 21, 24, 195
public expenditure 53
  arts 200–1; and equality 174–5,
    181–2; and full employment 72;
    levels 52, 62, 248–9, 262–3;
    and Keynesianism 50; in
    planning period 59; New Right
    policy 9; social 151, 155, 158,
    160, 163; under Thatcher 154,
    156
public opinion 256, 282, 295
  media and 279–80; on welfare
    state 154–5, 157–8, 161–2
public sector
  inclusion 195–6; market forces in
    185; new public management in
    159–60; social democracy and
    181–2; trades unions 104, 116
Public Sector Borrowing Requirement
  241
public service ethic
  erosion of 161; and Keynesianism
    63; amongst officials 181, 185;
    private/public ethos 30–5

Question of Leadership, A (Clarke)
  275
Quinlan, Michael 275
Quinton, Tony 267

radio 206, 208, 257
Raison, Timothy 148
Rathbone, Eleanor 128
Rawls, John 170–2, 186, 190, 267
reactionaries 36–40, 70, 199–200
Reagan, Ronald 36, 242
recession 152, 156, 246–7, 277

Redcliffe-Maud committee 270
redistribution 125, 130, 132, 135,
  147, 174–5, 182
redundancy 100, 118
Redwood, John 250
Rees-Mogg, Lord 203
Reflections (Burke) 34
Reid, Lord 274
Reith, Lord 205
Representation of the People Act
  (1918) 227–8
retirement pension 143–4, 155, 160,
  164
  private provision 159, 164
Review of Overseas Representation
  287
Rhetoric of Reaction, The
  (Hirschman) 2, 29, 36
Rhodes-James, Robert 98
rights 191–3
  citizenship 122, 124, 126, 130,
    133–4, 190; and duties 9, 21, 23,
    24; social 12, 127, 146, 182–3,
    190, 191–2, 295; welfare 154
Ritchie 178
Road to Serfdom (Hayek) 49, 75–6,
  266
Roberts, Andrew 98
Robertson, Denis 49
Robinson, Derek 270
Robinson, Joan 54
'Robot' plan 7, 259, 286
Roll, Eric 269
Rose, R. 262
Rostow, Walt 31
Rousseau, Jean-Jacques 32
Royal Commissions 272
  Donovan 103–4, 119; on Mental
    Illness 272; on Unemployment
    Insurance 134, 136
Royal Institute of International
  Affairs 287
Royal Institute of Public
  Administration 270
Royal Shakespeare Company 204
Russell, Bertrand 267, 288
Russia 256

Salisbury, Lord 90

Samuelson, Paul 64
Sandys, Duncan 261, 288
Scanlon, Hugh 102
Schottland, Charles 146
science policy 262, 270
Scotland 221–2, 252
Scottish Nationalist Party (SNP) 255
Scruton, Roger 267
SDP 255
Second World War
    and culture of continuity 230–1;
        and full employment 48; impact
        of 277; industrial relations
        during 92–6; and post-war
        consensus 35–6; and role of state
        18, 135
self-help 140
self-interest 11, 224, 226
Shanks, Michael 101
shareholding 294–5, 299
Sharp, Evelyn 275
Shifting Involvements (Hirschman) 2,
    29–36
Shonfield, Andrew 12
shop steward movement 98, 103–4,
    108, 119
Shore, Peter 273
Single European Act 244
Skidelsky, Robert 11, 19, 41–66, 278
Skinner, Quentin 133
Slessor, John 288
Smith, Adam 11, 16, 32, 264
Smith, John 175
social administration 146
social citizenship 94, 300
    activism of 22; erosion of 98; in EU
        social policy 114; New Right
        and 14; and welfare state 12,
        122–3; working class and 154
social cohesion 9, 191, 295
social contract 106–8, 112, 119, 180
social democracy 231
    Croslandite 3, 165–94; and culture
        212–13; Keynesian 6–17, 21–2,
        28, 65, 184; moral basis of
        179–80, 186–91; neo-liberal
        critique of 176–94
Social Democracy in Europe
    (Crosland) 175

social equality 175–6, 181–2, 184
social insurance
    Beveridge's scheme 22, 94,
        129–31, 133, 141–3; and
        citizenship 133–4; as 'defence of
        capitalism' 125; and gender
        127–9; Labour Party and 124,
        136; popular attitudes to 155;
        theoretical underpinning of
        123–38; Webbs and 122–3,
        136–7
social justice 268
    Croslandite 166–8, 186–7,
        190–1; and liberty 178, 187;
        neo-liberal attack on 176–81,
        184, 186–9
social policy 260
    influences on 285–6; Fig. 1, 2;
        inter-war 123; post-war 3, 122,
        139–64
social progress 13–14
social rights 12, 127, 146, 182–3,
    190, 191–2, 295
social scientists 271
social security 160, 185, 297
    see also social insurance
Social Security, Department of 160–1
Social Security Act (1986) 260
social services 139
social stratification 297
social values 294
social workers 203
socialism 125, 291
    and Keynesianism 48–9, 65, 74;
        liberal 12, 76; and modern
        capitalism 169; trades unions
        and 91–2; and welfare state
        139
Socialism Now (Crosland) 170, 172
sociologists 268–9
South Africa 243
sovereignty 217–18, 244, 254, 257
Soviet Union 18, 38, 242–3, 258
stakeholding 10, 265, 299–308
Stalin, Joseph 20
state
    collectivism 96; concentrated 8;
        disempowerment of 17, 18;
        industrial relations role of

89–94, 96–7, 100–1, 103–8, 116; interventionism 11–12, 14–16, 65, 135, 198, 265, 286, 295, 301; and Keynesianism 49; New Labour and 9; patronage role of 196; role in EU 220

State We're In, The (Hutton) 290, 292, 303, 307–8

statecraft 224–30

Steel, David 210

Stein, Herbert 48

Strachey, John 80, 83

strikes 93, 98–9, 108, 120

student protests (1968) 29–31

subsidiarity 217–18, 247

subsidy, arts 199, 203, 208–9

Suez crisis 234–5, 258, 270, 277

supply-side 49, 154, 184, 229, 242

syndicalism 119, 264

Tate Gallery 207

Tawney, R.H. 20, 21, 178

taxation 249, 298

New Right policy 9; and social democracy 173–5, 185; Thatcher Government and 154

Taylor, A.J.P. 205–6, 288

Taylor, Charles 188

Taylor, Robert 88–121

Taylor-Gooby, Peter 148, 155

Ten Years' Rule 230

Thatcher, Margaret 269, 275–6, 282, 288

and Hayek 111–12, 268; memoirs 28; and moral activism 26; and New Right 152, 163; resignation 244, 246; rift with Lawson 244; Thatcherism 25, 35–6; and trade unions 59

Thatcher Government, *see* Conservative Governments 1979–90

theatre 204, 207

Theory of Justice, A (Rawls) 170

think tanks 272, 273–4, 285

Thinking the Unthinkable (Cockett) 273

Third World 38

Thompson, E.P. 288

Thorneycroft, Peter 7, 53, 148, 235, 260, 266, 285–6

Times Literary Supplement 267

Titmuss, Richard 123, 127, 137, 146, 150

Tomlinson, Jim 50

Tooley, Sir John 199

Tourist Boards 208

Townsend, Peter 150, 268

Trade Disputes Act (1906) 111

trade liberalisation 52–3

Trade Union Reform Act (1993) 260

trade unions

of arts professionals 202, 208; and Conservative governments 98, 99, 106, 240; curbs 53, 59, 110, 112, 296; hostile to price and wage controls 136; and Labour governments 93–7, 106–9; in modern capitalism 169; as pressure group 279; Thatcher and 110–13, 240–2, 279; voluntarism and regulation 89–121

Trades Union Congress 114–15, 206

concordat with Labour 109; favours interventionism 117; national insurance proposals 129; nationalisation call 92, 94, 117; and NEDC 100; and public agencies 106; social contract 106–7; on state role in industrial relations 89, 117; and voluntary wage restraint 97

training 95, 100, 113, 118

Training and Enterprise Councils 113

transport, public 196

Treasury 50, 131, 134, 235, 245, 270, 280, 295

'Robot' plan 7, 259, 286; Treasury View 228–9, 266

Trends in British Public Policy (Hogwood) 263

Trollope, Anthony 34

True, Nick 272

trust 9–10

Tyrie, Nigel 272

UN Security Council 262

unemployment 9, 134, 247, 286
    and Beveridge Report 70–2; and
    Employment White Paper (1944)
    72; and inflation 55–7, 60–1,
    63, 77, 83–5, 240; and
    Keynesianism 41–2, 44–5, 46,
    53, 70, 74; and planning 74, 77,
    79; popular attitude to 161–2;
    and social expenditure 156;
    structural (natural rate of) 56,
    60–1, 63; under Conservatives
    7, 51, 60–1, 112–13, 278
*Unemployment: a Problem of
    Industry* (Beveridge) 134
Unemployment Assistance Board
    126–7
unemployment benefit 100, 161, 285,
    300
unemployment insurance 129
    Royal Commission 134, 136
United States 18, 306, 307
    capitalism in 292–3; culture in
    210; and full employment 48,
    50; reactionary politics in 36;
    relationship with Britain 232,
    234–6, 238, 242–3, 247;
    student protests 30–1; and trade
    liberalisation 52; Union 254
Universal Subsistence Allowance 136
universalism 122–4, 127, 132, 137,
    145, 158, 260, 300
universities 196, 203, 267, 268
Unprincipled Society, The
    (Marquand) 305

Vallance, Ian 302
Vietnam War 30, 60
Viner, Jacob 44
Virginia School 15, 20, 45
voluntarism 3, 88–117, 259, 265
    and training 95, erosion of
    98–101; workplace 96
wages
    call for national policy 96; freeze
    259; minimum 90, 113; restraint
    97, 99–100, 103, 108–10,
    117–18; wage inflation 53,
    98–9, 100, 103, 131–2
wages councils 90, 113

Waldegrave, William 258
Wales, 221, 252
Wallace 178
Walters, Sir Alan 47, 269
war 277
Warnock, Baroness Mary 203,
    267–8
Wealth of Nations (Smith) 32
Webb, Beatrice 122–3, 136–7
Webb, Sidney 122–3, 137
Weber, Max 20
welfare
    anti-welfarist agenda 140, 154–5;
    collectivism 23; pre-war schemes
    125–7; private 265
welfare state 22, 52, 76, 139–64,
    257, 265, 283
    antecedents of 142; consensus
    139–40, 145–9, 152, 163; crisis
    in 151–8; expenditure 151,
    154–7, 285; middle class and
    196; and modern capitalism 169;
    neo-liberal view of 182, 184–5,
    189–90, 192–3; popular
    attitudes towards 154–5,
    157–8; reforms 159–64, 242,
    285, 300; restructuring of 300–1;
    as social contract 12, 65; social
    insurance 123–38, 141–3; and
    socialism 139; TUC and 92, 117;
    and welfare rights 123
Wiener, Martin 33
White Paper (1956) 99; (1992) 112
    Defence (1957) 261, 288;
    Employment: (1944) 48, 72–3,
    75, 78–9, 82, 87, 147, 259;
    (1985) 41–2; *In Place of Strife*
    (1969) 105
Whitehall, *see* Civil Service
Williams, Bernard 267–8
Williams, Lady Juliet Rhys 128
Williams, Philip 167
Wilson, Harold 50, 58–9; 269
Wilson Government, *see* Labour
    Governments: 1964–70;
    1974–9
winter of discontent 62, 108, 110,
    240
Wolfenden, Sir John 272

women 127–8, 257, 258, 277
Wood, Kingsley 143
Wootton, Barbara 135
working class 98, 154–5
Writers and Arts Council 201

Young, Hugo 271
Young, Michael 268, 273
Young, Wayland 288

Zuckerman, Solly 270
Zweig, Ferdinand 97

Harold Wilson

Ben Pimlott

'One of the great political biographies of the century.'
A. N. Wilson, *Evening Standard*

'The rehabilitation of Wilson has begun – and Ben Pimlott, the best British political biographer now writing, has made a hugely impressive job of it . . . His narrative of the young Wilson, from sickly boy scout to academic pupil of the formidable William Beveridge, and then to chirpy junior minister is quite outstanding – clear, thoughtful and gripping. This early part of the book is central to its larger achievement, since Pimlott shocks the reader out of basic anti-Wilson prejudice by demanding a human sympathy for him. The little, blinking, stubborn boy, hiding his hurt with cocky self-confidence, lives on as a permanent presence within the powerful politician . . . Some biographies enter the political discourse at once, thanks to their innate qualities and lucky timing. There are so many echoes of the Wilson years in the politics of today that this happy fate must surely belong to Pimlott's book. Wilson's soured relationship with the press (and the terrible problems it caused for him) – the conflict within him between national leadership and good party management – even the growing debate about national decline – are all suggestive and worth lingering over. As, indeed, are almost all of these 734 well-researched and finely written pages.' Andrew Marr, *Independent*

'A masterly piece of political writing.'
Bernard Crick, *New Statesman*

'The narrative gallops along, sweeping the reader with it in a rush of excitement. A mass of complex detail is marshalled with the art that conceals art.' David Marquand, *Times Literary Supplement*

'Fascinating . . . Pimlott the X-ray has produced another work of formidable penetration.' Roy Jenkins, *Observer*

ISBN 0 00 637955 9

Frustrate Their Knavish Tricks

Ben Pimlott

'Witty, incisive and sometimes agreeably malicious . . . In all his writing, it is above all a love of liberty and a sympathy for the individual against the institution which shines through.'

PHILIP ZIEGLER, *Daily Telegraph*

'Ben Pimlott is an accomplished historian, biographer, and political journalist. All three worlds are well represented in this lively, often passionate collection of essays, reviews and occasional pieces written over the last twenty years. He is at his best in a fine introduction to George Orwell's 1984, a scintillating essay on "Future of Political Biography" and two evocative reports on unemployment in the North-East. . . . What unites his worlds is his politics. Pimlott has succeeded A.J.P. Taylor as Labour's best-known academic, and his preoccupations are distributed accordingly . . . As one would expect from an author of an outstanding biography of Hugh Dalton, he is good on character, always sensitive to the connections between public and private lives . . . Throughout the book Margaret Thatcher appears as the devil incarnate . . . Those who want to understand Labour's contemporary dilemmas should read these reflections of a humane, but puzzled, mind.'

ROBERT SKIDELSKY, *Guardian*

'Most enjoyable . . . always incisive . . . The approach is civilised, moderate, liberal progressive . . . Pimlott embodies the best instincts of the age of Blair. He is an inquiring, humane, mid-Atlantic post-Fabian.' KENNETH O. MORGAN, *Spectator*

'One of the very best of the current breed of journalist-academics . . . a master of brevity . . . Reading (his pieces) all together is an impressive experience, not least for a fellow practitioner. This is high-quality journalism, and undergraduate students of politics might save themselves a lot of work if they simply memorised his snappy characterisations of post-war politicians.'

IAN AITKEN, *New Statesman & Society*

ISBN: 0 00 638320 3

Law's Empire

Ronald Dworkin

In *Law's Empire* Ronald Dworkin reflects on the nature of the law, its given authority, its application in a democracy, the prominent role of interpretation in judgement, and the relations of lawmakers and lawgivers to the community on whose behalf they pronounce. For that community, *Law's Empire* provides a judicious and coherent introduction to the place of the law in our lives.

'As an advocate Dworkin is tirelessly fluent and endlessly inventive . . . and this is a surprisingly fraternal book, open, busy, engaging and teeming with ideas. It will give many readers a great deal of pleasure and instruction.'   John Dunn, *Times Literary Supplement*

'*Law's Empire* stands out for intellectual deftness, elegance and surprisingness.'   Alan Ryan, *New Society*

'*Law's Empire* is a rich and multilayered work . . . unusually accessible for a work dealing with abstract questions at such a high level. It is an ambitious book, and it does not disappoint the expectations appropriate to a major work by an important thinker.'   Thomas Nagel, *London Review of Books*

'Breaks new ground in a way that is both provocative and convincing.'   D. D. Raphael, *Times Higher*

ISBN 0 00 686028 1

The English
A Social History 1066–1945

Christopher Hibbert

'Christopher Hibbert writes so well, and presents a huge amount of material with such skill, that this 900 page volume can be read more quickly and enjoyably than many novels . . . an admirable evocation of the past and a lasting analysis of the English character'

JOHN MORTIMER *Sunday Times*

'From tournaments, pilgrims and kings through to bus conductors and summer holidays, he isolates the changing habits of successive generations. His greatest – and extraordinary – success is to have extracted from this mass of material the exact character of each century he touches'
The Independent

'Enthralling . . . Barons and peasants, contemporaries of Pepys and Boswell, a people revolutionised by technology – all leap from his pages like figures on a canvas by Lowry . . . How anyone can write as much and as well as Hibbert is a mystery. His big, rich book deserves a place on the shelves of anyone remotely interested in our history'
Mail on Sunday

'A glorious cavalcade of 900 years of life and death, work and play, sex and sensibility amongst the English . . . Christopher Hibbert blends erudition, energy and elegance to perfection . . . Get beyond the myths of history; treat yourself to this feast of a book'

ROY PORTER *The Standard*

'Compiled with flair and skill and with that flair for particularity and even oddity which no historian, "popular" or otherwise, can afford to dispense with'
Times Literary Supplement

0 586 08471 1

HarperCollins*Publishers*

Demanding the Impossible
A History of Anarchism

Peter Marshall

'To be governed means that at every move, operation or transaction one is noted, registered, entered in a census, taxed, stamped, priced, assessed, patented, licensed, authorized, recommended, admonished, reformed . . . exploited, monopolized, extorted, pressured, mystified, robbed; all in the name of public utility and the general good.'

So said Proudhon in 1851, and from the Ancient Chinese to today's rebel youth many have agreed – among their number Godwin and Kropotkin, Bakunin and Malatesta, Tolstoy and Gandhi, the Ranters and the Situationists, de Sade and Thoreau, Wilde and Chomsky, anarcho-syndicalists and anarcha-feminists. Peter Marshall, in his inclusive, inspirational survey, gives back to the anarchistic, undiluted and undistorted, their secret history.

'Reading about anarchism is stimulating and funny and sad. What more can you ask of a book?' Isabel Colegate, *The Times*

'Massive, scholarly, genuinely internationalist and highly enjoyable . . . this is the book Johnny Rotten ought to have read.'
David Widgery, *Observer*

'Large, labyrinthine, tentative: for me these are all adjectives of praise when applied to works of history, and *Demanding the Impossible* meets all of them. I now have a book – Marshall's solid 700 pages and more – to which I can direct readers when they ask me how soon I intend to bring my *Anarchism* up to date.' George Woodcock, *Independent*

'This is the most comprehensive account of anarchist thought ever written. Marshall's knowledge is formidable and his enthusiasm engaging . . . he organizes a mass of diverse material with great subtlety and skill, presenting a good-tempered critique of each position with straightforward lucidity.' J. B. Pick, *Scotsman*

ISBN 0 00 686245 4

Fontana Press

Whitehall

Peter Hennessy

'The thinking man's *Yes Minister*.'

Lord Hunt, ex-secretary of the Cabinet

'Mr Hennessy has at last produced his magnum opus – more than 800 pages chronicling the history of Whitehall from the Norman Conquest to Norman Strauss. Along the way we also get an analysis of present-day ministries, a reform tract and a succession of the Great and Good . . . It is the best account of the British Civil Service ever produced. More than that, it is also, to use Edward Bridges' favourite word, enormous fun.'

Robert Harris, *Observer*

'The most thorough examination of the civil service and her ways yet published. It is ambitious in intent, sweeping in scope, meticulous in detail and penetrating in analysis. His judgements are fair, and sure to disappoint the ideologies of both left and right. Whitehall looks set to beome the standard work on the ways and byways of a hugely important and underexposed part of national life.'

Jeremy Paxman, *Independent*

'This is an outstanding book by a political historian and journalist who has himself become something of a national institution . . . Present and future ministers, whether seeking to alter the machine or merely to comprehend its puzzling idiom and culture, are certain to regard Hennessy's brilliant investigation as the indispensable guide.'

Ben Pimlott, *Sunday Times*

'*Whitehall* is much the best book on the British civil service ever to appear. Everyone who claims the slightest acquaintance with British government will have to read the book, indeed own it.'

Anthony King, *Economist*

ISBN 0 00 686180 6

Fontana Press

The Crooked Timber of Humanity
Chapters in the History of Ideas

Isaiah Berlin

'Reading Isaiah Berlin is always exhilarating.'
Anthony Storr, *Independent on Sunday*

'Berlin's preoccupations are constant. His commitment is to individual and collective liberty and to moral and political pluralism. His writing is an extended exploration of the conditions in which those ideals blossom and flourish or wither and perish. The eight essays collected here are all concerned with manifestations of anti-rationalism: utopianism, fascism, romanticism and nationalism are all passed in magisterial review. To read them is to sit at an unlit window and see the landscape of European thought illuminated by a spectacular display of fireworks.'
Ian McIntyre, *Independent*

'To read Isaiah Berlin is above all to listen to a voice, effervescent, quizzical, often self-mocking, but always full of gaiety and amusement. These essays remind the reader on every page of the many thousands of listeners over the decades for whom that voice has brought the drama and passion and imaginative depth of the intellectual tradition to which they belong unforgettably alive.'
John Dunn, *Times Literary Supplement*

ISBN 0 00 686221 7

Fontana Press

The Politics of the Judiciary
Fourth Edition

J. A. G. Griffith

The furore caused by the initial publication of this book – described by the *Guardian* as 'an instant classic' – made front-page news in *The Times*. Since the third edition appeared much has happened – particularly concerning censorship of the media and freedom of speech, miscarriages of justice and police accountability, immigration policy, and labour injunctions – to reinforce Professor Griffith's controversial thesis that, given our legal system as it is now composed, the judiciary cannot act neutrally but must act politically. He shows, by examining specific cases, how the senior judiciary, constrained by their own self-imposed limitations, frequently fail sensibly to interpret the public interest.

'It is the achievement of Professor Griffith's book to lift the debate to an altogether better level . . . He has, in effect, thrown down the gauntlet to any believer in the neutrality of the judiciary, or in its independence from government.'

Michael Zander, *Guardian*

'Presents in detail, cogently and without hysteria, a controversial view. *The Times*

'A masterly analysis of the role of the judiciary . . . We are being warned: informatively, intelligently, forcefully.' *New Society*

ISBN 0 00 686222 5

Fontana Press

Governing Britain
Fifth Edition

A. H. Hanson & Malcolm Walles

Politically and administratively Britain is a highly developed country. For the performance of governmental functions she has well-established, clearly defined and widely respected institutions, run by men and women with a deep understanding of the roles they are expected to play. The emphasis throughout this book is on the way in which the political and administrative institutions of central government have responded to the challenge presented by the accelerating pace of social change. The result is a comprehensive account of the problems that face both people and government in Britain today.

This is the fifth edition of this book, and it has been extensively revised to take into account the particular convulsions which have altered the British political system during the 1980s.

ISBN 0 00 686208 X

Fontana Press

The Rise and Fall of the Great Powers

Economic Change and Military Conflict
from 1500 to 2000

Paul Kennedy

'One of the masterpieces of modern historical writing.'
CHRISTOPHER ANDREW, *Daily Telegraph*

'I doubt whether the story of the rise and fall of the great powers has ever been told so professionally, with such a command of sources, or with such close attention to the connections between economics, geography and politics.'   ROBERT SKIDELSKY, *Independent*

'Paul Kennedy has written a brilliantly original book which has become a best-seller in the US and made its author a pundit to be seen and heard. It is intended for the intelligent layman as well as the academic historian, combining in Toynbee-esque manner the sweeping conception with careful attention to historical detail.'
ZARA STEINER, *Financial Times*

'Despite the irresistible fascination of the subject, Paul Kennedy's outstanding new book is the first to tackle it with any real historical rigour. He ranges across five centuries and around the whole world. He seems to have read every relevant book in every possible language. And he has produced a general argument so deceptively simple that no politician, however busy, should ignore or misunderstand it.'
DAVID CANNADINE, *Observer*

'A masterpiece of exposition. It is erudite and elegantly written.'
LAWRENCE FREEDMAN, *New Society*

'A remarkable book, reported to be compulsory reading in exalted circles in Washington and Moscow. It is long, clever, often funny, and crammed with remarkable insights; it is tinged with the genius that unravels complexity.'   ANDREW WHEATCROFT, *Evening Standard*

ISBN 0 00 686052-4

FontanaPress
An Imprint of HarperCollins*Publishers*